Cosmetic English
化妆品专业英语

高瑞英 主编 党 志 主审

化学工业出版社

·北京·

全书分 5 个单元共 20 篇课文，内容选材来源于原版英文书刊、杂志、最新的化妆品著名企业站点信息、科技文献资料等，包括行业发展趋势，FDA（US Food and Drug Administration）职能，化妆品安全监管、产品简介、相关知识、标签、包装、广告、营销渠道，化妆品网站、著名企业介绍，美容知识等。全书由课文、课后练习、专业术语、辅助读物等部分组成，此外书后还设有附录，内容包括总词汇表，化妆品原料词典，参考文献英文刊名和缩写规则，化学常用词头和词尾的含义，常用词头和词尾含义，化学上常见的缩略语，化工常用英文缩写和颜色词汇中英文对照（彩妆用）等可供查阅。

本书内容通俗易懂，语言精练，趣味性强，选材新颖，覆盖面广。可供化妆品生产、管理、经营、销售及美容等从业人员阅读，也可作为高职高专化妆品专业教材。

图书在版编目（CIP）数据

化妆品专业英语/高瑞英主编 . —北京：化学工业出版社，2007.8（2022.9 重印）
ISBN 978-7-122-00976-0

Ⅰ. 化… Ⅱ. 高… Ⅲ. 化妆品-化学工业-英语Ⅳ. H31

中国版本图书馆 CIP 数据核字（2007）第 126602 号

责任编辑：旷英姿 于 卉 装帧设计：张 辉
责任校对：洪雅姝

出版发行：化学工业出版社（北京市东城区青年湖南街 13 号 邮政编码 100011）
印 装：北京建宏印刷有限公司
850mm×1168mm 1/32 印张 8½ 字数 227 千字
2022 年 9 月北京第 1 版第 13 次印刷

购书咨询：010-64518888 售后服务：010-64518899
网 址：http://www.cip.com.cn
凡购买本书，如有缺损质量问题，本社销售中心负责调换。

定 价：29.00 元 版权所有 违者必究

前　言

随着中国进入 WTO，化妆品的生产、监管、销售、服务等逐渐与国际接轨，中国的许多企业正在不断地吸收和引进国外的先进理念与先进技术，化妆品从业人员的英语素质亟待提高。《化妆品专业英语》旨在提高化妆品从业人员、高职高专化妆品专业学生专业英语的阅读能力，使读者了解国内外化妆品专业领域的基本知识和动向，扩充知识面，为专业学习服务，并着力于提高读者的综合素质及未来继续学习和发展的能力。

全书分 5 个单元共 20 篇课文，内容选材来源于原版英文书刊、杂志、最新的化妆品著名企业站点信息、科技文献资料等，包括行业发展趋势，FDA（US Food and Drug Administration）职能，化妆品安全监管、产品简介、相关知识、标签、包装、广告、营销渠道、化妆品网站、著名企业介绍，美容知识等。全书由课文、课后练习、专业术语、辅助读物等部分组成，此外书后还设有附录，内容包括总词汇表，化妆品原料词典，参考文献英文刊名的缩写规则，化学常用词头及词尾的含义，常用词头及词尾含义，化学上常见的缩略语，化工常用英文缩写和颜色词汇中英文对照（彩妆用）等可供查阅。

本书内容通俗易懂，语言精练，趣味性强，选材新颖，覆盖面广。可供化妆品生产、管理、经营、销售及美容等从业人员阅读，也可作为高职高专化妆品专业教材。

本书由高瑞英主编并统稿，党志主审。参加本书编写的其他人员（按姓氏笔画为序）有丁剑桥、刘纲勇、邹颖楠和张敏等。本书在编写过程中得到了有关院校领导和老师的大力支持和帮助，在此表示衷心感谢！

由于时间仓促，作者水平有限，加上化妆品领域发展日新月异，书中存在的不足在所难免，请读者批评指正。

编　者

2007 年 6 月

CONTENTS

UNIT ONE   MARKETING

Lesson 1   High-end Cosmetic Market in China

1. General Market Information

In 2004, the global cosmetic products market was mainly concentrated in North America, Western Europe, Pacific and Asian
region. China's cosmetic products market ranked the second largest
in Asia. Its high and mid-priced segments were dominated by
foreign and joint venture enterprises, but with no presence at all
by local firms. International giants including L'ORÉAL, P&G,
Shiseido and ESTĒE LAUDER formed a pattern of oligopolistic
competition. L'ORÉAL had the biggest market share in China in
2004. The remaining low-end market was shared by several
thousand local enterprises. However, there is a growing trend that
the international giants are entering the low-end market as well.

At present the beauty and cosmetics industry ranked the
fourth largest consumption zone in China after real estate, cars and
tourism. In 2004 revenue from China's beauty and cosmetics market
was 85 billion RMB (US $ 10.27 billion), with 16.5 million people
employed. By the end of 2004, there were 3,140 enterprises with business licenses to produce cosmetics in China, most of which are small
and medium-sized ones, producing more than 20,000 kinds of cosmetic
products. About 300 of them are foreign-invested companies. China's
lack of its own cosmetic companies with branded products is one of the

main factors behind the fact that more overseas investors are keen to enter the Chinese cosmetic market.

From general perspective, the regulatory standard to the beauty and cosmetic products market was not high, counterfeit and bad quality products as well as false advertisements were frequently seen in spite the continuous imposition of new regulations.

Over the last five years, the beauty and cosmetics industry in China has had an average growth rate of 20 to 25 percent per annum, benefiting both from the general rise of living standards and from the younger generations' disposable income spent on cosmetics. With the increasing number of young females in white-collar jobs ready to spend an increasing percentage of their income on cosmetics, the beauty industry is booming. According to estimates from the China Association of Fragrance, Flavor and Cosmetics Industry (CAFFCI), sales revenues are expected to reach 300 billion RMB (US$ 36.2 billion) by 2010.

Over the past two decades, foreign cosmetic companies successfully made their brands well-known among Chinese women. China Business Weekly reported that foreign brands and joint ventures represented 60 percent of the market in 2003. But Chinese brands offering a large range of products at cheaper price, still take up an important share of the overall market.

Most international cosmetic giants regard China as one of the major driving forces behind their international business. China's economy has shown strong growth, and there are positive indications that this strong growth will continue for the next few years. This will mean a relatively broader and wealthier group of customers. Chinese young people are full of curiosity and very dynamic. China's tremendous labor pool, including a great number of professionally educated people, will help draw in new investment into this industry. With more department stores and high-quality stores being built, high-end cosmetic brands can expand their business along with and in parallel to that growth.

Starting from April 1,2006, China scraped consumption taxes on skincare products and shampoo that had been 8% previously. China's consumption tax policy is different from the systems in the United States and most European Union countries. They are collected from domestic manufacturers, not from consumers. The customs authorities collect consumption taxes for imported goods. This means the new coming foreign cosmetic companies in the Chinese market will have a better price margin.

At present the following international cosmetic groups dominate high-end cosmetic market in China:

L'ORÉAL Group owns high-end brands LANCÔME, BIO-THERM, HELENA RUBINSTEIN, Shu Uemura.

LVMH Group owns high-end brands Dior and GUERLAIN.

CHANEL

Sisley Paris

CLARINS Paris

Elizabeth Arden

The ESTÉE LAUDER Companies Inc. owns high-end brands ESTÉE LAUDER, CLINIQUE, LA MER.

Procter & Gamble Co. (P&G) owns high-end brands SK-II and Max Factor.

Shiseido of Japan owns high-end brands Shiseido and Cle de Peau.

Beauty de Kose of Japan

LG Household & Health Care of Korea owns high-end brand

O HUI.

Amore Pacific of Korea owns high-end brand innisfree.

2. Market Trends

Skin care and make-up products account for the largest share of the cosmetic and toiletries market with 31% and 11% of the market respectively, and these categories have a huge potential for future increase in sales.

In order to maintain their position on the markets, big brands are diversifying their products, focusing on types of products enjoying a recent but growing popularity. Certain types of color cosmetics, such as eye shadow and nail polish, although they have quite a short history in China, are increasingly successful among Chinese women. Other types of products with a likely bright future in China include cleansing milk and anti-ageing and wrinkle creams. With China becoming an ageing society and the proportion of elderly population rising, they are expected to meet growing success.

Now 80% of cosmetic and toiletry sales are now through hypermarkets and mass retail outlets. However, the huge growth in specialty beauty stores such as Watson's, Mannings and SaSa is starting to threaten the larger retailers.

With about 3,700 companies crowding the market, competition is sharp. As the Chinese cosmetics market is highly brand-oriented, it is likely that only the biggest and most renowned brands will survive and thrive. As a result, brands launch increasingly intensive advertising campaigns. According to a CTR market study, cosmetics and toiletries were among the top five advertising categories in 2004, behind foodstuff, pharmaceuticals, retail, service and real estate. The overall advertising expenditure was almost 40 million RMB (US $ 4,8

4

million), 34% more than in 2003.

3. Competition

In 2005, China imported US $ 11. 86 million perfumes and toilet waters and US $ 207 million make-up and skincare products. France is the largest exporter of cosmetics to China. In China's import perfumes market (as shown in Table 1), France had a market share of 74. 92% in 2005. United States ranked No. 2 in China's import perfumes market with a market share of 9. 68% in 2005, up 120% over 2004. In China's import make-up and skincare products market (as Table 2 shows), France, United States and Japan formed a pattern of oligopolistic competition, with market shares of 29. 28%, 24. 36% and 22. 64% respectively in 2005. South Korea ranked No. 4 in China's import make-up and skincare products market with a market share of 5. 8% in 2005, up 229% over 2004.

French cosmetics giant L'ORÉAL has the largest market share in China. L'ORÉAL markets 17 skincare and hair care brands in China,

Table 1   World Trade Atlas
China-Imports-Total-3303/PERFUMES AND TOILET WATERS
Millions of US Dollars
January to December

Rank	Country	Share/%						Change/%
		2003	2004	2005	2003	2004	2005	05/04
0	World	6. 211864	11. 169648	11. 860703	100	100	100	6. 19
1	France	5. 383802	8. 332221	8. 885467	86. 67	74. 6	74. 92	6. 64
2	United States	0. 374124	0. 520498	1. 148289	6. 02	4. 66	9. 68	120. 61
3	United Kingdom	0. 145093	1. 684785	0. 632903	2. 34	15. 08	5. 34	−62. 43
4	Germany	0. 030628	0. 238795	0. 268127	0. 49	2. 14	2. 26	12. 28
5	Italy	0. 00485	0. 070233	0. 240158	0. 08	0. 63	2. 03	241. 94

Source of data: China Customs

Rank	Country	Share/%						Change/%
		2003	2004	2005	2003	2004	2005	05/04
0	World	78. 764569	138. 021574	207. 087814	100	100	100	50. 04
1	France	21. 974351	45. 278022	60. 627107	27. 9	32. 81	29. 28	33. 9
2	United States	27. 554277	27. 191373	50. 453189	34. 98	19. 7	24. 36	85. 55
3	Japan	13. 30146	31. 874895	46. 887435	16. 89	23. 09	22. 64	47. 1
4	South Korea	1. 812424	3. 647331	12. 002335	2. 3	2. 645	5. 8	229. 07
5	Italy	0. 132666	4. 236651	8. 694287	0. 17	3. 07	4. 2	105. 22

Source of data: China Customs

all imports except for products from Yue-Sai and Mininurse, which L'ORÉAL acquired from local cosmetics producers. In 2005 L'ORÉAL unveiled its Shanghai R & D center one of its 14 research facilities in the world covering 3,000 square meters.

Since the United States-based ESTĒE LAUDER Companies Inc. entered Chinese market in 1992, it has seen its fastest growth out of all its regional markets around the world. It has introduced three high-end brands into China, ESTĒE LAUDER, CLINIQUE and La Mer. The Asia Pacific headquarters of ESTĒE LAUDER Companies Inc. was also moved from Singapore to Shanghai in 2003. In 2005 The ESTĒE LAUDER Companies Inc. announced the opening of its first research facility in Shanghai's Zhangjiang High-Tech Park with the aim of exploring the benefits of traditional Chinese medicine.

The United States-based Procter &- Gamble Co. (P&-G) also has a large market share in China's high-end cosmetic market with two successful brands SK-Ⅱ and MAXFACTOR.

Japanese cosmetics giant Shiseido started investing in the Chinese market in 1981. The company has placed China, which accounts for about 12% to 14% of its overseas business, as the most important area in its global operation strategy. Shiseido also launched its new research and development center in Beijing in 2005.

Korean cosmetics giants Amore Pacific and LG Household &- Health Care launched massive and intensive advertising campaigns in China's high-end cosmetic market in 2005. As a result, the market share of South Korea in China's import make-up and skincare products market has jumped from 2. 645% in 2004 to 5. 8% in 2005, with a rise of 229%.

4. Market Access

The major task for all international cosmetic brands in China is to find prime retail space. There is plenty of retail space in China, but they are occupied by local brands, or the brand mix is incompatible. For the new-come high-end cosmetic brands that try to build up a strong customer base and high brand awareness in the Chinese market, it could better if they can find retail space in the most prestigious department stores or retail centers that have already gathered most high-end cosmetic brands, this will be easier to establish the brand image among the potential customers. Because usually the most prestigious department stores or retail centers all have stable customer sources that will easily become the potential customers of the new-come brands.

7

Words and Expressions

cosmetic [kɔz'metik] *n.* 化妆品；*a.* 化妆用的

high-end cosmetic market 化妆品高端市场

rank [ræŋk] *n.* 排名，等级，军衔，阶级；*a.* 繁茂的，恶臭的，讨厌的；*v.* 排列，归类于，列于

segment ['segmənt] *n.* 段，节，片断；*v.* 分割

foreign and joint venture enterprises 外资和合资企业

a pattern of oligopolistic competition 寡头垄断的格局

giants ['dʒaiənts] *n.* 巨人

the beauty and cosmetics industry 美容化妆品行业

revenue ['revinju:] *n.* 财政收入，税收

license ['laisəns] *n.* 执照，许可证，特许；*v.* 许可，特许

keen [ki:n] *a.* 锋利的，敏锐的，强烈的

counterfeit ['kauntəfit] *n.* 赝品，伪造品；*a.* 假冒的，假装的；*v.* 仿造，伪装，假装

annum ['ænəm] *n.* 年

disposable income 可支配收入

boom *n.* 繁荣，隆隆声；*v.* 急速发展

curiosity [,kjuəri'ɔsiti] *n.* 好奇，好奇心

dynamic [dai'næmik] *a.* 动态的，有动力的，有力的

tremendous [tri'mendəs] *a.* 巨大的，惊人的

scraped [skreip] *n.* 刮掉，擦掉；*v.* 刮掉，擦掉

dominate ['dɔmineit] *v.* 支配，占优势

account for *v.* 说明，占，解决，得分

category ['kætigəri] *n.* 种类，类别

diversify [dai'və:sifai] *v.* 使成形形色色，使多样化，使变化

focus on *vt.* 集中在

toiletry ['tɔilitri] *n.* 化妆品，化妆用具

hypermarket [ˌhaipəˈmɑːkit] n. 特大百货商场，特大超级商场

competition [ˌkɔmpiˈtiʃən] n. 比赛，竞争

renowned [riˈnaund] a. 有名的，有声誉的

survive [səˈvaiv] v. 生存，生还

thrive [triˈmendəs] a. 极大的，巨大的

intensive [inˈtensiv] a. 集中的，强化的，精细的，深入的

foodstuff [ˈfuːdstʌf] n. 食品，食料

pharmaceutical [ˌfɑːməˈsjuːtikəl] a. 药物的（医药的）；n. 药品（成药）

perfum [ˈpəːfjuːm] n. 香水，香气；v. 洒香水于，熏香

toilet [ˈtɔilit] n. 厕所，盥洗室

oligopolistic n. 寡头垄断的

unveiled pp. 公开

launch... campaign 发起……运动

market access 市场准入

it could better if 如果……，那就更好。

prestigious [ˌpresˈtiːdʒəs] a. 享有声望的，声望很高的

establish the brand image 建立品牌形象

certification [ˌsəːtifiˈkeiʃən] n. 证明，保证，鉴定

the Ministry of Health 卫生部

grant [grɑːnt] n. 拨款；vt. 授予，同意，承认

specify [ˈspesifai] v. 明确说明，叙述，指定，详细说明

convene [kənˈviːn] v. 集合，召集，召唤；v. 聚集，集合

submit [səbˈmit] v. 呈送，递交，主张；vt. （使）服从，（使）屈服

pertinent [ˌpəːtinənt] a. 相关的，中肯的，切题的

quarantine [ˈkwɔrəntiːn] n. 隔离，封锁交通，检疫期间；v. 检疫，停止交涉

procedure [prəˈsiːdʒə] n. 程序，手续，步骤

complicate [ˈkɔmplikeit] v. 弄复杂，使错综，使起纠纷

time-consuming [ˈtaimkənˌsjuːmiŋ] a. 耗费时间的

9

Relevant organizations of cosmetics in China
中国化妆品机构

The China Association of Fragrance，Flavor and Cosmetic industry	CAFFCI	中国香精香料化妆品工业协会(简称中国香化工业协会)
China Center for Diseases Control	CDC	中国疾控中心
China Hairdressing & Beauty Association	CHBA	中国美发美容协会
the Ministry of Health	MOH	卫生部
State Environment Protection Administration	SEPA	国家环境保护总局
State Food and Drug Admistration	SFDA	国家食品药品监督管理局
General Administration of Quality Supervision，Inspection and Quarantine	AQSIQ	国家质量监督检验检疫总局
The State Administration for Industry & Commerce	SAIC	国家工商行政管理总局

小 知 识

一、什么是 OEM？

OEM 是英文 Original Equipment Manufacturer 的缩写，直译为原始设备制造商，实际上就是委托生产。它最早起源于国外服装行业，伴随世界经济的快速发展，OEM 服务迅速辐射到各个行业，目前已经成为包括微软、IBM 许多国际品牌青睐的经营模式。对于正处于发展阶段的中小型化妆品企业来说，企业经营的成败在很大程度上依赖于上游加工厂家的专业水平。一家成熟和规范的 OEM 服务商，不仅能够为其品牌客户提供质量上乘的专业产品，还应该能够提供全面完善的专业服务。

二、什么是 ODM？ ODM 与 OEM 的区别是什么？

ODM，是 Original Design Manufacture（原始设计厂商）的缩写，早为业内所熟知的 OEM（原始设备制造商），主要是指按照厂商的设计进行制造，随着加工厂商逐渐掌握核心技术，开始出现自主知识产权的产品设计，原先用在电子行业的词借用到其他的行业。ODM 进入了人们的视野。OEM 的流行与 ODM 的兴起，反映了国内制造业发展的过程。从 OEM 到 ODM（Original Design Manufacturing，设计生产）再到 OBM（Original Brand Manufacturing，原创品牌），这是一条国际化 OEM 企业发展的必由之路。

通俗地说：

OEM 是品牌企业开发品牌包装设计，生产商供应产品，品牌企业出品。

ODM 是生产商供应产品、开发品牌、包装设计，企业出品。凡称是 ODM 者就是有开发的能力。

说到底 OEM 就是代加工，收加工费，要求自带配方；而 ODM 就是配方和加工都由厂商完成。

After-Reading Task

1. Which of the following was the global cosmetic products market mainly concentrate in from paragraph 1?

   A. North America   B. Western Europe

   C. Pacific and Asian region   D. all of the above

2. Which statement of this passage is true?

   A. Chinese local firms dominated high and mid priced segments

   B. The beauty and cosmetics industry ranked the second largest consumption zone in China

   C. Counterfeit and bad quality products as well as false advertisements were frequently seen in spite the continuous imposition of new regulations

   D. From general perspective, the regulatory standard to the beauty and cosmetic products market was high

3. Chinese consumption tax policy is different from the systems in the United States and most European Union countries, because ____ .

   A. They are collected from domestic manufactures

   B. They are collected from consumers

   C. Consumption taxes are collected for imported goods

   D. Consumption taxes are collected for exported goods

4. According to the text, which brands weren't owned by L'ORÉAL group?

   A. LANCÔME   B. LA MER

   C. HELENA RUBINSTEIN   D. SHU UEMURA

5. Why big brands are diversifying their products?

   A. In order to maintain their position on the markets

   B. In order to grow their popularity

   C. In order to increase their types of products

   D. In order to enjoy a recent popularity

6. Now ____ percent of cosmetic and toiletry sales are now through hypermarkets

11

and mass retail outlets

   A. 20%   B. 40%   C. 60%   D. 80%

7. In 2005, the largest exporter of cosmetics to China is ?

   A. the United State   B. France   C. European   D. Japan

8. From the passage, we can get the message that L'ORÉAL markets ____ skincare and hair care brands in China.

   A. 17   B. 18   C. 19   D. 20

9. Which brands has been introduced into China by EST Ē E LAUDER Companies Inc?

   A. CLINIQUE   B. L'ORÉAL   C. Olay   D. SK-II

10. When did Japanese cosmetics giant Shiseido started investing in the Chinese market?

   A. 1988   B. 1992   C. 1981   D. 2005

11. What is the major task for all international cosmetics brands in China?

   A. to find prime retail space   B. building up a strong customer base

   C. establishing the brand   D. building up high brand awareness

12. Before the cosmetics produts are allowed to sell in China, the Chinese laws require that they must complete ____ ?

   A. Safety Quality Test   B. Certificate for Imported Cosmetics

   C. Health Quality Test   D. all of the above

Further Reading

China Association of Fragrance Flavor and Cosmetic Industry

China Association of Fragrance Flavor and Cosmetic Industry (CAFFCI), established on August 21, 1984, is a mass organization composed, on a voluntary bases, of enterprises and institutions, of all kinds of ownership, engaged in manufacture and aca-

demic research of fragrances and flavors, as well as cosmetics in China. It is a nationwide, transregional and transdepartmental industrial organization as well as an association of the state level under the instruction of China National Council of Light Industry. The aim of

CAFFCI is to serve the enterprises within the industry sectors; promote the development of the industry sectors and protect the legal rights of the enterprises. Entrusted by the concerning governmental agencies, it is also responsible for part of the administration fraction of the industry sectors. It acts as a bridge and tie between the government and enterprise as well as among the enterprises.

The supreme authority body of CAFFCI is the Member's Representative Assembly with its standing office—the secretariat located in Beijing, China. Currently, CAFFCI has 478 organization members, among them 191 members are fragrance and flavor manufacturers, 222 members are manufacturers of cosmetics, and 65 members are institutions concerning academic research, engineering design and education in the industry sectors. Guided by CAFFCI, there are 5 professional committee (namely: Natural Perfume Committee; Aroma Chemical Committee; Fragrance and Flavor Committee; Cosmetics Committee as well as Science and Technology Committee) and a Center (The Information and statistics Center for Fragrance Flavor and Cosmetic Industry).

Main Tasks and Activities of CAFFCI:

1. to exploit the investigation, collection, statistics and study of the basic datum of the industry sectors; to put up suggestions for the development plans and programs of the industry sectors;

2. to convey the wishes and requests of the member organizations to the government; to protect the legal rights and benefits of the members; to mediate disputes between the management; to co-ordinate the benefits among the same industry sector;

3. to carry out the activities entrusted by the governmental organs as well as others bodies; to organize the management of natural perfume bases and the co-ordination of the development of per-

fumes;

    4. to promote the connections among the members; to organize the communication with respect to the experiences in business management and production technologies; to organize exhibition activities; to provide technical, economical and marketing information, both domestic and international, for the members; to edit and publish journals and books;

    5. to perform personnel training for the enterprises; to provide instructions for the enterprises improving the business management; to hold public welfare activities and all other activities which are beneficial to the industry sectors.

Lesson 2   Self-Introduction of a Famous World-Leading Cosmetics Company

▶ Who We Are

Three billion times a day, P&G brands touch the lives of people around the world. Our corporate tradition is rooted in the principles of personal integrity, respect for the individual, and doing what's right for the long-term.

▶ Purpose, Values and Principles

Our core values and principles guide us in everything we do. Learn more about what drives our purpose of providing products and services of superior quality and value to the world's consumers.

▶ Global Operations

The P&G community consists of over 135,000 employees working in almost 80 countries worldwide. What began as a small, family-operated soap and candle company now provides products and services of superior quality and value to consumers in 140 countries.

Product Spotlight

Designed with you in mind, Charmin® Fresh Mates are flushable, premoistened adult wipes that offer a cleaner clean than dry alone. And with the Charmin FreshWash™ gentle cleanser, Charmin Fresh Mates are perfect for everyday use.

▶ Learn More

▶ Our Products

Our company has one of the largest and strongest portfolios of trusted brands, including Pampers, Tide, Ariel, Always, Pantene, Bounty, Folgers, Pringles, Charmin, Downy, Iams,

Crest, Actonel and Olay.

▶ Employee Spotlight

Spotlight On: Our New Orleans, Louisiana, Folgers® Employees

What They've Done: In the aftermath of Hurricane Katrina's devastation, these employees—many of them suffering great losses of their own—banded together to help their city get back on its feet. Watch this inspirational video and discover how P&G employees have risen above this tragedy and are now reaching out to help others do the same.

▶ Diversity

P&G honors and values diversity. As our organization grows, we continue to build a culture that appreciates differences even as it reflects common values.

▶ Our History: From 1837 to Today

If James Gamble and William Procter hadn't married the Norris sisters, P&G might not exist.

Did You Know?

In the 1970s, P&G was one of the first companies to put its safety testing data in a computer database, helping to avoid duplicative testing.

▶ Science Behind the Brands

Many people think of P&G as simply a marketing company and are surprised by the enormous depth and breadth of our science capability.

▶ Product Innovations

It's Not Just Toothpaste

Ever pause to consider the mystery of it all while brushing your teeth in the morning? P&G did, and we came up with a sur-prising discovery: The key to stopping bone loss in women could be found in the calcium technology of Crest? Tartar Control toothpaste. The result? Actonel? a product that helps prevent osteoporosis.

As the producer of products in nearly 50 categories, rom toothpaste to bone disease therapies the breadth of P&G's business has allowed us to connect technology across categories in some unexpected ways. Here you can learn the secrets behind the P&G discoveries you use every day. From the invention of diapers that prevent diaper rash, to the mystery of shampoo and conditioner in one, this is your home for the science behind the brands.

Product Innovation Articles

Personal & Beauty

From Always? High Protection Feminine Pads

From Pert: Do You Wash and Go?

From Olay? What Would You Do for Younger-Looking Skin?

Hair Care

Skin Care

House & Home

From Tide? Detergent with Activated Bleach

From Bounty? Structured Tissues and Towels

Health & Wellness

From Crest: Tartar Control Toothpaste

Baby & Family

From Pampers? Don't Spring a Leak

Pet Nutrition & Care

From Eukanuba? What's Behind Your Pet's Smile?

From Iams? Does Your Pet Need a Daily Dose of Omega-3 Just Like You?

▶ Our Commitment

Improving the lives of consumers worldwide is about more than just great products. It's about taking responsibility for improving our communities around the world through the work we do, as a Company and as individuals.

Words and Expressions

---

integrity [in'tegriti] *n.* 诚实，正直，完整，完善

enormous [i'nɔ:məs] *a.* 巨大的，庞大的

innovation ['inəu'veiʃən] *n.* 创新，革新

explore [iks'plɔ:] *v.* 探险，探测，探究，[计算机] 探讨

perform [pə'fɔ:m] *v.* 执行，表演，做

commitment [kə'mitmənt] *n.* 委托，实行，承诺，保证（律）拘禁令，
  奉献，献身

long-term *a.* 长期的

core [kɔ:] *n.* 果心，核心，要点；*vt.* 挖去（水果的）果心

soap [səup] *n.* 肥皂

candle ['kændl] *n.* 蜡烛

spotlight ['spɔtlait] *n.* 照明灯，车头灯，公众注意中心

aftermath ['ɑ:ftəmæθ] *n.* 不幸事件之后果，余波

hurricane ['hʌrikən] *n.* 飓风，快速强烈的事物

devastation [,devəs'teiʃən] *n.* 破坏，劫掠

inspirational [,inspə'reiʃənl] *a.* 带有灵感的，给予灵感的，灵感的

video ['vidiəu] *a.* 录像的；*n.* 录像（机）；*vt.* 制作

tragedy ['trædʒidi] *n.* 悲剧，惨事，灾难

diversity [dai'və:siti] *n.* 差异，多样性

reflect [ri'flekt] *v.* 反射，反映，表现，反省，细想

duplicative *a.* 加倍的，二重的，复制的

Tartar ['tɑ:tə] *n.* 酒石，[医] 牙垢，鞑靼人，凶悍的人，难对付的人

osteoporosis [,ɔstiəupɔ:'rəusis] *n.* 骨质疏松症

therapy ['θerəpi] *n.* 疗法，治疗（名词复数：therapies）

diaper ['daiəpə] *n.* 尿布；*vt.* 换尿布

rash [ræʃ] *a.* 轻率的，匆忙的，鲁莽的；*n.* 疹子，皮疹

pad［pæd］ *n.* 衬垫，填补，印色盒，信笺簿；*v.* 填补，徒步，夸大

bleach［bliːtʃ］ *n.* 漂白剂；*v.* 变白，漂白

tissue［'tisjuː］ *n.* （动、植物的）组织，薄的纱织品，餐巾纸，手巾纸

towel［'tauəl，taul］ *n.* 毛巾；*v.* 用毛巾擦；*vt.* 用毛巾擦或擦干

leak［liːk］ *n.* 漏洞；*v.* 漏，泄漏；*vi.* 漏，渗

pet［pet］ *a.* 宠爱的；*n.* 宠物；*vt.* 抚摸，轻抚

omega［'əumigə］ *n.* 希腊字母的最后一个字，终了，最后

take responsibility for 对……负有责任，负起对……的责任

Glossary

The famous brands of cosmetics
著名化妆品牌

综 合 类			
ANNA SUI	安娜苏	JUVEN	柔美娜
AVON	雅芳	Kanebo	嘉纳宝
AVène	雅漾	KOSE	高丝
BIOTHERM	碧欧泉	Lancôme	兰蔻
BORGHESE	贝佳斯	L'ORÉAL	欧莱雅
CHANEL	香奈尔	Max Factor	蜜丝佛陀
Christian Dior(CD)	迪奥	MAYBELLINE	美宝莲
CLARINS	娇韵诗	Nina Ricci	莲娜丽姿
CLINIQUE	倩碧	OLAY	玉兰油
DeBON	蝶妆	REVLON	露华浓
DECLÉOR	思妍丽	RMK RMK rutina	若缇娜（KOSE 的
ESTĒE LAUDER	雅诗兰黛		一个系列产品）
evian	依云	Shiseido	资生堂
GUERLAIN	娇兰	Sisley	希思黎
HELENA RUBINSTEIN	郝莲娜	SK-Ⅱ	
H₂O	水芝澳	VICHY	薇姿
ÍPSA	茵芙莎	Yve Ssaint Laurent(ysl)	依夫·圣罗郎
		ZA	姬芮

护 肤 类			
ANELIN	颜婷	H$_2$O	水芝澳
BORGHESE	贝佳斯	Kanebo	嘉娜宝
CLARINS	娇韵诗	KOSE	高丝
CLINIQUE	倩碧	LADEFENCE	黎得芳
Elizabeth Arden	伊丽莎白雅顿	LANCÔME	兰蔻
ESTĒE LAUDER	雅诗兰黛	PRETTIEAN	雅姿丽
GIVENCHY	纪梵希	Samsara	姗拉娜
GUERLAIN	娇兰	Shiseido	资生堂

彩 妆 类			
ESTEE LAUDER	雅诗兰黛	LANCÔME	兰蔻

Websites of Top 80 brand of cosmetic worldwide
世界 80 强化妆品品牌网址

ANNA SUI	安娜苏	www. annasuibeauty. com	
AVEDA	艾凡达	www. aveda. co. jp	www. aveda. com
Avène	雅漾	www. avene. co. jp	
AVON	雅芳	www. avon. com	
BIOTHERM	碧欧泉	www. biotherm. com	
BOBBI BROWN	芭比布朗	www. bobbibrowncosmetics. com	
BodyShop	美体小铺	www. bodyshop. com	
BORGHESE	贝佳斯	www. borghese. com	
CAUDALÍE	泰奥菲	www. caudalie. com	
Cellex-C	左旋	www. cellex-c. com	
CHANEL	香奈尔	www. chanel. com	
Christan Dior(CD)	迪奥	www. dior. com	
CLARINS	娇韵诗	www. clarins. fr	
CLINIQUE	倩碧	www. clinique. com	
COVERGIRL	封面女郎	www. covergirl. com	
Covermark	傲丽	www. covermark. com	
DARPHIN	达芬	www. darphin. com	
Debon	蝶妆	www. lgdebon. com	www. lgdebon. com. cn
DECLÉOR	思妍丽	www. decleor. com	
DHC	蝶翠诗	www. dhccare. com	
Dove	多芬	www. dove. com	
Elizabeth Arden	伊丽莎白雅顿	www. elizabetharden. com	

ESTÉE LAUDER	雅诗兰黛	www. esteelauder. com
Ettusais	艾杜纱	www. ettusais. co. jp
ÉTUDE	爱丽	www. etude. co. kr
FANCL	芳凯尔	www. fancl. com
GLYCEL	卡诗儿	www. glycel. com
GUERLIAN	娇兰	www. guerlain. fr
H_2O	水芝澳	www. h2o plus. com
HELENA RUBINSTEIN	赫莲娜	www. helenarubinstein. com
ÍPSA	茵芙莎	www. ipsa. co. jp
Johnson	强生	www. yourbaby. com
JUVENA	柔美娜	www. juvena. com
Kanebo	佳丽宝	www. kanebo-cos metics. com
KOSE	高丝	www. kose. co. jp
La prairie	蓓丽	www. laprairie. com
LANCÔME	兰蔻	www. lancome. com
LA MER	海洋拉娜	www. cremedelamer. com
L'OCCITANE	欧舒丹	www. loccitane. net
L'ORÉAL	欧莱雅	www. lorealparis. com
MAC	魅可	www. maccosmetics. com
MARY KAY	玫琳凯	www. marykay. com
Max Factor	蜜斯佛陀	www. maxfactor. com
MAYBELLINE	美宝莲	www. maybelline. com
Neutrogena	露得清	www. neutrogena. com
NINA RICCI	莲娜丽姿	www. ninaricci. com
NIVEA	妮维雅	www. nivea. com
NU SKIN	如新	www. nuskin. net
NUXE		www. nuxe. com
NOXZEMA		www. noxzema. com
OLAY	玉兰油	www. olay. com
ORIGINS	品木宣言	www. origins. com
ORLANE	幽兰	www. orlane. fr
Pola	宝丽	www. pola. com
Proactive	高伦雅芙	www. proactive. com
REVLON	露华浓	www. revlon. com
ROC		www. roc skincare. com
RMK		www. rmkrmk. com
Shiseido	资生堂	www. shiseido. co. jp
Sisley	希思黎	www. sisley. com

SK-II		www. sk2. com
SOFINA	苏菲娜	www. sofina. co. jp
SONIA RYKIEL	索妮亚丽奈尔	www. soniarykiel. fr
Shu Uemura	植村秀	www. shu-uemura. co. jp
Tony & Tina	托尼蒂娜	www. tonytina. com
VICHY	薇姿	www. vichy. fr
Yves Rocher	伊夫罗谢	www. yvesrocherusa. com
Za	姬芮	www. za-ny. com

Further Reading

China Beauty Industry Investment Report, 2007

As people's living standard improves, people pay much more attention to appearance and figure except for health. After 20 years of development since 1980s until now, China beauty industry's total output value has rose from RMB 2 billion to current RMB 200 billion, increasing by 100 times. During the evolvement, beauty industry experienced two ages: the first was from mid-1980s to later 1990s (the age of industrialized product economy) and the second was from later 1990s to 2004 (the age of sci-tech economy). The third age from 2005 until now (the age of operation-oriented knowledge-capital economy) is under the way.

In recent years, China beauty industry has been keeping a rapid growth at more than 15%. For China beauty industry in 2006, output value reached RMB 240 billion, population joining in this area exceeded 16 million and beauty institution amount approached 1.8 million which rose 20% from 2005 and 93% are private-operated. However, per capita spending on beauty stays at a lower level compared to the developed countries; China beauty industry still sees huge potentials. An estimate shows total output value of China beauty industry will exceed RMB 300 billion by 2010. The market scale of China beauty industy（2001 to 2006）is illustrated diagrammatically in Figure 1.

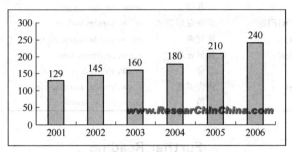

Figrue 1　Market scale of China beauty industry，
2001 to 2006（Unit：RMB billion）

Market competition is mainly focused on traditional beauty & hairdressing services such as whitening，macula removing，and breast enlargement，weight loss，hair dyeing，hair dressing and SPA. These services are closely related to people's life，so they are in enormous potentials. Investors can capture market shares as long as they constantly seek innovation based on strength and actuality.

As woman beauty market sees an increasingly fierce competition，man beauty has become one of the popular trends internationally. At present，male cosmetics include perfume，after shave lotion，shaving cream，and hair-care & skincare products，etc. Men's product has a foothold in cosmetic markets in recent 2 to 3 years but brands are mainly from Europe and U. S. As men get to love beauty，their demands will continuously grow towards beauty，nutrition，physical therapy，multi-purpose services and raw material naturalized instead of single products.

As beauty education gets orderly and developed，the demands for beauty education professionals further grow. Either education on life beauty skills or training on medical beauty talents needs to cultivate professional high-qualification teachers，which is also the only way for beauty education organizations to get upgraded and developed. Beauty professionals are supposed to master modern knowledge & skills on beauty, to understand beauty industry's development orientation and to turn experienced in operation and management.

Similar with catering industry, beauty & hairdressing industry has an extremely high elimination rate. Among some 1.8 million professional beauty institutions, over 1/3 was forced to be closed down each year; but even though, there are still a large number of new ones opened annually.

Beauty salon will carry out "star-level" management in the future, just like what the hotels are doing, and such policy is expected to be implemented from 2007. This system aims to regulate current beauty market by assessing whether or not beauty & hairdressing salon can reach standard or certain star level based on beauty & hairdressing salon's skills, services, health conditions and facilities.

Since 2005, the edge industries of drug & healthcare, fast consumer goods, medical devices and automobile, etc are developing to be scale-oriented, diversified and segmented, which awakes beauty industry. Beauty industry has formed an integrated industrial chain that stays with beauty services as major, production of materials, professional instrument and cosmetics as support; ornament, color service and image design as matched industry; exhibition, beauty newspapers & news communication, information consulting as media; and beauty education as base of talent resources. The training, service, culture and conference industries derived from beauty & hairdressing industry start enjoying a boom and they will witness greater potentials in economic benefits generating in 2007.

Lesson 3　Cosmetic Advertisements

　　Has the cosmetic industry made it a necessity to be young and beautiful? Has the industry used womens vulnerability as a marketing tool? The cosmetics industry is a very lucrative business catering to the female population and the entertainment industry and are geared towards targeting females- teenagers to the elderly. Viva Glam and COVERGIRL target age groups from late teens to late twenties and even late thirties while L'ORÉAL and OLAY target audiences from late twenties upwards.

　　The cosmetic industry is well aware of how conscious women are about beauty and their secret wish to look beautiful and youthful all the time— year after year. This industry preys on that vulnerability by using various appeals to tap into that subconscious desire to feel young, beautiful and wholesome. Almost all cosmetic companies commonly use appeals to reach out to desires such as the need to nurture (One's skin), the need for power (to be able to control the aging process), the need for affiliation (to be admired and accepted) and the need to be desired (look sexy, flirty and be cool).

　　Supermodels, celebrities and pretty women are used by cosmetic companies as a sales tactic to lure women to buy their products. These models are airbrushed to reveal flawless skin without a single blemish thereby conveying an unrealistic image and a false sense of hope to the vulnerable candidate. Beyonce Knowles, Heather Locklear and Claudia Schiffer among others were on L'ORÉAL advertisements conveying its slogan "You're worth it" while Pamela Anderson poses for MAC as a voluptuous model. Similarly Christie Brinkley, Queen Latifah, Brandy, Niki Talylor and other supermodels promoted COVERGIRL products.

The advertisement's messages are deceptive because it tells older women that they can eliminate wrinkles, which is untrue; misleading because it suggests to teenagers that they can look like supermodels, which unlikely; or simply false because it says that lipstick need only be applied once a day. These methods are used to clearly sell their products and exploit the vulnerable emotions of female candidate.

COVERGIRL

Ad created by COVERGIRL Cosmetics to promote a lipstick that is supposed to moisturize and last longer.

Pretty model is young, flirty and happy and in her mid twenties to early thirties. She wears pink lipstick that matchers her halter top as well as the flowers by her hair. The greenery indicates healing power, freshness, stability and endurance.

Targeted for females in their late teens to late thirties by appealing to romance, youth, look sexy, escape to have fun and the need for affiliation.

L'ORÉAL

Ad created by L'ORÉAL Paris to promote its new products that helps its consumers have a healthy summer skin tone. Model is pretty with a smooth suntan skin in a white robe, giving the impression of being in the sun or salon, looking squarely and confidently at the camera

Since 1997, L'ORÉAL Paris has proudly partnered with the Ovarian Cancer Research Fund(OCRF) to raise money for, and awareness of, the fight against ovarian cancer. This non-profit organization was created by Sol Schreiber to honor the memory of his wife Ann, a woman who valiantly fought ovarian cancer for five years. The OCRF provides support to patients, and their loved ones, living with ovarian cancer. This community of survivors, friends, family members, and doctors is devoted to early ovarian cancer diagnostic treatment programs and research. L'ORÉAL has established Women Of Worth-a grassroots program and award that celebrates, recognizes, and supports women who actively help others in their communities. And L'ORÉAL has created a Triangle of Giving to help connect the personal commitment, community and well-being of women everywhere.

Wrinkles and pimples.
What's next, bifocals and ripped jeans?

new total effects anti-aging
anti-blemish moisturizer

OLAY

Olay

Ad created by Olay Cosmetics to promote products that help fight multiple signs of aging.

The model is a middle aged woman, wearing bifocals and ripped jeans. Her skin looks quite smooth, especially her face and neck. She looks happy and confident.

Ad implies that the model feels happy and confident with her skin, and thanks to Olay Total Effects, she has such a beautiful skin at her age and that users of this product can be equally confident and look youthful.

Targeted audience is women over 40 who are very conscious of how they look as they approach middle age.

Multiple signs of aging are what people don't want to have but they still come, nobody can avoid them. Total perfect product promises to help people fighting signs of aging, makes people look much better and more confident. The product appeals to the need of nurturing skin and the need of escaping from the fear of aging.

The cosmetics industry makes up a large part of our economy. Ten billion dollars a year is spent on cosmetics and skin-care products alone. Unfortunately, the industry uses deceptive advertising practices such as COVERGIRL's false claim that its lipstick endures without additional applications. Cosmetics companies routinely play on the fears and anxieties of women. For example, Olay tells women consumers they must look like teenagers, despite the realistic impossibility of doing so. In addition, some companies promote promiscuity, leading to very serious consequences including deadly sexually transmitted diseases. The super model Pamela Anderson is an unfortunate example of this trend. Young girls are persuaded to spend money on unnecessary beauty products by an appeal, such as the one used by COVERGIRL, to their love of popular music and performers.

The advertising tactics used to influence such consumers vary by company and by product, however, most of the models used by these companies tend to be celebrities or young, pretty women. All these models are airbrushed to appear to have flawless skin, without so much as a single blemish to convey unrealistic images and a false sense of hope to the vulnerable consumer.

Most of people have the desire to be more beautiful or more attractive because the more beautiful people are the more confident and happier they feel. This is a very basic and huge non-stopping demand of people, and also one of the biggest markets for manufacturers making money. That is why top cosmetic manufacturers constantly produce a variety of new products that satisfy this need for each range of age. Cosmetics really help people looking more beautiful, attractive and confident. However, most of the cosmetic products are exaggerated by the producers on media. People spend a lot of time and money but what the products can really do for people is not that much as said on the media. According to statistics, ten billion dollars were spent a year on cosmetics and skin-care products alone. Nothing is wrong with trying to be more beautiful but we should know that good personality is much more important and valuable than good appearance, and success is not based on good appearance but based on our hard work and achievements. Remember that we are judged by our personality, hard work, and achievements not by what we put on.

Words and Expressions

vulnerability [ˈvʌlnərəˈbiləti]   *n.* 弱点，攻击
cater (to) [ˈkeitə]   *v.* 备办食物，投合，迎合
female population   （全体）女居民，妇女人口

gear　n. 齿轮，传动装置；v. 调整，（使）适合，换挡

conscious（of）［ˈkɔnʃəs］a. 神志清醒的，意识到的，自觉的，有意的

all the time　一直

prey on　vt. 捕食（掠夺，折磨）

subconscious［ˈsʌbˈkɔnʃəs］a. 潜在意识，模糊的意识

wholesome［ˈhəulsəm］a. 有益健康的，合乎卫生的，健全的

reach out　vt. 伸出（伸展，招揽）

affiliation［əˌfiliˈeiʃn］n. 加入，联盟，友好关系

tactic［ˈtæktik］n. 战略，策略

lure［ljuə］n. 饵，诱惑；v. 引诱，诱惑

airbrush［ˈɛəbrʌʃ］n. & v. 喷枪

flawless［ˈflɔːlis］a. 完美的，无瑕疵的

blemish［ˈblemiʃ］n. 污点，缺点；v. 弄脏，污损，损害

among others　除了别的以外，其中

slogan［ˈsləugən］n. 标语，口号

voluptuous［vəˈlʌptʃəs］a. 撩人的，沉溺酒色的

deceptive［diˈseptiv］a. 迷惑的，虚伪的，诈欺的

halter［ˈhɔːltə］n. 缰绳，绞索，女性三角背心的颈部系带

endurance［inˈdjurəns］n. 忍耐，忍耐力，耐性

partner with　做伙伴

ovarian［əuˈvɛəriən］a. 卵巢的

valiantly［ˈvæljəntli］ad. 勇敢地，英勇地

bifocals［baiˈfəukəlz］远近视两用眼镜

routinely［ruːˈtiːnli］ad. 通常

impossibility［imˌpɔsəˈbiləti］n. 不可能之事，不可能

In addition　另外

consequence［ˈkɔnsikwəns］ad. 因而，所以；n. 结果，后果

persuade［pəˈsweid］a. 空闲的，有闲的；v. 说服；vt. 劝说，说服

performer［pəˈfɔːmə(r)］n. 表演者，执行者

so much as　和……一样（甚至）

30

make money　挣钱

according to　根据

personality [ˌpəːsəˈnæliti] *n.* 个性

eye shadow　眼影

hue [hjuː] *n.* 色，色彩，叫声，[计算机] 色调

misconception[ˈmiskənˈsepʃən] *n.* 误解，错误想法

break from　决裂

combine（with）[kəmˈbain] *n.* 集团，联合收割机；*v.* 化合，结合，联合

perfection [pəˈfekʃən] *n.* 完美，完善

evolve into　*vt.* 发展成（进化成）

Glossary

Makeup
彩妆

cosmetics	彩妆	sponge puffs	海绵扑
concealer	遮瑕膏	brow brush	眉刷
Shading powder	修容饼	lash curler	睫毛夹
foundation(compact/stick)	粉底	eye shadow brush/shadow(applicator)	眼影刷
pressed powder	粉饼		
loose powder	散粉	lip brush	口红刷
shimmering powder/glitter	闪粉	blush brush	胭脂扫
brow powder	眉粉	pencil sharpener	转笔刀
brow pencil	眉笔	electric shaver-for women	电动剃毛器
liquid eye liner/eye liner	眼线液（眼线笔）		
eye shadow	眼影	electric lash curler	电动睫毛卷
mascara	睫毛膏		
lip liner	唇线笔	brow template	描眉卡
lip color/lipstick	唇膏	facial tissue	纸巾
lip gloss/lip color	唇彩	oil-Absorbing Sheets	吸油纸
blush	腮红	cotton pads	化妆棉
makeup remover	卸妆水	Q-tips	棉签
manicure/pedicure	指甲	body art	贴在身上的小亮片
nail polish	指甲油		
cosmetic applicators/accessories	工具	makeup removing lotion	卸妆乳
cosmetic brush/face brush	粉刷	nail polish remover	去甲油
powder puffs	粉扑	Nail saver	护甲液

After-Reading Task

1. What's the meaning of "lucrative" in paragraph 1 ?
   A. damage   B. profitable   C. complex   D. big
2. Almost all cosmetic company use appeals to reach out to the following desires except ____ .
   A. the need to the nature   B. the need for power
   C. the need to affiliation   D. the need to be desired
3. Which is the correct expression of paragraph 3?
   A. Supermodels, celebrities and pretty women help cosmetic company to sell their product.
   B. Those all have flawless skin.
   C. Beyonce Knowles does the ad for L'OREAL.
   D. Christive Brinkley, Queen Latifah, Brandy, Heather Locklear promoted COVERGIRL products.
4. The advertisement's message are misleading because ____ .
   A. It tells older women that they can eliminate wrinkles
   B. It suggests to teenagers that they can look like supermodels
   C. It says that lipstick need only be applied once a week
   D. It exploits the vulnerable emotions of female candidates
5. What's Ovarian Cancer Research Fund ?
   A. It's a profit organization created by Sol Scherber.
   B. Its aim is to honor a woman valiantly fought ovarian cancer.
   C. It provides support to people who living with ovarian cancer.
   D. It's a cosmetic company.
6. The ad created by Olay Cosmetic tells that ____ .
   A. Its target audience is women over 30
   B. the product can help fight multiple signs of aging
   C. the model has such a beautiful skin at her age because of COVERGIRL
   D. the middle aged women won't be confident without Olay
7. The cosmetic industry makes up a large part of our economy, but ____ .
   A. the industry uses reasonable advertising practices
   B. cosmetics company don't exploit the fears and anxieties of women
   C. some companies' promotion lead to very serious consequence
   D. all of the above

8. Which of the following is false for COVERGIRL Cosmetics?

 A. Its target age groups from teens to late thirties.

 B. It promotes a lipstick that is supposed to moisturize and last longer.

 C. It tells women consumers they must look like teenagers.

 D. It claims that its lipsticks endures without additional applications.

9. Why cosmetic manufacturers constantly produce a variety of new products?

 A. Because most people have the desire to be more beautiful.

 B. Because the demand of cosmetics is one of the biggest market for manufacturers making money.

 C. Because the new product can satisfy the need for each range of age.

 D. Because the more beautiful people are the more confident and happier they feel.

10. What do you think of cosmetic?

 A. Cosmetics do nothing helpful to people's beauty and confidence.

 B. What cosmetics product can do for people is as much as said on the media.

 C. Most of cosmetics products are exaggerated by the producers on the media.

 D. People spend too much money on cosmetics.

11. If you want to be more beautiful, you can _____ .

 A. develop your personalities and work hard

 B. do more exercise but not eat too much

 C. put on various of cosmetics

 D. all of the above

Further Reading

A Brief History Of Cosmetics

There is archaeological evidence of cosmetics usage in Ancient Egypt around 4,000 BC. Romans and the Ancient Greeks also used cosmetics. Interestingly, both the Ancient Egyptians and Romans used cosmetics that contained lead and mercury.

In the West, cosmetics use was mostly restricted to the upper classes throughout the medieval period. Cosmetics were also used in what is today the Middle East as well as in Persia. Though Islam has so explicit restriction against the use of cosmetics, the rise of Islam seems to have inspired various restrictions against the use of cosmetics in that part of the world.

Likewise, in various eras cosmetics usage was restricted or disapproved in general. In the 19th century Queen Victoria, for example, officially declared that the wearing of cosmetics was impolite. It was during this era in the western world that cosmetics were first seen as crude, or something that only prostitutes and actors wore.

It wasn't until right around World War II that cosmetics achieved wide appeal that was cross-class. During the 1930s and 1940s both lower and upper classes used cosmetics on a regular basis. It was during this period of time that makeup became so popular as to be advertised in magazines and other publications of the day.

In Japan geishas wore cosmetics made of natural resins and plants. These cosmetics were used to paint the lips, eyebrows and eye lid areas. A mixture of white paste and a very soft wax called bintsuke wax was used to paint the face of a geisha.

Today, the cosmetics manufacturing industry is dominated by a very small number of multinational corporations that were each started in the early 20th century. Eugene Shueller founded the L'ORÉAL makeup company in 1909. Back then the company was named French Harmless Hair Colouring Company and has since split up into Liliane Bettencourt, Nestle and others. L'ORÉAL is the largest of today's multinational cosmetics manufacturing companies.

Though small independents like Lip-Ink International try to break into the cosmetics manufacturing industry with unique products, there haven't been many successful breaches since those of Revlon just prior to World War II and ESTĒE LAUDER just after the war. Until then the industry was invented largely by the original trio of Elizabeth Arden, Max Factor and Helena Rubinstein.

Lesson 4　Practical Guide to Brand Promotion in China

Hongkong Trade Development Council

Advertising promotion is developing rapidly on the mainland, with advertising expenses of enterprises showing an annual growth of nearly 40% between 2000 and 2004. The following diagram (as shown in Figure 2) are some statistics on advertising expenses:

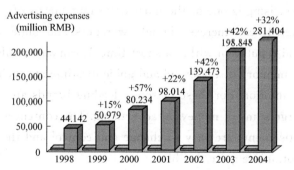

Figure 2　Annual Advertising Expenses of Enterprises

Source: Nielsen Media Research

The following statistics (as Figure 3 shows) show which products and sectors rely more heavily on advertising promotion. A comparison between 2003 and 2004 shows that professional services, health food, and shampoos and conditioners are the top three users of advertising promotion. Professional services spent 83% more on advertising in 2004 than in 2003.

35

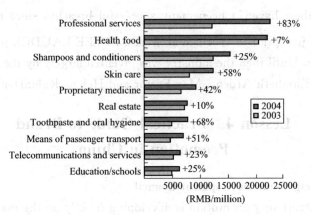

Figure 3　Advertising Expenses of Top 10 Users
of Advertising Promotion （2003 and 2004 Comparison）
Source：Nielsen Media Research

Characteristics and Functions of Advertising

Advertising is one of the most important means of promotion for brands. It can increase brand awareness and build up brand image and reputation within a short time. It can also reinforce consumers' memory of the brand and guide or stimulate their demand and consumption. For these reasons, leading brands are willing to spend large sums of money on advertising. The content and timing of advertisements are easy to change and control and the methods of promotion are quite flexible.

There are many different types of advertising media (as Table 3 shows), each with its own effects. Enterprises should choose their advertising media according to their own needs, and it is particularly important for SMEs with limited resources to choose media that are cost effective. Different media have different characteristics. For instance, TV advertising, combining sound with image, is the most influential of all media. However, since TV commercials cannot be preserved and are complicated and costly to pro-

Table 3   Characteristics of Different Advertising Media

Advertising Media	Characteristics	National Total (2005)	Market Penetration (2004)
Newspapers	Wide coverage, high circulation, can carry complicated advertising content, but it is quite difficult for newspaper advertisements to project a sharp image	2000 + titles	90%
Magazines	Have specific target readers and great influence and can be kept for a long time, but are slow in dissemination	9000 + titles	21%
Broadcasting	Quick dissemination, simple and quick production, low cost, and can reach audiences at different levels	800 + stations	25%
Internet	Simple production, extremely low cost, and no time or space restrictions	—	33%
Direct mailing	Very target specific as they can directly reach designated consumers	—	—
Outdoor ads	Great variety of forms and choices, targeted at specific regions, and can easily attract pedestrian attention	—	92%
Means of transport	Vast scope of dissemination and simple to produce, but advertising content must be clear and wording must be simple and precise	—	—

duce, they are more suitable for large enterprises. By comparison, advertising on means of transport is more suitable for SMEs as it has a wide coverage and is simple and inexpensive to produce. As for direct mailing, care must be taken not to make excessive use of this media as it can easily arouse customers' resentment and affect the brand image.

With the development of communications technology, fewer people now rely on the radio to obtain information. To the contrary, the utilisation rate of the Internet on the mainland is steadily increasing and online advertising is showing strong growth (as Figure 4 shows), with sales revenue soaring from less than RMB 100 mil-

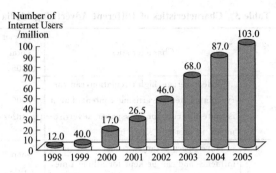

Figure 4   Number of Internet Users in China

(June 1998 to June 2005)

Source: China Internet Information Centre

lion in 1999 to nearly RMB 400 million in 2000. According to the figures published by the renowned US financial magazine *Barron's* in 2004, 70% of the Internet users in China were people under 30 years of age in 2003. Enterprises opting to use the Internet as their promotion tool should target young people in keeping with the Internet user age distribution.

The geographical coverage of different advertising media varies. There are national and local media. National advertising media include national newspapers, magazines and TV stations. However, national advertisements are costly and are more suitable for large companies. SMEs cannot afford to bear the risks involved. Local advertising media include provincial newspapers, magazines and TV stations and they target consumers in particular areas. Regional advertisements are more target-specific and sometimes can be more influential than national advertisements. Thus, enterprises should choose their advertising media according to their product characteristics and target market.

Local Advertising Media

Conwell Property Investment Consultancy Co Ltd (with parent company in Hong Kong) was incorporated in Beijing in 1996. Its business mainly covers market research, planning and consultancy. As the mainland property market was not quite mature at that time, Conwell decided to target expatriate tenants right from the start. With limited resources, the company decided to make use of regional advertising by running advertisements in free magazines for foreigners and distributing leaflets containing company profile and property rentals and sales information at various embassies in a bid to achieve the best advertising and publicity effects. With a well-defined target market and appropriate methods of promotion, Conwell has established its brandname and is doing great business.

Choosing the Right Advertising Media Combination

Advertising media combinations involve the use of more than one advertising medium to promote the same category of product within the same period of time. A common strategy is to make use of one main medium and several other supporting media. Different advertising media have different targets and advantages. The right choice of combination will enable an enterprise to achieve the best advertising effect with the lowest cost. In order to choose the optimum combination, it is necessary to understand the performance and effects of different media.

The following (as shown in Table 4) is a comparison of the effects of major media made by the American author Margaret Riel in Memorandum on Media Choice:

Table 4　Comparison of the effects of major media

Item	Newspaper	Magazine	TV	Broadcasting	Outdoor
Delivery to targets	√	√√√	√√√	√√√	√
Emotional Appeal	√	√√	√√√	√	
Visual effects	√	√√	√√√		√√
Market elasticity	√√√	√√	√√√	√√√	√√√
Seasonal elasticity	√√√	√√√	√√	√√√	√√

Note: Blank denotes "not applicable"; √ denotes "effective"; √√ denotes "very effective"; √√√ denotes "extremely effective".

The following are some of the more common advertising media combinations and their characteristics.

(1) Combination of newspapers and TV with on-site media

This combination first uses newspapers ads for promotion to create an impression of the brand in the consumers' mind and then makes use of TV and on-site media to prompt consumers to make purchases. This combination is suitable for products that do not require much consideration in the buying process, such as snacks and articles of daily use. On-site advertising can stimulate people's purchasing desire. Since sales venues on the mainland are much larger than in Hong Kong and enterprises can conduct massive on-site publicity at sales venues, this combination is easier to implement on the mainland.

(2) Combination of direct mailing with on-site advertising or posters

This combination can be used for advertising promotion in particular areas and is useful for market consolidation and development. Take Pizza Hut for example. Apart from opening restaurants serving pizzas, it also introduced takeaway and delivery services many years ago. Pizza Express is an independent brand of Pizza Hut China and provides delivery service only. In addition to putting up posters outside Pizza Hut restaurants and other outdoor media, it regularly mails the latest promotional leaflets to residential and business clients.

(3) Multimedia combination

This combination combines the advantages of different media and can help enterprises reduce risk by diversifying their advertising expenses. The use of multimedia increases the coverage of advertisements and helps reach more consumers of different groups.

40

How Enterprises Allocate Resources in Multimedia Advertising Combination

Betu is a Hong Kong fashion brand. It opened its first store in Shanghai in February 1989 and had over 80 outlets in the mainland by 2005. The company has been spending 5% to 8% of its annual sales on promotion in recent years. It runs advertisements in magazines (20%), on underground trains (15%) and buses (10%), on light boxes at shopping centres (10%), and in other media (45%) such as the Internet, sponsoring the clothing of actresses on TV dramas and programmes, and sponsoring beauty pageants.

Betu targets women in their 20s. As mainland women have the habit of finding out about products of different brands from what they read, online advertising (such as 21cn. com and 163. com) and soft advertising are ideal for disseminating brand information and telling brand stories. This advertising combination, offering easily accessible media and combining reading, mobility with information technology, can effectively increase brand awareness and penetration, leave a deep impression on consumers and stimulate their purchasing desire.

Evaluation of Advertising Effects

Evaluation of advertising effects can contribute to improving advertising campaigns by finding out the inadequacies of the advertisements and the gap between actual implementation and the target. However, as hiring professional research companies to conduct evaluations involves huge expenses, SMEs may not be able to afford it. Desirable advertising effects should embody three aspects: cognitive effect (how many people have heard or seen the advertisement?), persuasive effect (how many people understand the message of the advertisement and to what extent do they understand it?), and purchase effect (to what extent has the advertisement helped promote product sale?).

While SMEs may have limited funds, they should not overlook the evaluation of advertising effects. In fact, they can create their own indirect means of evaluation. The following is the method devised by Betu to evaluate the effects of its advertising media:

How Enterprises Devise their own Methods for
Evaluating Advertising Effects

Betu invests considerable amounts every year on brand promotion in the advertising media. Its method for evaluating the effects of advertising is to have shop attendants conduct a simple questionnaire survey with consumers to find out how they come to know Betu products. In this way, they can get a clear picture of the effects of different advertising media. For example, Betu spent several hundred thousand yuan advertising its products at a certain bus stop. After finding out from the survey that very few customers actually paid any attention to that advertisement, it decided to stop advertising at that bus stop. Sometimes customers would come to its shops with magazines showing Betu products and ask for those products. After a period of observation and referring to the results of the questionnaire surveys, it is not difficult to find out which magazine has better advertising effects.

Words and Expressions

---

guide [gaid] *n.* 引导者，指南，路标
flexible ['fleksəbl] *a.* 灵活的，易弯曲的，柔韧的
media ['mi:djə] *n.* 媒体，新闻媒介，传播媒介
Characteristics *n.* 特性，特征
coverage ['kʌvəridʒ] *n.* 涉及范围
circulation [sə:kju'leiʃən] *n.* 流通，循环，发行量

dissemination [diˌsemiˈneiʃən] *n.* 传播，宣传，传染（病毒）

designate [ˈdezigneit] *v.* 指定，标示

pedestrian [peˈdestriən] *a.* 徒步的，缺乏想像的；*n.* 行人

SMEs（Small and Medium Enterprises） 中小型企业

resentment [riˈzentmənt] *n.* 怨恨，愤恨

revenue [ˈrevinjuː] *n.* 财政收入，税收

expatriate [eksˈpætrieit] *n.* 亡命国外者；*v.* 逐出国外，脱离国籍，放逐

tenants [ˈtenənt] *n.* 房客，佃户

leaflet [ˈliːflit] *n.* 小叶，传单

profile [ˈprəufail] *n.* 侧面，轮廓，人物素描；*v.* 描绘……轮廓，评论人物；*n.* 概要，人物简介

category [ˈkætigəri] *n.* 种类，类别

snack [snæk] *n.* 小吃，点心；*v.* 吃零食，吃点心

On-site 现场

venues [ˈvenjuː] *n.* 犯罪地点，审判地，管辖地，发生地点，集合地点

implement [ˈimplimənt] *n.* 工具，器具；*vt.* 实现，执行，使……生效

posters [ˈpəustə] *n.* 海报，招贴，脚夫

allocate [ˈæləukeit] *v.* 分派，分配，分配额

multimedia [ˈmʌltiˈmiːdjə] *n.* 多媒体

awareness *n.* 认识（了解，知道）

penetration [peniˈtreiʃən] *n.* 渗透，侵透，侵入

inadequacy [inˈædikwəsi] *n.* 不适当，不十分，不完全

implementation [implimenˈteiʃən] *n.* 安装启用，实行，履行

cognitive [ˈkɔgnitiv] *a.* 认知的，认识的，有认识力的

questionnaire [kwestiəˈneə,-tʃə-] *n.* 调查表

After-Reading Task

1. Which of the following is the top users of advertising promotion shown by

the statistic?

    A. professional services   B. health food

    C. shampoos   D. All of the above

2. Which of the following statement is not ture about Characteristics and Functions of Advertising?

    A. Advertising is one of the most important means of promotion for brands.

    B. Advertising can decrease brand awareness.

    C. Advertising can reinforce consumers' memory of the brand.

    D. Advertising guide or stimulate their demand and consumption.

3. About the following advertising medias, which one had the maximum market penetration?

    A. Magazines   B. Internet   C. Outdoor ads   D. Newspapers

4. Which of the following statement is wrong about the TV advertising?

    A. TV advertising is the most influential of all media.

    B. TV commercials cannot be preserved and are complicated and costly to produce.

    C. TV advertising are more suitable for large enterprises.

    D. TV advertising is more suitable for SMEs.

5. Which of the following statement is true about the Internet advertising?

    A. Fewer people now rely on the Internet to obtain information.

    B. The utilisation rate of the Internet on the mainland is steadily increasing and online advertising is showing strong growth.

    C. 70% of the Internet users in China were people above 30 years of age in 2003.

    D. Enterprises opting to use the Internet as their promotion tool should target old people in keeping with the Internet user age distribution.

6. Which of the following statement is not true about the national and local media?

    A. National advertising media include national newspapers, magazines and TV stations.

    B. National advertisements are costly and are more suitable for large companies.

    C. Local advertising media include provincial newspapers, magazines and TV stations and they target consumers in particular areas.

    D. Regional advertisements are less target-specific and can be less influential than national advertisements.

7. The characteristic of combination of newspapers and TV with on-site media is
____ .
   A. This combination first uses newspapers ads for promotion to create an
   impression of the brand in the consumers' mind and then makes use of
   TV and on-site media to prompt consumers to make purchases
   B. This combination is suitable for products that require much consideration
   in the buying process
   C. On-site poster can stimulate people's purchasing desire
   D. This combination combines the advantages of different media and can help
   enterprises reduce risk by diversifying their advertising expenses

8. The characteristic of combination of direct mailing with on-site advertising or
posters is ____ .
   A. This combination is suitable for products that require much consideration
   in the buying process
   B. This combination combines the advantages of different media and can help
   enterprises reduce risk by diversifying their advertising expenses
   C. This combination can be used for advertising promotion in particular areas
   and is useful for market consolidation and development
   D. The use of direct mailing increases the coverage of advertisements and
   helps reach more consumers of different groups

9. Desirable advertising effects should embody the aspects: ____ .
   A. cognitive effect   B. persuasive effect
   C. purchase effect   D. all of the above

10. How do you undersatang the "persuasive effect" of advertising?
   A. how many people have heard or seen the advertisement?
   B. how many people understand the message of the advertisement and to
   what extent do they understand it?
   C. to what extent has the advertisement helped promote product sale?
   D. None of the above

Further Reading

Shelf-Life of Cosmetics

If you think you're being thrifty by keeping that foundation

long after the case is broken and the sponge is weathered, you could be putting yourself at risk of contamination. Unlike the U. S. , where products often state an expiry date, in Canada it's difficult to tell when products expire because there's no law requiring that the expiration date be listed.

"Most products remain effective for two years from their manufacturing date," says Dr. Tom Y. Woo, a dermatologist at Laser Rejuvenation Clinics & Spa in Calgary. But unless the products have all-natural ingredients, like Lush, for example, it's not often that the packaged date is listed.

If your products have active ingredients, such as acne creams or some moisturizers, they need to be kept in a cool and dark place. "Otherwise, they can decompose and cause severe irritation to the skin," says Dr. Woo.

However, most cosmetics are inert products, which means they don't have active ingredients. In most cases, they just lose their effectiveness if you keep them too long. But sometimes, they're a haven for bacteria. To find out how long you should keep your cosmetics, read on.

Mascara: 3 to 6 months

These should be used quickly because they're easily contaminated. Every time you push the brush back into the container, you're pushing air in too, and bacteria. The wet consistency of mascara makes it a breeding ground for bacteria. Don't open more than one bottle of the same colour at a time. Start a new tube of mascara on the first of a month, or circle the three-month date on your calendar to remind you to pick up a new one.

Moisturizer: 3 months to a year

Moisturizers with oils and botanicals should be used quickly, since over time they lose their effectiveness. Don't freeze moisturizers because the ingredients will separate. Use one day-formula and one night-formula at a time so you use them up promptly and don't have waste.

Oil-free foundation: 1 year

Without the oils, they dry out more quickly and become clumpy. They can also become darker, giving you a tan you don't want! If the foundation starts to look strange or smell bad, or if the ingredients start to separate, throw it out.

Products with SPF: 1 season

When the summer ends, toss that bottle of sunscreen. They lose their effectiveness to block out UVA and UVB rays and can stain skin and clothes.

Blush or foundation sponges: 1 week

You don't need to throw sponges out, but you do need to wash them every week. Use soapy water and allow them to dry naturally and fully before you place it back in the compact to avoid encouraging bacteria.

Concealer: 12 to 18 months

Liquid based concealers may start to separate when they're going bad. Once this happens, toss it. Like mascara, pushing the brush back into the container can cause bacteria to start, so wipe the brush after each use. If you're covering a blemish that may be infected or contain bacteria, use your finger to apply the concealer instead of a brush so you keep the germs from spreading.

Powder foundation or blush: 2 years

Over time, they get cakey and dried out, making them difficult to apply.

Eyeshadow: powder: 2 years; cream 12 to18 months

Cream eye shadows have emulsions that break down over time. Avoid touching the inner part of your eye with the brush. Wash brushes at least once a week. Don't use shadow if you have an eye infection, and if you discover an eye irritation, discard any eye shadows you were using for the few weeks prior.

Eyeliner: 2 years

Sharpening them helps with bacterial growth, so they're actually fairly safe to use. If you get an eye infection, throw it out.

Lip liner: 2 years

Like eyeliner, sharpening helps them. However, if you get a cold sore or another irritation, do not use the lip liner again, instead it's time to throw it out. Keep out of sunlight to preserve it.

Lipstick: 2 years

The pigment and oils preserve lipstick. If you get a cold sore, throw out the lipstick. If you use a lip brush, wash it twice a week.

Lip gloss: up to 2 years

Throw it out if you get a cold sore. If you get lipstick on the applicator, wipe it clean to avoid mixing ingredients.

Fragrance: up to 2 years

They contain alcohol, a natural preservative. When it starts to smell unpleasant or strong, discard it. Prolong its life by keeping it in the fridge or out of direct sunlight. Fragrances are a common cause of allergies and irritations, so if you notice one, stop using the fragrance.

UNIT TWO ADMINISTRATION AND REGULATIONS

Lesson 5 FDA's Authority over Cosmetics

FDA (US Food and Drug Administration) is only able to regulate cosmetics after products are released to the marketplace. Neither cosmetic products nor cosmetic ingredients are reviewed or approved by FDA before they are sold to the public.

FDA cannot require companies to do safety testing of their cosmetic products before marketing. If, however, the safety of a cosmetic product has not been substantiated, the product's label must read:

"WARNING: The safety of this product has not been determined. "

FDA does not have the authority to require manufacturers to register their cosmetic establishments, file data on ingredients, or report cosmetic-related injuries. To keep abreast of such information, FDA maintains a voluntary data collection program. Cosmetic companies that wish to participate in the program forward data to FDA.

Recalls are voluntary actions taken by the cosmetic industry to call back products that present a hazard or that are somehow defective. FDA is not permitted to require recalls of cosmetics but does monitor companies that conduct a product recall. If FDA wishes to remove a cosmetic product from the market, it must first prove in

49

a court of law that the product may be injurious to users, improperly labeled, or otherwise violates the law.

FDA collects cosmetic product samples as part of its plant inspections, import inspections, and follow-ups to complaints of adverse reactions. The agency does not, however, function as a private testing laboratory. FDA is prohibited from recommending private laboratories to consumers for sample analysis. Consumers may consult their local phone directory for testing laboratories.

FDA can inspect cosmetics manufacturing facilities, collect samples for examination, and take action through the Department of Justice to remove adulterated and misbranded cosmetics from the market. Domestic and foreign manufacturers must follow the same regulations. Foreign products that appear to be adulterated or misbranded may be refused entry into the United States.

Regulating Cosmetics

The Federal Food, Drug, and Cosmetic Act defines cosmetics as "articles other than soap which are applied to the human body for cleansing, beautifying, promoting attractiveness, or altering the appearance. "

FDA has classified cosmetics into 13 categories: fragrances, eye makeup, manicure products, makeup other than eye (e. g. , lipstick, foundation and blush), hair coloring preparations, shampoos, permanent waves, and other hair products, deodorants, shaving products; baby products (e. g. , shampoos, lotions and powders), bath oils and bubble baths, mouthwashes, tanning products.

It is against the law to distribute cosmetics that contain poisonous or harmful substances that might injure users under normal conditions. Manufacturing or holding cosmetics under insanitary conditions, using non-permitted colors, or including any filthy, putrid or decomposed substance is also illegal.

Except for color additives and a few prohibited ingredients, a cosmetic manufacturer may use any ingredient or raw material and market the final product without government approval. The prohibited ingredients are: biothionol, hexachlorophene, mercury compounds (except under certain conditions as preservatives in eye cosmetics), vinyl chloride and zirconium salts in aerosol products halogenated salicylanilides, chloroform, methylene chloride.

Manufacturers must test color additives for safety and gain FDA approval for their intended use.

Cosmetic firms may voluntarily register their manufacturing plants with FDA, file cosmetic formulas, and report adverse reactions.

Cosmetics sold to consumers must bear labels that list ingredients in descending order of predominance. Trade secrets (as defined by FDA) and the ingredients of flavors and fragrances do not have to be specifically listed.

Words and Expressions

authority [ɔːˈθɔriti]   *n.* 权力，权威，当局，职权

regulate [ˈregjuleit]   *v.* 有系统的管理，规定，调节

substantiate [sʌbsˈtænʃieit]   *v.* 证实，实体化

establishment [isˈtæbliʃmənt]   *n.* 公司，确立，制定，设施

keep abreast of   了解……的最新情况

participate in   *v.* 参加，参与，分享

forward [ˈfɔːwəd]   *vt.* 转寄，促进，运送；*a.* 早的，迅速的，前进的；
   ad. 向前地，向将来

recall [riˈkɔːl]   *n.* 召回，回忆，取消；*v.* 回想起，召回，恢复

defective [diˈfektiv]   *a.* 有缺陷的，欠缺，不完全变化动词；*n.* 有缺陷

的人，不完全变化动词

monitor ['mɔnitə] v. 监视，监听，监督，（计算机）监视；n. 监督器，级长，监听员

conduct ['kɔndʌkt,-dəkt] n. 行为，举动，品行；vt. 引导，指挥，管理；vt. 导电，传热

injurious [in'dʒuəriəs] a. 有害的

improperly [im'prɔpəli] ad. 不正确地，不适当地

inspection [in'spekʃən] n. 检查，视察

follow-up n. 追踪调查，追踪报道，后续产品；a. 继续的，作为重复的

take action 采取行动（进行活动），提起诉讼

Department of Justice 律政司

misbrand ['mis'brænd] vt. 贴错标签，贴假商标于

After-Reading Task

1. According to FDA's duty, which one is not ture?
   A. FDA is only able to regulate cosmetics after products are released to the marketplace.
   B. Cosmetic products aren't reviewed or approved by FDA before they are sold to the public.
   C. Cosmetic ingredients aren't reviewed or approved by FDA before they are sold to the public.
   D. FDA can require companies to do safety testing of their cosmetic products before marketing.

2. How did FDA collect the information about the cosmetic products?
   A. FDA has the authority to require manufacturers to register their cosmetic establishments, file data on ingredients, or report cosmetic-related injuries.
   B. FDA maintains a voluntary data collection program.
   C. Cosmetic companies must participate in the program forward data to FDA.
   D. FDA can recommend private laboratories to consumers for sample analysis.

3. If FDA wishes to remove a cosmetic product from the market, it must _____ .
   A. first prove in a court of law that the product may be injurious to users,

improperly labeled, or otherwise violates the law

B. call back products that present a hazard or that are somehow defective

C. remove a cosmetic product from the market

D. collects cosmetic product samples

4. According to FDA's definition of the term "Cosmetics", which one is the part of cosmetics?

 A. skin care   B. fragrances

 C. hair coloring preparations   D. all of the above

5. which of the following is ture from the article?

 A. Manufacturing or holding cosmetics under insanitary conditions, using non-permitted colors, or including any filthy, putrid or decomposed substance is also illegal.

 B. Manufacturers needn't test color additives for safety and gain FDA approval for their intended use.

 C. Cosmetic manufacturer can't use any ingredient or raw material and market the final product without government approval.

 D. biothionol and hexachlorophene aren't the prohibited ingredients.

Further Reading

Drug Administration Law of the People's Republic of China

SDA Regulation; Order No. 13; Effective Date: 1999-09-01; Repeal Date: 2003-09-01

(Promulgated by Order No. 13 of the State Drug Administration on September 1, 1999, effective as of the date of promulgation, and abolished on September 1, 2003)

Chapter I -General Provisions

Article 1 The China GCP is formulated to ensure the clinical trial process standardized, the results scientific and credible, and the rights, benefits and safety of trial subjects protected. It is established pursuant to the Drug Control Law of People's Republic of China and refering to the international recognized principles.

Article 2 The China GCP is a standard regarding the whole

53

process of clinical trials including protocol designing, organizing, implementing, monitoring, auditing, recording, analyzing, and reporting.

Article 3 The clinical trials of all drugs, in various phases, including human bioavailability or bioequivalance study must be performed according to the China GCP Guidelines.

Chapter Ⅱ-Preparations and Prerequisites for a Clinical Trial

Article 4 All research involving human subjects should be conducted in accordance with the ethical principles, contained in "Declaration of Helsinki" (see Annex 1), namely justice, respect for persons, beneficence (to maximize benefits and to minimize harms and wrongs) and non-maleficent (to do no harm), as defined by the current revision of "International Ethical Guidelines for Biomedical Research Involving Human Subjects" issued by the Council for International Organizations of Medical Sciences (CIOMS). All individuals involved in the conduct of any clinical trial must be fully informed of the trial.

People involved must comply with these principles, and adhere to Chinese laws and regulations relating to the drug control.

Article 5 To initiate a clinical trial, sufficient scientific rationale should be provided. Prior to planning of a clinical trial in humans, the specific aims, the problems to be solved, anticipated efficacy and possible risks must be considered carefully. Anticipated benefits should prevail over possible risks. The chosen clinical trial methods must conform to the scientific and ethical standard.

Article 6 Investigational product (s) should be prepared and provided by the sponsor. Before conducting clinical trials, the sponsor is responsible for providing pre-clinical data of the investigational product, including composition of the formula, manufacturing process, and quality analysis reports. The pharmaceutical, pre-clinical, and existing clinical data should meet the requirements for conducting respective phases of the clinical trial. In addition, the information on safety and efficacy collected in completed and ongoing clinical trials elsewhere with the investigational product should be also provided to prove that the investigational product is appropriate for clinical trials, so as to indicate its safety and possible clinical application.

Article 7 The facilities and conditions of the study sites involved in the clinical trial should comply with the requirements for conducting the trial safely and efficiently. Each investigator should have appropriate expertise, qualifications and competence as well as training in the GCP to undertake a proposed study. Prior to the trial, the investigator (s) and the sponsor should reach an agreement on the protocol, the monitoring and auditing, standard operating procedures (SOP), and the allocation of trial-related responsibilities.

Lesson 6   Hypoallergenic Cosmetics

Hypoallergenic cosmetics are products that manufacturers claim produce fewer allergic reactions than other cosmetic products. Consumers with hypersensitive skin, and even those with "normal" skin, may be led to believe that these products will be gentler to their skin than non-hypoallergenic cosmetics.

There are no Federal standards or definitions that govern the use of the term "hypoallergenic." The term means whatever a particular company wants it to mean. Manufacturers of cosmetics labeled as hypoallergenic are not required to submit substantiation of their hypoallergenicity claims to FDA.

The term "hypoallergenic" may have considerable market value in promoting cosmetic products to consumers on a retail basis, but dermatologists say it has very little meaning.

Ever since the days when "She's lovely, she's engaged, she uses Ponds" became one of the best known advertising slogans in America, cosmetics manufacturers have pursued consumers with promises of everything from new beauty to a new lifestyle. Indeed, with cosmetics-perhaps more than with any other type of product-promotion is the key to sales success. Recognizing this, manufacturers have used a wide variety of appeals to break into or increase their share in this lucrative market.

For many years, companies have been producing products which they claim are "hypoallergenic" or "safe for sensitive skin" or "allergy tested. " These statements imply that the products making the claims are less likely to cause allergic reactions than competing products. But there has been no assurance to consumers that this actually was the case.

For the past four years, the Food and Drug Administration has been working to clear up this confusion of claims by establishing testing requirements that would determine which products really are "hypoallergenic. " But late last year, the U. S. Court of Appeals for the District of Columbia ruled that FDA's regulation defining "hypoallergenic" was invalid. This means there is now no regulation specifically defining or governing the use of the term "hypoallergenic" or similar claims. And because of the lengthy procedural steps required to establish a new regulation, that is likely to be the situation for some time to come.

Where does that leave consumers?

Consumers concerned about allergic reactions from cosmetics should understand one basic fact: there is no such thing as a "non-allergenic" cosmetic-that is, a cosmetic that can be guaranteed never to produce an allergic reaction.

56

But are some cosmetics less likely to produce adverse reactions than competing products?

By and large, the basic ingredients in so-called "hypoallergenic" cosmetics are the same as those used in other cosmetics sold for the same purposes. Years ago, some cosmetics contained harsh ingredients that had a high potential for causing adverse reactions. But these ingredients are no longer used. FDA knows of no scientific studies which show that "hypoallergenic" cosmetics or products making similar claims actually cause fewer adverse reactions than competing conventional products.

FDA's ill-fated regulation on "hypoallergenic" cosmetics was first issued as a proposal in February 1974. It said that a cosmetic would be permitted to be labeled "hypoallergenic" or make similar claims only if scientific studies on human subjects showed that it caused a significantly lower rate of adverse skin reactions than similar products not making such claims. The manufacturers of cosmetics claiming to be "hypoallergenic" were to be responsible for carrying out the required tests.

Numerous comments on the proposal were received from consumers, consumer groups and cosmetic manufacturers. Some people urged a ban on the use of the term "hypoallergenic" on grounds that most consumers don't have allergies. Others suggested that the term be banned because allergic individuals cannot use "hypoallergenic" products with any assurance of safety. A number of cosmetic manufacturers complained about the requirement for product comparison tests to validate claims of hypoallergenicity. Among other things, they said the tests would pose an undue economic burden on them.

In responding to the comments, FDA pointed out that the proposed regulation was not intended to solve all problems concerning cosmetic safety. The primary purpose of the regulation, the Agency said, was to clear up confusion about the term "hypoallergenic" and to establish a definition that could be used uniformly by manufacturers and understood by consumers.

FDA issued its final regulation on "hypoallergenic" cosmetics on June 6, 1975. Although the final regulation did require comparative tests, procedures for carrying out the tests were changed to reduce the costs to the manufacturers.

The new regulation was quickly challenged in the U. S. District Court for the District of Columbia by Almay and Clinique, makers of "hypoallergenic" cosmetics. The two firms charged that FDA had no authority to issue the regulation, but the court upheld FDA.

The firms then appealed to the U. S. Court of Appeals for the District of Columbia, which ruled that the regulation was invalid. The appeals court held that FDA's definition of the term "hypoallergenic" was unreasonable because the Agency had not demonstrated that consumers perceive the term "hypoallergenic" in the way described in the regulation.

As a result of the decision, manufacturers may continue to label and advertise their cosmetics as "hypoallergenic" or make similar claims without any supporting evidence. Consumers will have no assurance that such claims are valid.

However, cosmetics users who know they are allergic to certain ingredients can take steps to protect themselves. FDA regulations now require the ingredients used in cosmetics to be listed on the product label, so consumers can avoid substances that have caused them problems.

Words and Expressions

allergic [əˈləːdʒik]   *a.* 过敏的

58

substantiation [sʌbs'tænʃieitʃən] n. 实体化，证实，证明

demonstrate ['demənstreit] v. 示范，演示，证明，示威

ingredient [in'gri:diənt] n. 成分，因素

standard ['stændəd] a. 标准的；n. 标准

pursue [pə'sju:] v. 追求，追捕，继续从事

promotion [prə'məuʃən] n. 促进，提升

appeal（to）[ə'pi:l] n. 恳求，上诉，吸引力；v. 求助，诉请，呼吁

lucrative ['lu:krətiv, lju:-] a. 有利益的，获利的，合算的

assurance n. 保证，确信，保险

clear up 整顿，清理，收拾；说明，澄清；解决；（天气）转晴；消除，解除（疑虑等）

invalid [in'vælid] a. 无效的，伤残的；n. 病人，残疾者

specifically [spi'sifikəli] ad. 特定地，明确地

lengthy ['leŋθi] a. 冗长的，漫长的

guarantee [ˌgærən'ti:] v. & n. 保证，担保；vt. 保证

harsh [hɑ:ʃ] a. 粗糙的，刺耳的，严厉的

ban [bæn] n. 禁令；v. 禁止；vt. 禁止，取缔

validate ['vælideit] v. 使……有效，确认

undue ['ʌn'dju:] a. 过分的，不适当的

challenge ['tʃælindʒ] n. 挑战；v. 向……挑战

upheld [ʌp'held] v. 支持

Glossary

Relevant organizations of cosmetics abroad
国外化妆品相关机构

全　　称	缩　写	中　文　名
American Society of Perfumers	ASP	美国调香师学会
Chemical Abstracts Service	CAS	化学文摘社
Code of Federal Regulations	CFR	联邦法规代码（美国）
Cosmetic Ingredient Review	CIR	化妆品成分评估（美国）

全　称	缩　写	中　文　名
European Cosmetic. Toiletry and Perfumery Association	Colipa	欧洲化妆品，盥洗用品和香料协会
European Economic Community	EEC	欧洲经济共同体
European Inventory of Existing Chemical Substance	EINECS	欧洲现有化学品目录
European Union	EU	欧共体
Food and Drug Administration	FDA	食品和药品管理局(美国)
Fragrance Materials Association of the U. S	FMA	美国日用品香料协会
International Fragrance Association	IFRA	国际日用香料香精协会
International Nomencalture Cosmetic Ingredient	INCI	化妆品成分国际名称
International Nomenclature Committee	INC	国际命名委员会(属 CIFA)
International Organization for Stantardization	ISO	国际标准化组织
Japanese Cosmetic Ingredients Codex	JCIC	日本化妆品成分法典
Japanese Standards of Cosmetic In gredients	JSCI	日本化妆品成分标准
Research Institute for Fragrance Materials	RIFM	国际日用香料研究所
Society of Flavor Chemists	SFC	美国食品香料化学师学会
The Comprehensive Licensing Standards of Cosmetics by Category	JCIS	化妆品分类综合发证标准(日本)
the Cosmetic，Toiletry and Frarance Association	CTFA	化妆品、盥洗用品和香精协会(美国)
Flavor and Extract Manufactures Association of the United States	FEMA	美国食品香料与萃取物制造者协会
Council of Europe and Experts on Flavoring Substances	CoE-EFS	欧洲理事会及食品香料物质专家委员会
International Federation of Essential oil and Aroma Trades	IFEAT	国际精油和香料贸易联合会
International Organization of the Flavor Industry	IOFI	国际食品香料香精工业组织
Joint FAO/WHO Codex Alimentarius Commission	FAO/ (WHO-CAC)	联合国粮农组织/世界卫生组织联合食品法典委员会
Soap and Detergent Association	SDA	肥皂和洗涤剂协会

After-Reading Task

1. In the sentence "The two firms charged that FDA had no authority to issue the regulation, but the court *upheld* FDA." the italicized word cannot be replaced by ____ .
   A. upset   B. hold   C. support   D. backup
2. In the sentence "they said the tests would pose an *undue* economic burden on them." the italicized word can be replaced by ____ .
   A. not proper   B. excessive
   C. not sufficient   D. not yet payable or due
3. Which of the following probably believes the hypersensitive cosmetics?
   A. Consumers   B. Dermatologists
   C. Manufacturers   D. FDA
4. About hypoallergenic cosmetics, which one is true?
   A. All consumers believe that hypoallergenic cosmetics will be gentler to their skin than non-hypoallergenic cosmetics.
   B. FDA cannot regulate the "hypoallergenic" cosmetics
   C. Manufacturers may advertise their cosmetics as "hypoallergenic" without any supporting evidence.
   D. A new regulation of hypoallergenic cosmetics will be established soon.
5. Why did the U. S. Court of Appeals not uphold the regulation? Because the U. S. Court of Appeals think that ____ .
   A. "hypoallergenic" cosmetics are less likely to cause allergic reactions than competing products
   B. "hypoallergenic" cosmetics will be gentler to their skin than non-hypoallergenic cosmetics
   C. Product comparison tests would pose an undue economic burden on the manufacturers
   D. FDA had no sufficient relative evidence

Further Reading

Do cosmetics cause allergies?

Overuse of some cosmetics can cause allergies and other skin problems. Ingredients such as fragrance and preservatives can cause

61

allergic reactions in some people. Skin reactions, which doctors call contact dermatitis, should be taken seriously. Even if you've used a cosmetic for years with no problems, you can develop an allergic reaction as you become sensitized to one or more of the ingredients.

Some cosmetics are labeled "allergy-tested" or "hypoallergenic," but products with these claims don't always offer a solution to cosmetic allergies. "Hypoallergenic" means only that the manufacturer feels that the product is less likely to cause an allergic reaction. Before placing this claim on the label, some companies conduct tests, and others simply don't include perfumes or other common problem-causing ingredients in their products. The claim "dermatologist-tested" on some cosmetic products only means that a skin doctor has tested the product to see if it will generally cause allergenic problems. Other label claims that carry no guarantee that they won't cause reactions include "sensitivity-tested" and "non-irritating."

"Natural" ingredients are extracted directly from plants or animal products as opposed to being produced synthetically. Natural ingredients can cause allergic reactions. If you have an allergy to certain plants or animals, you could have an allergic reaction to cosmetics containing those ingredients. For instance, "lanolin," extracted from sheep wool, is an ingredient in many moisturizers and is a common cause of allergies.

Lesson 7   Is It a Cosmetic, a Drug, or Both?

The legal difference between a cosmetic and a drug is determined by a product's intended use. Different laws and regulations apply to each type of product. Firms sometimes violate the law by marketing a cosmetic with a drug claim, or by marketing a drug as if it were a cosmetic, without adhering to requirements for drugs.

How does the law define a cosmetic?

The Food, Drug, and Cosmetic Act (FD&C Act) defines cosmetics by their intended use, as "articles intended to be rubbed, poured, sprinkled, or sprayed on, introduced into, or otherwise applied to the human body... for cleansing, beautifying, promoting attractiveness, or altering the appearance". Among the products included in this definition are skin moisturizers, perfumes, lipsticks, fingernail polishes, eye and facial makeup preparations, shampoos, permanent waves, hair colors, toothpastes, and deodorants, as well as any material intended for use as a component of a cosmetic product.

How does the law define a drug?

The FD&C Act defines drugs by their intended use, as "(A) articles intended for use in the diagnosis, cure, mitigation, treatment, or prevention of disease and (B) articles (other than food) intended to affect the structure or any function of the body of man or other animals".

How can a product be both a cosmetic and a drug?

Some products meet the definitions of both cosmetics and drugs. This may happen when a product has two intended uses. For example, a shampoo is a cosmetic because its intended use is to cleanse the hair. An antidandruff treatment is a drug because its intended use is to treat dandruff. Consequently, an antidandruff shampoo is both a cosmetic and a drug. Among other cosmetic/drug combinations are toothpastes that contain fluoride, deodorants that are also antiperspirants, and moisturizers and makeup marketed with sunprotection claims. Such products must comply with the requirements for both cosmetics and drugs.

What about "cosmeceuticals"?

The FD&C Act does not recognize any such category as "cosmeceuticals." A product can be a drug, a cosmetic, or a combination of both, but the term "cosmeceutical" has no meaning under the law.

How is a product's intended use established?

Intended use may be established in a number of ways. Among them are:

Claims stated on the product labeling, in advertising, on the Internet, or in other promotional materials. Certain claims may cause a product to be considered a drug, even if the product is marketed as if it were a cosmetic. Such claims establish the product as a drug because the intended use is to treat or prevent disease or otherwise affect the structure or functions of the human body. Some examples are claims that products will restore hair growth, reduce cellulite, treat varicose veins, or revitalize cells.

Consumer perception, which may be established through the product's reputation. This means asking why the consumer is buying it and what the consumer expects it to do.

Ingredients that may cause a product to be considered a drug because they have a well known (to the public and industry) therapeutic use. An example is fluoride in toothpaste.

This principal also holds true for essential oils in fragrance products. A fragrance marketed for promoting attractiveness is a cosmetic. But a fragrance marketed with certain "aromatherapy" claims, such as assertions that the scent will help the consumer sleep or quit smoking, meets the definition of a drug because of its intended use.

How are the laws and regulations different for cosmetics and drugs?

The following information is not a complete treatment of cosmetic or drug laws and regulations. It is intended only to alert you to some important differences between the laws and regulations for cosmetics and drugs in the areas of approval, good manufacturing practice, registration, and labeling. You should direct questions regarding laws and regulations for drugs to CDER (Center for Drug Evaluation and Research).

How approval requirements are different

FDA does not have a premarket approval system for cosmetic products or ingredients, with the important exception of color additives. Drugs, however, are subject to FDA approval. Generally, drugs must either receive premarket approval by FDA or conform to final regulations specifying conditions whereby they are generally recognized as safe and effective, and not misbranded. Currently, certain— but not all—over-the-counter (OTC) drugs (that is, non-prescription drugs) that were marketed before the beginning of the OTC Drug Review (May 11, 1972) may be marketed without specific approval pending publication of final regulations under the ongoing OTC Drug Review. Once a regulation covering a specific class of OTC drugs is final, those drugs must either be the subject of an approved New Drug Application (NDA), or comply with the appropriate monograph, or rule, for an OTC drug.

What do these terms mean?

An NDA is the vehicle through which drug sponsors formally propose that FDA approve a new pharmaceutical for sale and marketing in the U. S. FDA only approves an NDA after determining, for example, that the data are adequate to show the drug's safety and effectiveness for its proposed use and that its benefits outweigh the risks. The NDA system is also used for new ingredients entering the OTC marketplace for the first time. For example, the newer OTC products (previously available only by prescription)

65

are first approved through the NDA system and their 'switch' to OTC status is approved via the NDA system.

FDA has published monographs, or rules, for a number of OTC drug categories. These monographs, which are published in the Federal Register, state requirements for categories of non-prescription drugs, such as what ingredients may be used and for what intended use. Among the many non-prescription drug categories covered by OTC monographs are acne medications, treatments for dandruff, seborrheic dermatitis, and psoriasis, sunscreens.

A note on "new drugs": Despite the word "new," a "new drug" may have been in use for many years. If a product is intended for use as a drug, no matter how ancient or "traditional" its use may be, once the agency has made a final determination on the status of an OTC drug product it must have an approved NDA or comply with the appropriate OTC monograph to be marketed legally in interstate commerce. Certain OTC drugs may remain on the market without NDA approval pending final regulations covering the appropriate class of drugs.

Where to learn more about NDAs and OTC monographs: If you have questions about NDAs and OTC monographs, you should address them to CDER. The CDER Handbook provides an introduction to the drug approval and OTC monograph processes. Other resources, also available on CDER's Web site, provide additional information on these subjects.

How good manufacturing practice requirements are different

Good manufacturing practice (GMP) is an important factor in assuring that your cosmetic products are neither adulterated nor misbranded. However, no regulations set forth specific GMP requirements for cosmetics. In contrast, the law requires strict adherence to GMP requirements for drugs, and there are regulations specifying minimum current GMP requirements for drugs. Failure to follow GMP requirements causes a drug to be adulterated.

How registration requirements are different

FDA maintains the Voluntary Cosmetic Registration Program, or VCRP, for cosmetic establishments and formulations. As its name indicates, this program is voluntary. In contrast, it is mandatory for drug firms to register their establishments and list their drug products with FDA.

How labeling requirements are different

A cosmetic product must be labeled according to cosmetic labeling regulations. See the Cosmetic Labeling Manual for guidance on cosmetic labeling. OTC drugs must be labeled according to OTC drug regulations, including the "Drug Facts" labeling, as described in 21 CFR 201. 63. Combination OTC drug/cosmetic products must have combination OTC drug/cosmetic labeling. For example, the drug ingredients must be listed alphabetically as "Active Ingredients," followed by cosmetic ingredients, listed in order of predominance as "Inactive Ingredients. "

And what if it's "soap"?

Soap is a category that needs special explanation. That's because the regulatory definition of "soap" is different from the way in which people commonly use the word. Products that meet the definition of "soap" are exempt from the provisions of the FD&C Act because—even though Section 201 (i) (1) of the act includes "articles. . . for cleansing" in the definition of a cosmetic—Section 201 (i) (2) excludes soap from the definition of a cosmetic.

How FDA defines "soap"

Not every product marketed as soap meets FDA's definition of the term. FDA interprets the term "soap" to apply only when the bulk of the nonvolatile matter in the product consists of an alkali

67

salt of fatty acids and the product's detergent properties are due to the alkali-fatty acid compounds, and the product is labeled, sold, and represented solely as soap.

If a product intended to cleanse the human body does not meet all the criteria for soap, as listed above, it is either a cosmetic or a drug. For example:

If a product consists of detergents or primarily of alkali salts of fatty acids and is intended not only for cleansing but also for other cosmetic uses, such as beautifying or moisturizing, it is regulated as a cosmetic.

If a product consists of detergents or primarily of alkali salts of fatty acids and is intended not only for cleansing but also to cure, treat, or prevent disease or to affect the structure or any function of the human body, it is regulated as a drug.

If a product is intended solely for cleansing the human body and has the characteristics consumers generally associate with soap, does not consist primarily of alkali salts of fatty acids, it may be identified in labeling as soap, but it is regulated as a cosmetic.

Words and Expressions

adhere to   坚持，依附

sprinkle ['spriŋkl]   *v.* 洒，散置，微雨

spray on   喷射

alter   *v.* 改变

lipstick ['lipstik]   *n.* 口红

fingernail polish   *n.* 指甲油

permanent wave   电烫发

toothpaste ['tu:θpeist]   *n.* 牙膏

68

deodorant［diːˈəudərənt］ n. 除臭剂

diagnosis［ˌdaiəgˈnəusis］ n. 诊断

mitigation［ˌmitiˈgeiʃən］ n. 缓和，减轻，镇静

antidandruff a. 去头屑的

fluoride［ˈflu(:)əraid］ n.（护齿的）氟化物

antiperspirant n. 止汗药

comply with vi. 应允，同意，遵照，根据

restore［risˈtɔː］ v. 回复，恢复，归还

cellulite［ˈseljəlait］ n.（胖女人臀腿部的）脂肪团

varicose vein 静脉曲张

revitalize［riːˈvaitəlaiz］ v. 使复活，使重新充满活力；vt. 使复兴，使苏醒，便复活，使恢复

essential oil n. 香精油

fragrance［ˈfreigrəns］ n. 芬芳，香气，香味

aromatherapy 用香料按摩

scent［sent］ n. 气味，香味，痕迹；(v. 闻出，循着遗臭追踪，发觉)

good manufacturing practice GMP 良好生产规范

registration［ˌredʒisˈtreiʃən］ n. 登记，注册

monograph［ˈmɔnəugrɑːf］ n. 专题论文

seborrheic［ˌsebəuˈtrəufik］ a.［生理］刺激泌脂的

dermatitis［ˌdəːməˈtaitis］ n.［医］皮炎

psoriasis［psɔ(:)ˈraiəsis］ n.［医］牛皮癣，银屑癣

sunscreen［ˈsʌnskriːn］ n.（防晒油中的）遮光剂

interstate［ˌintə(:)ˈsteit］ a. 洲际的

pending［ˈpendiŋ］ a. 未决定的，待决的；(prep. 直到，当……的时候)

address［əˈdres］ n. 住址；n. 致词，讲话；vt. 发表演说，写地址（图书、文章等）讨论（某主题）

adulterate［əˈdʌltəreit］ v. 搀……使品质变劣

the Voluntary Cosmetic Registration Program CVRP 化妆品自愿登记程序

mandatory ['mændətəri]   *a.* 命令的，强制性的

alphabetically   *ad.* 按字母表顺序地

in order of predominance   静脉曲张

alkali salt of fatty acids   *n.* 脂肪酸碱盐

criteria [krai'tiəriə]   *n.* 标准

Glossary

Multi-	多元	Moisturisor	保湿面霜
Normal	中性(皮肤)	Cream	霜
Oily	油性(皮肤)	Lotion	水、露
Dry	干性(皮肤)	Milk	乳
Combination	混合性(皮肤)	Pack	剥撕式面膜
Balancing	平衡酸碱	Peeling	敷面剥落式面膜
Oil-control	抑制油脂	Acne/Spot	青春痘用品
Nutritious	滋养	Clean-/Purify-	清洁用
Anti-	抗、防	Whiten	美白用
Anti-wrinkle	抗老防皱	Sunblock	防晒用
Firm	紧肤	Facial	脸部用
Sensitive	敏感性皮肤	Hydra-	保湿用
Aftersun	日晒后用品	Scrub	磨砂式(去角质)
Alcohol-free	无酒精	Waterproof	防水
Essence	精华液	Fast/Quickdry	快干
Toner	化妆水	Gentle	温和的
Toning lotion	化妆水	Foam	泡沫
Pressed powder	粉饼	Longlasting	持久性
Foundation	粉底	Repair	修护
Makeup	粉底、彩妆	Trentment	修护
Remover	去除、卸妆	Active	赋活用
Correct	遮瑕膏	Day	日间用
Eye gel	眼胶	Night	夜用
Eye mask	眼膜	Revitalite	活化
Eye shadow	眼影	Nutritious	滋养
Eyeliner	眼线(笔、刷)		

After-Reading Task

1. According to FD & C Act's definition, which one is not true?
   A. Cosmetic has its intended use, such as cleansing, promoting attractiveness and so on.
   B. Cosmetics are only applied to the facial beauty.
   C. Cosmetic products include the products of polishing fingernail and cleansing teeth.
   D. Material may also can be a cosmetic product.

2. About a drug, which one is untrue?
   A. The drug can affect the structure of the body of a man.
   B. The drug can be used to cleanse human body.
   C. The drug can be used to prevent a disease.
   D. The drug is impossible to be a cosmetic.

3. Product intended use may be established in a number of ways except ____ .
   A. state the definition of a drug or a cosmetic
   B. state certain claims to cause a cosmetic to be considered a drug
   C. ask consumer about the reason and expectation
   D. state the component, which has a well known especial use

4. Which statements of the terms is true?
   A. FDA doesn't have a pre-market approval system for cosmetic products including color additives.
   B. NDA only approves an FDA after determining the benefits outweigh the risk.
   C. The newer OTC products' switch to OTC status is approved via the NDA system.
   D. Once a regulation covering a specific class of OTC drugs is final those drugs must not be the subject of an approved NDA.

5. If people have questions about NDAs and OTC monographs, they should turn to ____ .
   A. FD&C Act   B. NDA's web site
   C. OTC's web site   D. CDER

6. A GMP is ____ .
   A. to assure your cosmetic products are misbranded
   B. set for cosmetics and drugs with the same requirements
   C. strictly set for cosmetic, otherwise, it can cause cosmetic to be adulterated

71

D. none of the above

7. In the sentence "the drug ingredients must be listed *alphabetically*" the italicized word can be replaced by ____ .

   A. simultaneously   B. in the order of importance

   C. randomly   D. in the order of letters

8. What is a "soap" in regulatory definition?

   A. the word people commonly use

   B. the "soap" products are the same in the provisions of FD&C Act.

   C. soap is the articles for cleansing.

   D. as it stated in section 201 (i) (1), soap is not a cosmetic.

9. How labeling requirements ate different?

   A. A cosmetic must be labeled according to OTC Labeling regulations.

   B. A OTC drugs must be labeled according to CLM for guidance.

   C. Combination OTC drug/cosmetic products must have combination OTC drug/cosmetic labeling.

   D. All of the above

10. According to FDA's definition of the term "soap", when is it regulated as a drug?

    A. when it consists of detergents.

    B. when it is intended solely for cleansing the human body.

    C. when it is intended not for cleansing but for other uses, such as beautifying or moisturizing.

    D. when it does not consist primarily of alkali salts fatty.

11. Which statement is true?

    A. The articles for cleansing are always regulated as a cosmetic.

    B. Sunscreens, antidandruff shampoo and acne medications are among the many non-prescription drug categories covered by OTC monographs.

    C. A cosmetic and drug are the same in the registration requirements but different in labeling requirements.

    D. A product can be either a cosmetic or a drug but not be the combination of cosmetic and a drug.

Further Reading

Cruelty Free—Not Tested on Animals

Some cosmetic companies promote their products with claims

such as "CRUELTY-FREE" or "NOT TESTED ON ANIMALS" in their labeling or advertising. The unrestricted use of these phrases by cosmetic companies is possible because there are no legal definitions for these terms.

Some companies may apply such claims solely to their finished cosmetic products. However, these companies may rely on raw material suppliers or contract laboratories to perform any animal testing necessary to substantiate product or ingredient safety. Other cosmetic companies may rely on combinations of scientific literature, non-animal testing, raw material safety testing, or controlled human use testing to substantiate their product safety.

Many raw materials, used in cosmetics, were tested on animals years ago when they were first introduced. A cosmetic manufacturer might only use those raw materials and base their "cruelty-free" claims on the fact that the materials or products are not "currently" tested on animals.

Lesson 8   Cosmetic Labeling

How can you be sure your shampoo that claims to have all natural ingredients does not also contain some synthetic chemicals? Or that your hand lotion actually does contain the vitamin hit claims? The logical response should be, "Read the ingredient label on the back of the product. " Logical, if you happen to be a chemist or a cosmetic scientist. Perplexing, if you are the average cosmetic consumer.

A quick glance at the back of the cosmetic label is all it takes to see that the ingredients are written in the language of chemistry. Unless you know that one of the shampoo ingredients—methyl paraben—is a synthetic preservative derived from a petroleum base, or that tocopherol is vitamin E, you may never be able to check the claims against the contents.

Most of us don't recognize the names of the ingredients listed. But there's no way to change that and still accurately identify the ingredients.

Chemical names are the only way ingredients can be listed because that's what they are. Most are cosmetic formulations, but in some products, such as an underarm deodorant that also claims to stop perspiration, the first chemical listed may be a drug ingredient and FDA would classify the product as a drug as well as a cosmetic.

Many ingredients are marketed with trade names, but these often provide little clue to the identity and intended use of the material. Trade names in the ingredient list could be confusing to consumers purchasing a cosmetic because they would have no way to compare similar ingredients in similar products. Also, some trade names include mixtures of raw materials—for example, an ingredient could be combined with a preservative.

Despite the highly technical language of the ingredient list, it's entirely possible for consumers to get valuable information about a product by checking the label-front and back. To decode the cosmetic label, here's what you need to know.

Image vs. Reality Don't be fooled by claims made for certain cosmetic ingredients. Their presence in the products could be pure puffery because the law does not require cosmetic manufacturers to substantiate performance claims.

"Image is what the cosmetic industry sells through its products," Bailey says, "and it's up to the consumer to believe it or not."

FDA considers the labeling of vitamins in cosmetics a separate issue, however, and does not recognize health claims for them in cosmetics. A product that features a vitamin—for example, vitamin E—must list it by its chemical name TOCOPHEROL on the ingredient list. Listing it as a vitamin in the ingredient statement would give the misleading impression that vitamin E in the product offers a nutrient or health benefit (Vitamin E is usually added as an antioxidant to prevent chemical deterioration of the product).

Consumers can get important health and value information by checking the ingredient list. For example, if you need fragrance-free hair spray because you have a sensitivity, a product containing a fragrance—even one that just masks the chemical odors of the raw materials—could be a waste of money if you can't use it.

Ingredient statements on cosmetics were first required in 1973 under the Fair Packaging and Labeling Act (FPLA), enforced by FDA. Before then, consumers could only guess what was in a cosmetic product or if the product contained what it claimed. That requirement is especially valuable today with the industry competition for new ingredients.

The law allows a manufacturer to ask FDA to grant "trade secret" status for a particular ingredient. FDA grants this status under vary limited circumstances and after careful review of the manufacturer's data. The manufacturer must prove that the ingredient imparts some unique property to a product and that the ingredient is not well-known in the industry. If trade secret status is granted, the ingredient does not have to be listed on the label, but the list must end with the phrase "and other ingredients."

Consumers can also check value by comparing ingredient lists of similar products. Ingredients are listed in descending order, starting with the greatest amount in the product. A lotion with a featured ingredient close to the beginning of the list, for example, would have more of that ingredient than any other ingredient. A featured ingredient listed close to the end suggests that not much of that ingredient is present.

Anyone curious about an ingredient in a cosmetic can find answers in the International Cosmetic Ingredient Dictionary, published by the Cosmetic, Toiletries, and Fragrance Association. The dictionary provides a complete list of the most widely known cosmetic ingredients and their definitions and trade names.

Cosmetic ingredient declaration regulations apply only to retail products intended for home use. Products used exclusively by beauticians in beauty salons or cosmetic studios, and cosmetic samples such as those distributed free at hotels are not subject to the ingredient labeling rules. They must, however, state the name and address of the manufacturer, packer or distributor, and give an accurate statement of quantity and all necessary warning statements, as do all other cosmetics that weigh over one-fourth ounce or one-eighth fluid ounce.

Cosmetics That Are Also Drugs Cosmetics making therapeutic claims that they may affect the structure or function of the body are regulated as drugs and cosmetics and must meet the labeling requirements for both. One way you can tell if you're dealing with such a product is if the first entry in the ingredient list says "Active Ingredient. " However, active ingredients are not legally required to be identified by this term. The law does require the active ingredient (s) to be listed first, followed by a list of all inactive cosmetic ingredients.

Examples of products that are both cosmetics and drugs are shampoos that treat dandruff, fluoride toothpastes to prevent dental decay, and sunscreens and sunblocking cosmetics, including foundations that contain sunscreens.

A product with a drug and cosmetic classification must be scientifically proven safe and effective for its therapeutic claims before it is marketed. If the product is not, FDA considers it to be a misbranded drug and can take regulatory action.

Preventing Problems Under FDA's good manufacturing practice guidelines, even cosmetic products that are not regulated as drugs should be thoroughly tested for safety and subject to quality control during manufacture. But the law does not require the agency to review these tests before the cosmetics are marketed. Nevertheless, FDA does require safety warnings when problems become apparent.

Misuse of some cosmetic products can cause problems that range in severity from a mild rash to skin burns, or from burning eyes to blindness.

Look for warnings about the consequences of misuse required on products that could be hazardous, in addition to the detailed directions for use that appear on almost all cosmetics.

For example, products containing halocarbon or hydrocarbon propellants, such as aerosol hairsprays or deodorants, must bear the exact wording:

"Warning—Use only as directed. Intentional misuse by deliberately concentrating and inhaling the contents can be harmful or fatal." All cosmetics in self-pressurized containers, such as shaving creams, must have specifically worded warnings against spraying near the eyes, puncturing, incinerating, storing, and intentionally misusing.

"Keep out of the reach of children" is also required for all products in pressurized containers. In the case of products intended for use by children, such as foaming soap, the phrase "except under adult supervision" may be added.

Words and Expressions

perplexing ［pə'pleksiŋ］ *a.* 令人费解的，使人困惑的

tocopherol ［təu'kɔfərəul］ *n.* ［生化］生育酚，维生素 E

dilemma ［di'lemə,dai-］ *n.* 困境，进退两难

underarm ［'ʌndərɑːm］ *a.* 手臂下的，腋下的

clue ［kluː］ *n.* 线索；*v.* 提示

decode ［,diː'kəud］ *vt.* 解码，译解

trade secret *n.* 商业秘密，行业秘密

impart ［im'pɑːt］ *vt.* 给予，传授，告知

unique ［juː'niːk］ *a.* 独一无二的，独特的，稀罕的

descend ［di'send］ *v.* 下来，下降，遗传，突击

compendium ［kəm'pendiəm］ *n.* 简要，概略，提纲

beautician ［bjuː'tiʃən］ *n.* 美容师

entry ［'entri］ *n.* 进入，入口，登记

active ingredient　活性组分，有效成分

dental ［'dentl］ *a.* 牙齿的，牙科的

decay ［di'kei］ *n.* 衰退，腐败；*v.* 衰退，腐败

sunblock *n.* 防晒霜，紫外线防护霜

guideline ［'gaid,lain］ *n.* 指引

misuse ［'mis'juːz］ *vt.&n.* 误用，滥用

skin burn　皮肤烧伤

halocarbon ［,hæləu'kɑːbən］ *n.* 卤代烃（卤化碳）

hairspray *n.* 头发定型剂

inhale ［in'heil］ *v.* 吸入

puncture ［'pʌŋktʃə］ *n.* 刺穿

incinerate ［in'sinəreit］ *v.* 焚化，毁弃

intentionally ［in'tenʃənəli］ *a.* 企图地，策划地，故意地

78

hydratant/hydra/ mois-turize	保湿	waterproof	防水
hydra-move	动态保湿	soin/peau/teint	修饰肤色
hydra-balance	平衡保湿	anti-oxidant	抗氧化
poreminimizing /pore-re-ducer	收缩、细致毛孔	SPF/PA	防晒指数
lift/firming /contou-ring	紧实、提拉	exfoliant/gommage/scrub	去角质
sebum/shine/brilliance	控制皮脂分泌	repair/anti-age	修复、抗衰老
nutri/nutritive /nour-ishing	丰富营养、滋润	dual/3d/multi	两种、三种或多种功能

小　知　识

一、什么是化妆品的防晒指数 SPF

　　市售的防晒化妆品上一般都标有 SPF 三个英文字母及一个阿拉伯数字。所谓 SPF（英文："Sun Protection Factor" 的缩写），即防晒指数。如 SPF15 是指 15 倍的防晒强度，假设一个人在没有抹防晒霜的情况下晒 15 分钟皮肤开始出现红斑，那么抹上 SPF15 的防晒霜后，可保证她在 15×15 分钟后才会晒伤皮肤，这里 "15" 是倍数，一个倍数为 15 分钟至 20 分钟。目前市场上的防晒产品系从 6 倍到 40 倍不等，倍数越大，防晒时间越长，防晒效果越好；但系数高的产品往往含有大量物理或化学防晒剂，对皮肤的刺激较大一些，容易堵塞毛孔，甚至滋生暗疮和粉刺。

　　以前，防晒化妆品的系数越高，质地和触感越是黏腻、不透气，油性皮肤唯恐避之不及。现在好了，虽然防晒新品的系数日渐偏高，但大部分品牌都很好地消灭了油腻的缺陷，顾客再不必担心不透气。

二、如何选择合适的 SPF 值

　　防晒剂有两种：紫外线吸收剂和紫外线屏蔽剂（如二氧化钛和氧化锌的超微细粉末）。SPF 达到 20 以上的产品不含二氧化钛是不可能的。防晒剂在吸收紫外线的同时，对皮肤存在一定的刺激作用，如果紫外线吸收剂过量，还会成为皮肤的负担，因此，选择什么样的防晒品，要根据你的工作场所、时间及阳光的强度来决定。

　　如果你的工作在室内，外出活动不多，则使用 SPF 值以 15～20 的防晒产品即可；如果工作需要在外奔波或者节假日外出旅游，可用 SPF20 以上的产品；假如到海滨浴场或热带地区旅游，那就应该选择 SPF30 以上的防晒品了。具体来说：一般类型皮肤的人，SPF 值以 8～12 为宜；对光敏感的人，SPF 值以 12～20 为宜；敏感性皮肤应挑选植物配方的防晒品或是含有二氧化钛的太阳油，还可使用含有维生素 E 及不含防腐剂的产品，维生素 E 抗晒效能相当高，其拥有的润滑成分及净化作用，可中和因日晒造成的细胞损伤。使用果酸护肤品时，应配合防晒系数较高的物理性防晒品，防止新生的皮肤受到伤害。因为果酸护肤品会使皮肤变薄、较脆弱，不耐紫外线。

此外，选择防晒品还应视肤色而定。肤色白皙者最好选用 SPF 超过 30 的防晒品，防止斑点的产生；皮肤偏深者，平日用 SPF15 的防晒品即可。

After-Reading Task

1. What do you think of cosmetic labeling?

   A. If you are the average cosmetic consumer, you will be perplexed by the cosmetic label.

   B. If you are the chemist, you will be perplexed by the cosmetic label.

   C. The ingredients at the back of the cosmetic label are written in the language of chemistry.

   D. Most of us can recognize the names of the ingredients listed at the back of the cosmetic label.

2. Which statement is ture about decoding the cosmetic label?

   A. Most of us can recognize the names of the ingredients listed.

   B. There's no way to change that and still accurately identify the ingredients.

   C. Few ingredients are marketed with trade names.

   D. Trade names often provide much clue to the identity.

3. Chemical names are the only way ingredients can be listed because _____ .

   A. That's what they are.

   B. They are cosmetic formulations.

   C. They are drug ingredient.

   D. They are marketed with trade names.

4. Consumers can get valuable information about a product by _____ .

   A. checking the label-front and back and decoding the cosmetic label

   B. claims made for certain cosmetic ingredients

C. being a chemist

D. being a cosmetic scientist

5. Why vitamin E must list it in the ingredient statement by its chemical name TOCOPHEROL on the ingredient list?

A. Because health claims for them in cosmetics.

B. Listing it as a vitamin would give the misleading impression.

C. Vitamin E in the product offers a nutrient or health benefit.

D. Vitamin E is usually added as an antioxidant to prevent chemical deterioration of the product.

6. Consumers can get ____ by checking the ingredient list

A. a sensitivity

B. fragrance-free hair spray

C. chemical odors of the raw material

D. important health and value information

7. Which of the following is wrong about the Ingredient statements on cosmetics?

A. Ingredient statements on cosmetics were first enforced by FDA.

B. Ingredient statements on cosmetics were first required in 1973.

C. Ingredient requirement has none of value today with the industry competition for new ingredients.

D. Important value information can be get by checking the ingredient list.

8. According to the passage, which of the following statement about the "trade secret" status for a particular ingredient is not true?

A. The law allows a manufacturer to ask FPLA to grant "trade secret" status for a particular ingredient.

B. FDA grants this status under vary limited circumstances and after careful review of the manufacturer's data.

C. The manufacturer must prove that the ingredient imparts some unique property to a product.

D. The manufacturer must prove that the ingredient is not well-known in the industry

9. Anyone curious about an ingredient in a cosmetic can find answers in ____ .

A. the Cosmetic, Toiletries, and Fragrance Association

B. the International Cosmetic Ingredient Dictionary

C. the Fair Packaging and Labeling Act

D. FDA

10. Which statement is not ture about decoding the cosmetic ingredient declaration regulations?

   A. Cosmetic ingredient declaration regulations apply not only to retail products but also to beauty salons.

   B. Products used exclusively by beauticians in beauty salons or cosmetic studios, are not subject to the ingredient labeling rules.

   C. Cosmetic samples such as those distributed free at hotels are not subject to the ingredient labeling rules.

   D. Products intended for home use are subject to the ingredient labeling rules.

11. Which examples of products are neither cosmetics nor drugs?

   A. shampoos that treat dandruff

   B. normal foundations

   C. sunscreens and sunblocking cosmetics

   D. fluoride toothpastes to prevent dental decay

12. Which of the folowing statement is wrong about the product that both a drug and cosmetic?

   A. A product with a drug and cosmetic classification must be scientifically proven safe and effective for its therapeutic claims before it is marketed.

   B. If the product is not scientifically proven safe and effective, FDA considers it to be a misbranded drug and can take regulatory action.

   C. Misuse of some cosmetic products can cause problems that range in severity from a mild rash to skin burns, or from burning eyes to blindness.

   D. Cosmetic products that are not regulated as drugs shouldn't be tested for safety and subject to quality control during manufacture.

13. Some products required specific wording except ____ .

   A. Detergent bubble bath products

   B. Coal-tar color-containing hair-dye products

   C. Depilatories and hair straighteners

   D. Feminine deodorant sprays

14. Which of the following statement is wrong about the detergent bubble bath products?

   A. Excessive use or prolonged exposure may irritate skin and the urinary tract.

B. The labeling of detergent bubble bath products instructs users to continue the product if rash, redness or itching occur.

C. The labeling of detergent bubble bath products instructs users to consult a physician if imitation persists.

D. The labeling of detergent bubble bath product instructs users to keep out of reach of children.

15. According to the passage, which of the following statement is true about the coal-tar color-containing hair-dye products?

A. Coal-tar color-containing hair-dye products contain ingredients that may cause skin irritation on certain individuals.

B. A preliminary test according to the product's accompanying directions should last be made.

C. Users are cautioned to dye eyelashes or eyebrows because doing so may can't cause blindness.

D. The ammonia, detergents, conditioning agents, and dyes in hair-dye products are all weak eye irritants and could also cause allergic reactions in other areas.

16. Why the nail builders can cause irritation, inflammation and infection of the nail bed and nail fold?

A. Nail hardeners often contain formaldehyde and formaldehyde-releasing preservatives.

B. Enamels often contain formaldehyde and formaldehyde-releasing preservatives.

C. Because of residual traces of the methacrylate monomers.

D. Because of the high resin content or low concentration of plasticizer sealing the nail surface to air.

17. The label of flammable product usually cautions about avoiding _____ during use until the product is fully dry.

A. heat, fire and smoking   B. lighting a cigarette

C. igniting an engine   D. catching a fire

Further Reading

Differences between an OTC drug and a cosmetic

The Food, Drug & Cosmetic Act defines cosmetics as articles

intended to be applied to the human body for cleansing, beautifying, promoting attractiveness, or altering the appearance without affecting the body's structure or functions. Among the products included in this definition are skin creams, lotions, perfumes, lipsticks, fingernail polishes, eye and facial makeup preparations, permanent waves, hair colors, toothpastes, and deodorants, as well as any material intended for use as a component of a cosmetic product.

Products that intend to treat or prevent disease, or otherwise affect the structure or functions of the human body, are considered drugs. Over-the-counter drugs are drugs that can be purchased without a doctor's prescription. Examples of products that are over-the-counter drugs are fluoride toothpastes, hormone creams, sunscreen preparations, antiperspirants, and antidandruff shampoos.

UNIT THREE   SAFETY

Lesson 9   Are Hair Dyes Safe

The decision to change hair color has recently become more complicated because some recent studies have linked hair coloring with an increased risk of contracting certain cancers. To make matters more confusing other studies do not support those findings. Most hair dyes also don't have to go through pre-market testing for safety that other cosmetic color additives do before hitting store shelves. Consumers are often on their own consequently, when deciding whether hair dyes are safe.

FDA is responsible for overseeing the safety of cosmetics sold in this country and can prohibit the sale of any cosmetics found harmful—except most hair dyes. Although the adulteration provision of the Food, Drug, and Cosmetic Act enables FDA to seek removal of a cosmetic from the market if it is shown to be harmful under conditions of use, hair coloring made from coal-tar were given special exemption from bans when the act was passed in 1938.

The main ingredient in the coal-tar hair dyes manufactured at the time prompted an allergic reaction in some susceptible individuals. Fearing FDA would ban the sale of hair dyes because some users might develop a rash or have other allergic reactions, the industry successfully lobbied before the act passed to get coal-tar hair dyes exempted from the adulteration provision. Manufacturers were required, however, to include a warning in the labels that the products can cause skin irritation in certain allergic individuals. Most hair dyes in use today derive their ingredients from petroleum sources, but have been considered coal-tar dyes by FDA because they contain some of the same compounds found in these older dyes.

In 1978, FDA proposed to require a warning on the labels of hair dyes containing the compounds 4-methoxy-m-phenylenediamine (4MMPD) or 4-methoxy-m-phenylenediamine sulfate (4MMPD sulfate), two coal-tar ingredients. This followed findings by researchers at the National Cancer Institute in Bethesda, MD., that rodents fed either of the chemicals were more likely to develop cancer than animals not fed the substances.

The researchers put the compounds in the animals 'feed rather than on the animals' skin because they were trying to assess the effects of hair dye ingredients inside the body. (Other studies have shown that a small percentage of hair dye is absorbed from the scalp and passed into the bloodstream where it can travel to other organs and tissues.) To detect a cancer-causing effect of the compounds in a short period in a limited number of animals researchers fed the animals large doses of the hair dye ingredients.

Some researchers say that extrapolating results from ingested hair dye studies to absorbed hair dye use cannot accurately assess cancer risk because the compounds being tested are altered or are absorbed differently in the gut than they are when applied to the scalp. Moreover, tests of individual hair dye ingredients don't measure the health hazards of the highly reactive compounds that are formed when the various ingredients in a specific hair dye are mixed together and applied to hair.

In other studies, when investigators painted 4MMPD on the skin of rodents, there was no evidence that the compounds caused cancer in the animals. But critics claim that not enough of the chemical penetrates the skin from the small areas on which it's applied to accurately assess the compound's ability to prompt cancers in a limited number of animals.

After FDA adopted the requirement of a warning about 4MMPD and 4MMPD sulfate, manufacturers stopped using the chemicals in their hair dyes. In addition, the hair dye industry has stopped using several other ingredients found to cause cancer in animals. But some of the cancer-causing compounds have been replaced by similarly structured chemicals. However, some scientists feel that the similar structure of these ingredients makes it likely that their cancer-causing potential won't differ much from the chemicals they're replacing. The agency continues to monitor the situation and review studies as they are completed.

Several studies have tried to pinpoint the risk of various cancers to hair dye users by calculating the difference in frequency of cancer in people who color their hair and those who don't.

Some of these studies found an increased risk of cancer associated with hair dye use, but failed to consider the effects of other cancer-causing agents, such as cigarette smoke when comparing the two groups. In other studies the numbers of people included were too small to lend much statistical credence to the findings.

To minimize the chance of allergic reactions, before dyeing your hair, test the product by dabbing a bit behind your ear. Don't wash it off for two days. If itching, burning, redness, or rash occur, don't use the product.

Several studies found no risk of cancer. Few studies looked at long-term use of hair dyes (greater than 20 years).

The findings so far are inconclusive, to chemist John Bailey, Ph. D. , Director of FDA's colors and cosmetics program. "The studies raise some questions about the safety of hair dyes," he says, "but at this point there's no basis for us to say that hair dyes pose a definitive risk of cancer. In the final analysis, consumers will need to consider the lack of demonstrated safety when they choose to use hair dyes."

The less hair dye used over a lifetime, the less likely a person will be exposed to enough dye to cause cancer, according to Bailey. "My personal recommendation is that consumers use good judgment and exercise moderation," he says. "You may reduce the risk of cancer by exposing yourself to less hair dye—you probably shouldn't change your hair color every week, for example."

People can also reduce their risk by delaying dyeing their hair until later in life when it starts to turn gray, he adds.

Consumers might also want to consider using henna, which is largely plant-derived, or hair dyes that are lead acetate-based. These colorings don't fall into the coal-tar dye category and therefore any additive ingredients they contain have been tested for safety before marketing, in accordance with FDA requirements. Henna products on the market can give a range of colors, from dark brown through various reddish-brown and lighter red to reddish-blond shades. They cannot, however, lighten hair. Lead acetate dyes gradually darken hair and are commonly used in progressive type hair colorings, such as those advertised as being for men. None of these colors may be used on eye-lashes or eyebrows.

Words and Expressions

with the exception of　除……之外
aerosol ['ɛərəsɔl]　*n.* 气溶胶，气雾剂，喷雾器
chlorofluorocarbon　*n.* 氟氯碳

88

propellant [prə'pelənt] *n.* 推进剂，发射火药，推进燃料

injury ['indʒəri] *n.* 受伤处，损害，伤害

associate [ə'səuʃieit] *n.* 同伴，伙伴；*v.* 联合，联想；*a.* 副的

fingernail ['fiŋgəneil] *n.* 手指甲

extender [iks'tendə] *n.* 扩充器（延长器，增充剂）

methyl methacrylate *n.* 异丁烯酸甲酯

monomer ['mɔnəmə] *n.* 单体

dermatology [ˌdə:mə'tɔlədʒi] *n.* 皮肤（病）学

poisonous ['pɔiznəs] *a.* 有毒的

deleterious [ˌdeli'tiəriəs] *a.* 有害于，有毒的

proceedings [prə'si:diŋz] *n.* 公报，进程，过程，议程，诉讼（程序）

preliminary [pri'liminəri] *n.* 初步行动，准备，初步措施；*a.* 初步的，开始的，预备的

injunction [in'dʒʌŋkʃən] *n.* 命令，指令，劝告

seizure ['si:ʒə] *n.* 捕获，夺取，捕获物

ln addition to 除……之外（还）

eliminate [i'limineit] *v.* 除去，排除，剔除，［计算机］消除

Glossary

hair products
发用化妆品

焗油膏	conditioning hairdressing/hair-dressing gel/treatment	染发	hair color
摩丝	mousse	冷烫水	perm/perming formula
发胶	styling gel	卷发器	rollers/perm rollers

After-Reading Task

1. According to the first passage，which one is not ture?

    A. Some recent studies have linked hair coloring with an increased risk of contracting certain cancers.

B. Some studies do not support those findings that hair coloring had an increased risk of contracting certain cancers.

C. Most hair dyes have to go through pre-market testing for safety.

D. Other cosmetic color additives have to go through testing before hitting store shelves.

2. Which statement is ture about the FDA responsibility?

A. FDA is responsible for overseeing the safety of cosmetics sold in this country

B. FDA can't prohibit the sale of any cosmetics found harmful—except most hair dyes.

C. Food, Drug, and Cosmetic Act prohibits FDA to seek removal of a cosmetic from the market if it is shown to be harmful under conditions of use.

D. Hair coloring made from coal-tar were given special exemption from bans before the act was passed in 1938.

3. Which statement is wrong about the coal-tar hair dyes and it's manufactures?

A. The main ingredient in the coal-tar hair dyes manufactured at the time prompted an allergic reaction in some susceptible individuals.

B. The industry successfully lobbied before the act passed to get coal-tar hair dyes exempted from the adulteration provision.

C. Manufacturers were required to include a warning in the labels that the products can cause skin irritation in certain allergic individuals.

D. Less hair dyes in use today derive their ingredients from petroleum sources.

4. How can we take steps to minimize the chance of allergic reactions?

A. Before dyeing your hair, test the product by dabbing a bit behind your ear. Don't wash it off for two days. If itching, burning, redness, or rash occur, don't use the product.

B. People can also reduce their risk by advancing dyeing their hair when it starts to turn gray.

C. The less hair dye used over a lifetime, the more likely a person will be exposed to enough dye to cause cancer.

D. You should change your hair color every week.

5. According to the text, which of the following is wrong for "coal- tar ingredients"?

A. FDA proposed to require a warning on the labels of hair dyes containing the coal-tar ingredients.

B. The rodents fed the coal- tar ingredients were more likely to develop canc er than animals not fed the substances.

C. In other studies, when investigators painted 4MMPD on the skin of rodents, there was no evidence that the compounds caused cancer in the animals.

D. Other studies have shown that a large percentage of hair dye is absorbed from the scalp and passed into the bloodstream where it can travel to other organs and tissues.

6. According to the text, why the researchers say that extrapolating results cannot accurately assess cancer risk?

A. Because the ingested hair dye didn't absorbe hair dye.

B. Because the compounds being tested are altered or are absorbed differently in the gut than they are when applied to the scalp.

C. There was no evidence that the compounds caused cancer in the animals.

D. Because the compound has the ability to prompt cancers in a limited number of animals.

7. According to the text, which of the following is wrong for "henna"?

A. Henna is largely plant-derived.

B. Henna colorings don't fall into the coal-tar dye category.

C. Any additive ingredients the henna coloring contain can't be tested for safety before marketing.

D. Henna products on the market can give a range of colors, from dark brown through various reddish-brown and lighter red to reddish-blond shades.

Further Reading

What Ingredients are Prohibited from Use in Cosmetics?

With the exception of color additives and a few prohibited ingredients, a cosmetic manufacturer may use almost any raw material as a cosmetic ingredient and market the product without an approval from FDA. The Federal Food, Drug, and Cosmetic Act requires that color additives used in cosmetics must be tested for safety and be listed by the FDA for their intended uses.

Regulations restrict or prohibit the use of the following ingredients in cosmetics: bithionol, mercury compounds, vinyl chloride, halogenated salicyanilides, zirconium complexes in aerosol cosmetics, chloroform, methylene chloride, chlorofluorocarbon propellants and hexachlorophene.

In the early 1970s, FDA received a number of complaints of personal injury associated with the use of fingernail extenders containing methyl methacrylate monomer, on the basis of its investigations of the injuries and discussions with medical experts in the field of dermatology, FDA concluded that liquid methyl methacrylate was a poisonous and deleterious substance that should not be used in fingernail preparations. The agency chose to remove products containing 100% liquid methyl methacrylate monomer through court proceedings, which resulted in a preliminary injunction against one firm as well as several seizure actions and voluntary recalls.

In addition to the ingredients that are controlled by regulation or were the subject of a court ruling, cosmetic and fragrance trade associations have recommended eliminating or limiting the use of certain ingredients associated with health risks.

Lesson 10   Cosmetic Safety: More Complex Than at First Blush

The European cosmetic known as ceruse was used faithfully—and fatally, because it was mainly white lead—by wealthy women from the second century until well into the 19th century to make their faces look fashionably pale.

Nothing on the market today approaches ceruse's deadliness. But many consumers wonder about the eye makeup, lipsticks, foundations, and nail products that are on the shelves. Are there any risks in using these cosmetics? Are long lashes, even skin tone, and brightly colored nails worth any risk at all?

Serious injury from makeup is a "pretty rare event," says John E. Bailey, Ph. D. , director of FDA's Office of Colors and Cosmetics. "We don't see it happen that often. "

Even one of the most serious problems, eye infections from a scratch on the eyeball with a contaminated mascara wand, has become rare. January 1989 was the last time an infection of this type was reported to FDA.

In 1994, FDA headquarters received approximately 200 reports of adverse reactions to cosmetics. Skin-care products and makeup accounted for about 65. Of those, at least 22 concerned products containing the chemical alpha hydroxy acid (AHA), used in so-called "skin peelers. " Most of the 65 reports were either allergic reactions or skin irritations. The other complaints were about hair products, soaps, toothpastes, and mouthwashes.

Although industry probably received about 50 reports for every one made to FDA, says Bailey, the problems reported to the companies are along the same lines—allergies and skin irritation.

The agency can't do much about isolated allergic reactions or irritation problems. It's up to the individual to avoid the product that caused the reaction and any other products that contain the offending ingredient. But that doesn't mean reporting the problem isn't important.

"We look for clusters," says Bailey. "If we see we're getting a number of complaints for the same product, then that is cause for concern. "

Unlike reports of allergic or irritation reactions, even one report of an acute injury, usually caused by a contaminated

93

product, results in quick action by the agency. "We'll inspect the establishment, talk to the consumer, talk to the doctor, collect samples, and analyze them to determine the extent of contamination," says Bailey.

Moldy Oldies

Contaminated makeup is the result of either inadequate preservatives or product misuse. But contamination doesn't necessarily translate into serious injury for the user.

"Cosmetics are not expected to be totally free of microorganisms when first used or to remain free during consumer use," according to a 1989 FDA report on contamination of makeup counter samples in department stores. The report was based on a survey which found that over 5 percent of samples collected were seriously contaminated with such things as molds, other fungi, and pathogenic organi sms.

Every time you open a bottle of foundation or case of eye shadow, microorganisms in the air have an opportunity to rush in. But adequately preserved products can kill off enough of the little bugs to keep the product safe.

Occasionally, however, a product will be seriously contaminated. According to FDA data, most cases of contamination are due to manufacturers using poorly designed, ineffective preservative systems and not testing the stability of the preservatives during the product's customary shelf life and under normal use conditions.

Driving and Making Up Don't Mix

Consumers must take an active role in keeping product contamination and potential infection to a minimum once they take a product home, says Gerald McEwen, Ph. D. , vice president for science for one of the cosmetic industry's trade associations, The Cosmetic, Toiletry and Fragrance Association.

94

"You need (to follow) good personal hygiene—clean hands, clean face," he says. "And common sense."

One of the riskiest things a woman can do is put on mascara while she's driving, says McEwen. "You hit a bump and you scratch your eyeball," he explains. "Once you've scratched your eyeball, you have all kinds of possibilities of contamination. We're not talking about disease germs here. We're talking about normal bacteria that are all over the air. Those get into that kind of a cut, and without proper medical attention you can go blind."

Testing the Testers

There's something else that is definitely taboo when using makeup—sharing.

"Never share, not even with your best friend," says Irene Malbin, CTFA's vice president of public relations. Sharing cosmetics means sharing germs, and the risk, though small, isn't worth it, says Malbin.

Shared-use cosmetics—the testers commonly found at department store cosmetic counters—are even more likely to become contaminated than the same products in an individual's home, according to the 1989 FDA report.

FDA followed its 1989 report on makeup testers with a survey of corresp onding unopened retail packages. The survey found only negligible contamination, and the agency concluded that the preservatives couldn't handle the challenge of constant use.

"At home, the preservatives have time—usually a whole day—to kill the bacteria that is inevitably introduced after each use," says Bailey. "But in a store, there may be only minutes between each use. The preservatives can't handle it."

If you really want to test a cosmetic before you buy, "you should insist—must insist—on a new, unused applicator," says

95

CTFA's Malbin. She says that some companies use cotton swabs for that purpose.

Allergic Reactions

Do the preservatives themselves pose any safety risk?

According to a study of cosmetic reactions conducted by the North American Contact Dermatitis Group, preservatives are the second most common cause of allergic and irritant reactions to cosmetics. Fragrances are number one. Although the study is more than 10 years old, the results can still be considered valid today, says Harold R. Minus, M. D. , an associate professor of dermatology at Howard University Hospital.

People who have had allergic reactions to cosmetics may try hypoallergenic or allergy-tested products. These are, however, only a partial solution for some and no solution at all for others.

"Hypoallergenic can mean almost anything to anybody," says Bailey.

"Hypo" means "less than," and hypoallergenic means only that the manufacturer feels that the product is less likely than others to cause an allergic reaction. Although some manufacturers do clinical testing, others may simply omit perfumes or other common problem-causing ingredients. But there are no regulatory standards on what constitutes hypoallergenic.

Likewise, label claims that a product is "dermatologist-tested," "sensitivity tested," "allergy tested," or "nonirritating" carry no guarantee that it won't cause reactions.

"FDA tried to publish regulations (in 1975) defining hypoallergenic to mean a lower potential for causing an allergic reaction," says Bailey. "In addition, we were going to require that companies submit information to FDA establishin g that in fact their products were hypoallergenic. " However, two cosmetic manufacturers, Almay and Clinique, challenged the proposed regulations in court, claiming that consumers already understood that hypoallergenic products were no panacea against allergic reactions. In July 1975, the U. S. District Court for the District of Columbia upheld FDA's regulations, but the two companies appealed. On Dec. 21, 1977, the U. S. Court of Appeals for the District of Columbia reversed the district court's ruling. "

What's 'Natural'?

Like hypoallergenic, "natural" can mean anything to anybody.

"There are no standards for what natural means," says Bailey. "They could wave a tube (of plant extract) over the bottle and declare it natural. Who's to say what they're actually using?"

Revlon, Inc. , uses natural plant extracts in its New Age Naturals cosmetics line, says Dan Moriarity, Revlon's director of public relations. "But the base formulas are the same as our conventional products," he says. In addition, because these products contain fragrances, they don't fit Revlon's definition of hypoallergenic, he explains.

Anyone who has ever had poison ivy knows that "natural" and "hypoallergenic" are not necessarily interchangeable terms. For example, some manufacturers of cosmetics marketed as natural products use naturally occurring vitamins E and C as preservatives. But, according to Alexander Fischer, M. D. , author of Contact Dermatitis, "Topical vitamin E is a potent sensitizer which can produce both delayed allergic contact dermatitis and immediate allergic hives. "

In addition, natural doesn't mean pure or clean or perfect either. According to the cosmetic trade journal Drug and Cosmetic Industry, "all plants (including those used in cosmetics) can be heavily contaminated with bacteria, and pesticides and chemical fertilizers are widely used to improve crop yields. "

Safety Testing

Whether driven by altruism, liability, or the bottom line, most companies see the need for safety testing. But safety testing can rarely be mentioned without bringing up the controversy surrounding the use of animals for those tests.

Many companies have begun to label their products with statements indicating that no animals have been used in testing.

"As far as we know," says Neil Wilcox, D. V. M. , director of FDA's Office of Animal Care and Use, "what these companies do is use, for the most part, old reliable ingredients that have been proven safe (based on past animal data and a history of safe use) and then test the final product on people. "

"There's kind of a fine point here," says CTFA's McEwen. "These companies that say they don't test on animals are skirting the issue. Practically every ingredient that's used in cosmetics was at some point tested on animals. Probably a statement like 'no new animal testing' would be more accurate. "

But what if a company wants to use a new ingredient?

Unlike drugs, FDA does not require pre-market approval for cosmetics. However, if a safety problem with a cosmetic product arises after it's been marketed, FDA can take action to obtain the manufacturer's safety data on the product. Because there is not yet enough information on alternatives to animal testing to validate their use in ensuring human safety, FDA, at this point, would only accept animal safety data.

The most widely used, and possibly most controversial, animal test, the Draize Eye Irritancy Test, involves putting drops of the substance in question into the eye of an albino rabbit. Investigators then note if any redness, swelling, cloudiness of the iris,

98

or corneal opacity occurs. In addition, the ability of the eye to repair any damage is noted.

"Draize may be impossible to replace with a single alternative test," says Sidney Green, Ph. D. , a toxicologist with FDA's Center for Food Safety and Applied Nutrition.

He explains that because the Draize test measures three different areas of the eye, replacing Draize will probably take a combination of alternative tests, "but we've not seen that combination yet. "

Wilcox explains that for FDA to approve other methods, those methods will have to produce test results that can be reproduced in other labs. In addition, databases will have to correlate historical animal test results with newer lab results.

"Database development and cooperation (between industry and FDA) is pivotal to the validation process," says Wilcox.

The cosmetics industry has taken one step towards database development—the Cosmetic Ingredient Review. The basic purpose of the review is to gather information from the scientific literature and from company files on the safety of cosmetic ingredients and make that information publicly available.

FDA's division of toxicological review and evaluation is currently evaluating two alternatives for the Draize eye test. One is Eytex, manufactured by Ropak Corp. , Irvine, Calif. , a chemical assay that produces opacity similar to that of an animal cornea upon exposure to irritants. The other is vertebrate cell cultures from humans and mice.

But until alternatives have been scientifically verified, the option for animal testing must be available for new ingredients and new products, says Wilcox. "No one wants to think of animals being used for anything other than kindness and human companionship," he says. "But it's important that we continue to recognize the risk to human health if unreliable tests are used."

Words and Expressions

blush [blʌf]　*v.* 脸红，羞愧，呈现红色，使成红色；*n.* 脸红，红色，红光

ceruse ['siəru:s]　*n.* 铅白

faithfully ['feiθfuli]　*ad.* 忠实，诚心诚意，深信着

fatally ['feitəli]　*ad.* 致命地，不幸地，宿命地

white lead [led]　*n.* ［化］铅白，铅粉，［矿］白铅矿

fashionable ['fæʃənəbl]　*a.* 时髦地，按照流行地

deadliness ['dedlinis]　*n.* 致命

wonder about　对……好奇，对……疑惑，想知道

lash [læʃ]　*n.* 鞭子，鞭打，睫毛；*v.* 鞭打，摆动，扎捆

contaminate [kən'tæmineit]　*v.* 弄脏，污染

wand [wɔnd]　*n.* 棒，棍，杖

headquarter [,hed'kwɔ:tə]　*n.* 总部，总局

adverse reaction　有害反应，逆反应

alpha hydroxy acid（AHA）　a-羟基酸

peeler ['pi:lə]　*n.* 削皮器

mouthwash ['mauθwɔʃ]　*n.* 漱口剂，洗口药

offending　*a.* 不愉快的，厌恶的

clusters ['klʌstə]　*n.* 串，丛，群；*v.* 聚合，成串，丛生，使……聚集

moldy ['məuldi]　*a.* 发霉的

oldy ['əuldi]　*n.* 老人，陈旧之物

inadequate [in'ædikwit]　*a.* 不充分的，不适当的

microorganism [maikrəu'ɔ:gəniz(ə)m]　*n.* 微生物

survey [sə:'vei]　*n.* 纵览，视察，测量；*v.* 审视，视察，通盘考虑，调查

fungi ['fʌndʒai, 'fʌŋgai]　*n.* 菌类，蘑菇

pathogenic [,pæθə'dʒenik]　*a.* 致病的，病原的，发病的

organism ['ɔ:gənizəm]　*n.* 生物体，有机体

kill off　消灭光，除去

occasionally [əˈkeiʒənəli]　ad. 偶尔地

customary [ˈkʌstəməri]　a. 习惯的，惯例的

use condition　使用条件

take an active role in　发挥积极作用

trade association　同业公会

The Cosmetic，Toiletry and Fragrance Association（CTFA）　化妆品，盥洗用品和香精协会（美国）

common sense　常识（尤指判断力）

taboo [təˈbuː]　n. 禁忌，禁止接近，禁止使用；a. 禁忌的；v. 禁忌，禁制，禁止

negligible [ˈneɡlidʒəbl]　a. 可以忽略的，微不足道的

inevitably [inˈevitəbli]　ad. 不可避免地

applicator [ˈæplikeitə]　n. 敷贴器（撒药机，扣环起子，高频发热电极）

panacea [ˌpænəˈsiə]　n. 万灵药

interchangeable [ˌintəˈtʃeindʒəb(ə)l]　a. 可互换的

altruism [ˈæltruizəm]　n. 利他主义，利他

skirting [ˈskəːtiŋ]　n. 裙料，壁脚板

toxicological　a. 毒物学的

Glossary

cosmetic applicators/accessories
化妆品工具/附件

cosmetic brush,face brush	粉刷	pencil sharpener	转笔刀
powder puffs	粉扑	electric shaver-for women	电动剃毛器
sponge puffs	海绵扑	electric lash curler	电动睫毛卷
brow brush	眉刷	brow template	描眉卡
lash curler	睫毛夹	facial tissue	纸巾
eye shadow brush/shadow applicator	眼影刷	oil-Absorbing Sheets	吸油纸
		cotton pads	化妆棉
lip brush	口红刷	Q-tips	棉签
blush brush	胭脂扫		

After-Reading Task

1. From the text we know that serious injury from makeup ____.
   A. often happen   B. seldom happen
   C. never happen   D. it doesn't mention
2. If FDA received 20 reports of cosmetic complaining, the industry will probably receive _____ reports like that?
   A. about 650   B. about 65   C. about 80   D. about 100
3. Which is not the cause of contamination?
   A. poorly designed   B. ineffectively preserved
   C. product misuse   D. irritations
4. According to Gerald McEwen, _____ .
   A. serious injury from makeup doesn't happen that often
   B. FDA can't do much about isolated allergic reactions or irritation problems
   C. Consumers should follow good personal hygiene
   D. Some companies use cotton swabs for that purpose
5. Why consumers should insist on a new, unused applicator?
   A. Cosmetics can be contaminated easily.
   B. In a store, the cosmetics are always used by everyone.
   C. In a store, there maybe not enough time for preservatives to work effectively.
   D. Some companies use cotton swabs for that purpose.
6. In the sentence "People who have allergic reactions to cosmetics may try *hypoallergenic* or allergy-tested product. " The italicized word means _____.
   A. the product will not cause an allergic reaction as likely as others
   B. the product will cause an allergic reaction as likely as others
   C. the product is not clinically tested
   D. the product is clinically tested
7. Which of the following is right according to the text?
   A. The preservatives themselves can pose any safety risk.
   B. Preservatives are the first common cause of allergic and irritant reactions to cosmetics.
   C. The standards on what constitutes hypoallergenic are not absolute.
   D. Label claims make sure that the product won't cause reactions.

8. What is "natural"?

   A. There are exact definition of "natural".

   B. "natural" can means anything to anybody.

   C. "natural" and "hypoallergenic" are necessarily interchangeable terms.

   D. "natural" means pure or clean or perfect.

9. Why a statement like "no new animal testing" would probably be more accurate?

   A. Because on some degree every ingredient was used animal test.

   B. Because the companies that say they don't test on animals are skirting the issue.

   C. Because some companies want to use a new ingredient.

   D. FDA would accepted animal safety data.

10. Which of the following is not right about "the Draize Eye irritancy Test"?

   A. It is used more frequently and possibly more disputed than other animal test.

   B. It tests three different areas of the eye.

   C. A combination of alternative test is used to replace Draize.

   D. All of the above

11. What's Wilcox's attitude towards animal test?

   A. Critical   B. Approved

   C. Objective   D. Indifferent

Further Reading

Are cosmetics safe?

   Serious problems from cosmetic use are rare, but sometimes problems arise with specific products. For example, FDA warned consumers about the danger of using aerosol hairspray near heat, fire, or while smoking. Until hairspray is fully dry, it can ignite and cause serious burns. Injuries and deaths have occurred from fires related to aerosol hairsprays.

   Another problem can occur with aerosol sprays or powders; If they are inhaled, they can cause lung damage.

   The most common injury from cosmetics is from scratching the eye with a mascara wand. Eye infections can result if the eye

103

scratches go untreated. Such infections can lead to ulcers on the cornea, loss of lashes, or even blindness. To play it safe, never try to apply mascara while riding in a car, bus, train or plane. Sharing makeup can also lead to serious problems. Cosmetics become contaminated with bacteria the brush or applicator sponge picks up from the skin—and if you moisten brushes with saliva, the problem is much more severe. Washing your hands before using makeup will help prevent exposing the makeup to bacteria.

Artificial nails can be a source of problems, especially when not applied correctly. Artificial nails must be completely sealed because any space between the natural nail and the artificial nail gives fungal infection an opportunity to begin. Such infections can lead to permanent nail loss.

Sleeping while wearing eye makeup can cause problems, too. If mascara flakes into your eyes while you sleep, you might awaken with itching, bloodshot eyes, and possibly infections or eye scratches. To avoid eye infections or injury, remove all makeup before going to bed.

Other safety tips are:

Keep makeup containers closed tight when not in use.

Keep makeup out of the sunlight to avoid destroying the preservatives.

Don't use eye cosmetics if you have an eye infection such as conjunctivitis (pink eye), and throw away any makeup you were using when you first discovered the infection.

Never add any liquid to a product unless the instructions tell you to.

Throw away any makeup if the color changes or an odor develops. Preservatives can degrade over time and may not be able to fight bacteria.

Lesson 11   Protecting Children from the Sun

It's never too early to save your skin—or your children's—from the sun. The sun produces invisible rays—ultraviolet A (UVA) and ultraviolet B (UVB)—that can cause short—and long-term skin damage.

The immediate effects of harmful sun rays—sunburn, photosensitive reactions (rashes), and cell and tissue damage—are bad enough. But medical experts believe that too much exposure to the sun in childhood or adolescence is a major cause of skin cancer and premature skin aging later in life. Health experts also believe that UVA may weaken the immune system.

You can take steps early and often to minimize the sun's harmful effects. Using sunscreens and sun-protective clothing can reduce your children's risk of skin damage later in life. It's important to understand the labeling information on sun protection products and shop carefully before heading to the beach, tennis court or park. The Federal Trade Commission (FTC) carefully monitors advertising claims in this area and offers this information to help you make wise purchasing decisions.

Sunscreens

Sunscreens provide some protection by blocking the sun's rays on the skin. They are labeled with a sun protection factor (SPF): the higher the SPF, the greater the protection against harmful sun rays. But no sunscreen totally blocks the sun's rays. Even people wearing high SPF sunscreens get some exposure. To minimize the damage:

Use water-resistant sunscreens that help protect skin from both UVA and UVB rays and that have SPF numbers of at

105

least 15.

Apply sunscreen liberally (at least one large handful) about 30 minutes before going outside. No matter what sunscreen product is used, reapply it after swimming, toweling or any vigorous activity that causes heavy perspiration. Toweling off can remove even water-resistant sunscreens.

Talk with camp counselors and others with child care responsibilities about reapplying sunscreens after children play hard, perspire or swim.

Remember to apply sunscreen to children's skin even when they are under a beach umbrella. The sun's rays can reflect off surrounding concrete or sand.

Sun-protective Clothing

Sun-protective clothing is another way to help protect children from the negative effects of the sun. Sun-protective fabrics differ from typical summer fabrics in several ways. Sun-protective fabrics typically have a tighter weave or knit, and usually are darker in color. And, garments made with these fabrics generally have a label listing the garment's Ultraviolet Protection Factor (UPF) value, that is, the level of protection the garment provides from the sun's harmful ultraviolet (UV) rays. The higher the UPF, the greater the UV protection.

The UPF rating indicates how much of the sun's UV radiation is absorbed by the fabric. For example, a fabric with a UPF rating of 20 allows 1/20th of the sun's UV radiation to pass through it. This means that this fabric will reduce your skin's UV radiation exposure by 20 times where it's protected by the fabric.

Garments with a rating over UPF 50 may be labeled UPF 50+; however, these garments may not offer substantially more protection than those with a UPF of 50. Also, a garment should not be labeled "sun-protective" or "UV-protective" if its UPF is less than 15. In addition, sun-protective clothing may lose its effectiveness if it's too tight or stretched out, damp or wet, and has been washed and worn repeatedly.

Protecting Kids

To help protect children from the sun's damaging effects:

Remember the sun is strongest from 10 a. m. to 3 p. m. Schedule children's outdoor activities accordingly.

Dress children for maximum protection. Hats with brims and tightly woven, long-sleeved shirts and pants offer the best defense. Look for the UPF to ensure sufficient protection.

Select sunglasses that help screen out both UVA and UVB rays. UV rays may contribute to the development of cataracts. Sunglasses that are close-fitting and have big lenses offer more protection.

Keep babies younger than six months out of the sun. Sunscreens may irritate baby skin, and an infant's developing eyes are especially vulnerable to sunlight.

Teenagers who work outside as lifeguards, gardeners or construction workers may be at special risk for skin damage, and need adequate protection before going out in the sun. Try to discourage teens from going to tanning parlors. Like the sun, tanning devices can damage the skin and eyes.

Skin Cancer

Skin cancer is the most common form of cancer in this country. Medical experts are diagnosing it more often than ever, especially in young people. They believe too much sun exposure in the early years may be responsible.

Two types of skin cancer, basal cell and squamous cell, usually are treatable if detected early. Basal cell often develops on the face, ears, lips and around the mouth of fair-skinned people.

Squamous cell usually appears as a scaly patch or raised, wart-like growth. Melanoma, another type of skin cancer, is the most dangerous. It can occur anywhere on the body. Early detection is crucial for successful treatment.

Factors associated with increased risk of developing skin cancer include several blistering sunburns as a child or teenager, a family history of skin cancer, light-colored skin, hair and eyes, and moles that are irregular in shape or color.

Words and Expressions

invisible [in'vizəbl] *a.* 看不见的，无形的
ray [rei] *n.* 光线，射线
ultraviolet ['ʌltrə'vaiəlit] *a.* 紫外线的
immediate [i'mi:djət] *a.* 直接的，紧接的，紧靠的，立即的，知觉的
sunburn ['sʌnbə:n] *n.* 日灼，晒伤；*v.* 晒黑
photosensitive [,fəutəu'sensitiv] *a.* 感旋光性的
adolescence [,ædəu'lesəns] *n.* 青春期
immune [i'mju:n] *a.* 免除的，免疫的；*n.* 免疫者
take steps 设法，采取措施
minimize ['minimaiz] *v.* 将……减到最少，[计算机] 最小化
The Federal Trade Commission (FTC) 联邦贸易委员会
blocking [blɔk] *n.* 街区，木块，石块；*v.* 阻塞
sun protection factor (SPF) 防晒系数
water-resistant ['wɔ:təri,zistənt, 'wɔ-] *a.* 抗水的
liberally ['libərəli] *ad.* 不受限制地，公平地，大方地
toweling ['tauəliŋ] *n.* 毛巾料
vigorous ['vigərəs] *a.* 精力充沛的，元气旺盛的，有力的
perspiration [,pə:spə'reiʃən] *n.* 汗，流汗，努力

toweling off　　　*v.* 擦干（……的）身子

camp ［kæmp］　　*n.* 露营，帐篷；*v.* 露营，扎营

counselor ［'kaunsɔlə］　　*n.* 顾问，参事，法律顾问

perspire ［pəs'paiə］　　*v.* 出汗，流汗

beach ［bi:tʃ］　　*n.* 海滩；*v.* 拖（船）上岸；*vt.* 使船冲上滩

fabric ［'fæbrik］　　*n.* 织物，布，结构

rating ［'reitiŋ］　　*n.* 等级

damp ［dæmp］　　*n.* 湿气；*a.* 潮湿的

brim ［brim］　　*n.* 边，边缘，（河）边；*v.* 满，使……盈

screen ［skri:n］　　*n.* 屏，幕，银幕，屏风；*v.* 选拔，掩蔽，遮蔽

sunglass　　*n.* 聚集日光引火的凸透镜，太阳眼镜

vulnerable ［'vʌlnərəb(ə)l］　　*a.* 易受伤害的，有弱点的

lifeguard ［'laifgɑ:d］　　*n.* 救生员

discourage ［dis'kʌridʒ］　　*v.* 使气馁，阻碍

tanning ［'tæniŋ］　　*n.* 硝皮，制革法，晒成褐色

parlor ［'pɑ:lə］　　*n.* 客厅，会客室，店

squamous ［'skweiməs］　　*a.* 有鳞的（多鳞的，鳞状的）

treatable ［'tri:təbəl］　　*a.* 能处理的（好对付的）

scaly ［'skeili］　　*a.* 鳞状的

wart ［wɔ:t］　　*n.* （皮肤上的）疣，瘊子

blistering　　起凸，形成气孔，爆皮，起泡

mole ［məul］　　*n.* ［医］胎块，痣

After-Reading Task

1. According to the first passage，which one is not true?

　　A. It's never too early to save your skin from the sun.

　　B. It's never too early to save your children's skin from the sun.

　　C. The sun produces invisible rays—ultraviolet A and ultraviolet B.

　　D. UVA and UVB can't cause short—and long—term skin damage.

2. The medical experts believe that too much exposure to the sun in childhood or adolescence is a major cause _____ of skin in life.

A. cancer and premature skin aging later

B. sunburn

C. photosensitive reactions (rashes)

D. cell and tissue damage

3. How can we take steps to minimize the sun's harmful effects?

A. Not use sunscreens and sun-protective clothing.

B. Apply sunscreen liberally about 30 minutes before going outside.

C. Not reapply sunscreen after swimming or toweling.

D. Not apply sunscreen to children's skin when they are under a beach umbrella

4. According to the text, which of the following is wrong for "sun-protective clothing"?

A. Sun-protective clothing is another way to help protect children from the negative effects of the sun.

B. Sun-protective fabrics differ from typical summer fabrics in several ways.

C. Sun-protective fabrics typically have a tighter weave or knit, and usually are brighter in color.

D. Garments made with sun-protective fabrics generally have a label listing the garment's UPF value

5. According to the UPF's definition of the garments made with sun-protective fabrics, which statement is not true?

A. The higher the UPF, the greater the UV protection

B. The UPF rating indicates how much of the sun's UV radiation is reflected by the fabric.

C. A fabric with a UPF rating of 20 allows 1/20th of the sun's UV radiation to pass through it.

D. Garments with a rating over UPF 50 may be labeled UPF 50+.

6. When should the garment not be labeled "sun-protective" or "UV-protective"?

A. its UPF is less than 15.

B. it may offer substantially more protection.

C. its UPF is more than 15.

D. it's too tight or stretched out.

7. Sun-protective clothing may lose its effectiveness if _____.

A. it's too tight or stretched out

B. it's too damp or wet

C. it has been washed and worn repeatedly

D. all of the above

8. How can we help protect children from the sun's damaging effects?

   A. Schedule children's outdoor activities accordingly

   B. Dress children for maximum protection.

   C. Select sunglasses that help screen out both UVA and UVB rays.

   D. All of the above

9. According to the text, we may _____?

   A. Keep babies younger than six months under of the sun

   B. Let teenagers work outside and dress them for adequate protection before going out in the sun

   C. Encourage teens from going to tanning parlors

   D. Remember not to apply sunscreen to children's skin when they are under a beach umbrella

10. Which statement is not true about skin cancer in this country?

    A. Skin cancer is the most common form of cancer in this country.

    B. Medical experts believe too much sun exposure in the early years may be responsible.

    C. Melanoma usually appears as a scaly patch or raised, wart-like growth.

    D. Melanoma can occur anywhere on the body.

Further Reading

Ultraviolet Radiation

Ultraviolet (UV) radiation is defined as that portion of the electromagnetic spectrum between x-rays and visible light, i. e. , between 40 and 400nm. The UV spectrum is divided into Vacuum UV (40 to 190nm), Far UV (190 to 220nm), UVC (220 to 290nm), UVB (290 to 320), and UVA (320 to 400nm). The sun is our primary natural source of UV radiation. Artificial sources include tanning booths, black lights, curing lamps, germicidal lamps, mercury vapor lamps, halogen lights, high-intensity discharge lamps, fluorescent and incandescent sources, and some types of lasers (excimer lasers, nitrogen lasers, and third harmonic Nd: YAG lasers). Unique hazards apply to the different sources depending on the wavelength range of the emitted UV radiation.

UVC is almost never observed in nature because it is absorbed completely in the atmosphere, as are Far UV and Vacuum UV. Germicidal lamps are designed to emit UVC radiation because of its ability to kill bacteria. In humans, UVC is absorbed in the outer dead layers of the epidermis. Accidental overexposure to UVC can cause corneal burns, commonly termed welders' flash, and snow blindness, a severe sunburn to the face. While UVC injury usually clears up in a day or two, it can be extremely painful.

UVB is typically the most destructive form of UV radiation because it has enough energy to cause photochemical damage to cellular DNA, yet not enough to be completely absorbed by the atmosphere. UVB is needed by humans for synthesis of vitamin D; however, harmful effects can include erythema (sunburn), cataracts, and development of skin cancer. Individuals working outdoors are at the greatest risk of UVB effects. Most solar UVB is blocked by ozone in the atmosphere, and there is concern that reductions in atmospheric ozone could increase the prevalence of skin cancer.

UVA is the most commonly encountered type of UV light. UVA exposure has an initial pigment-darkening effect (tanning) followed by erythema if the exposure is excessive. Atmospheric ozone absorbs very little of this part of the UV spectrum. UVA is needed by humans for synthesis of vitamin D; however, overexposure to UVA has been associated with toughening of the skin, suppression of the immune system, and cataract formation. UVA light is often called black light. Most phototherapy and tanning booths use UVA lamps.

112

The photochemical effects of UV radiation can be exacerbated by chemical agents including birth control pills, tetracycline, sulphathizole, cyclamates, antidepressants, coal tar distillates found in antidandruff shampoos, lime oil, and some cosmetics. Protection from UV is provided by clothing, polycarbonate, glass, acrylics, and plastic diffusers used in office lighting. Sun-blocking lotions offer limited protection against UV exposure.

Accidental UV overexposure can injure unaware victims due to the fact that UV is invisible and does not produce an immediate reaction. Labeling on UV sources usually consists of a caution or warning label on the product or the bulb packaging cover or a warning sign on the entryway. Some type of emission indicator as required with laser products is rarely found. Reported UV accident scenarios often involve work near UV sources with protective coverings removed, cracked, or fallen off. Depending on the intensity of the UV source and length of exposure, an accident victim may end up with a lost-time injury even though totally unaware of the hazardous condition. Hazard communication training is especially important to help prevent accidental exposures in the workplace.

Exposure guidelines for UV radiation have been established by the American Conference of Governmental Industrial Hygienists and by the International Commission on Non-Ionizing Radiation Protection. Handheld meters to measure UV radiation are commercially available, but expert advice is recommended to ensure selecting the correct detector and diffuser for the UV wavelengths emitted by the source.

In summary, UV radiation has numerous useful applications but increased awareness and control of UV hazards are needed to prevent accidental overexposures.

Lesson 12　Is Indoor Tanning Safe?

"Tan indoors with absolutely no harmful side effects"

"No burning, no drying, and no sun damage"

"Unlike the sun, indoor tanning will not cause skin cancer or skin aging"

Beware of claims like these. Ads that claim indoor tanning devices are a safe alternative to outdoor tanning may be false.

Tanning indoors damages your skin. That's because indoor tanning devices emit ultraviolet rays. Tanning occurs when the skin produces additional pigment (coloring) to protect itself against burn from ultraviolet rays. Overexposure to these rays can cause eye injury, premature wrinkling of the skin, and light-induced skin rashes, and can increase your chances of developing skin cancer.

Tanning Devices

The most popular device used in tanning salons is a clamshell-like tanning bed. The customer lies down on a Plexiglas surface as lights from above and below reach the body.

Many older tanning devices used light sources that emitted shortwave ultraviolet rays (UVB) that actually caused burning. Aware of the harmful effects of UVB radiation, salon owners began using tanning beds that emit mostly longwave (UVA) light sources. Some salons claim this is safe. While UVA rays are less likely to cause burning than UVB rays, they are suspected to have links to malignant melanoma and immune system damage.

Advertising Claims

Here are some claims commonly made about indoor tanning—and the facts.

"You can achieve a deep year-round tan with gentle, comforta-

114

ble, and safe UVA light. "

Ultraviolet light is divided into two wavelength bands. Short-wave ultraviolet rays called UVB can burn the outer layer of skin. Longwave ultraviolet rays called UVA penetrate more deeply and can weaken the skin's inner connective tissue.

Long-term exposure to the sun and to artificial sources of ul-traviolet light contributes to the risk of developing skin cancer. Two types of skin cancer, basal cell and squamous cell, are treat-able if detected early. Melanoma, another type of skin cancer, can be fatal.

"No harsh glare, so no goggles or eye shades are necessary. "

Studies show that too much exposure to ultraviolet rays, in-cluding UVA rays, can damage the retina. Overexposure can burn the cornea, and repeated exposure over many years can change the structure of the lens so that it begins to cloud, forming a cataract. Left untreated, cataracts can cause blindness.

The Food and Drug Administration requires tanning salons to direct all customers to wear protective eye goggles. Closing your eyes, wearing ordinary sunglasses, and using cotton wads do not protect the cornea from the intensity of UV radiation in tanning de-vices.

Long-term exposure to natural sunlight also can result in eye damage, but in the sun, people generally are more aware that their eyelids are burning. Under indoor UV lights, exposed skin remains cool to the touch. In addition, the intensity of lights used in tanning devices is much greater—and potentially more damaging to the eyes—than the intensity of UV rays in natural sunlight.

"Tan year-round without the harmful side effects often associ-ated with natural sunlight. "

Exposure to tanning salon rays increases the damage caused by

115

sunlight. This occurs because ultraviolet light actually thins the skin, making it less able to heal.

Unprotected exposure to utltraviolet rays also results in premature skin aging. A tan is damaged skin that is more likely to wrinkle and sag than skin that hasn't been tanned. Over time, you may notice certain undesirable changes in the way your skin looks and heals. According to some skin specialists, skin that has a dry, wrinkled, leathery appearance early in middle age is a result of UV exposure that occurred in youth.

"No danger in exposure or burning. "

Whether you tan indoors or out, studies show the combination of ultraviolet rays and some medicines, birth control pills, cosmetics, and soaps may accelerate skin burns or produce painful adverse skin reactions, such as rashes. In addition, tanning devices may induce common light-sensitive skin ailments like cold sores.

Protecting Yourself

1. Limit your exposure to avoid sunburn. If you tan with a device, ask whether the manufacturer or the salon staff recommend exposure limits for your skin type. Set a timer on the tanning device that automatically shuts off the lights or somehow signals that you've reached your exposure time. Remember that exposure time affects burning and that your age at the time of exposure is important relative to burning. Studies suggest that children and adolescents are harmed more by equivalent amounts of UVB rays than adults. The earlier you start tanning, the earlier skin injury may occur.

2. Use goggles to protect your eyes. Ask whether safety goggles are provided and if their use is mandatory. Make sure the goggles fit snugly. Check to see that the salon sterilizes the goggles after each use to prevent the spread of eye infections.

3. Consider your medical history. If you are undergoing treatment for lupus or diabetes or are susceptible to cold sores, be aware that these conditions can be aggravated through exposure to ultraviolet radiation from tanning devices, sunlamps, or natural sunlight. In addition, your skin may be more sensitive to artificial light or sunlight if you use certain medications — for example, antihistamines, tranquilizers or birth control pills. Your tanning salon may keep a file with information on your medical history, medications, and treatments. Make sure you update it as necessary.

A Word about Sunscreens

Chances are you spend some time in natural sunlight. You still could benefit from using sunscreens with sun protection factor (SPF) numbers of 15 or more. The SPF number gives you some idea of how long you can stay in the sun without burning. For example, if you normally burn in 10 minutes without sunscreen, you should be protected from burn for 150 minutes using SPF 15. Swimming and perspiration reduce the actual SPF value for many sunscreens, so be sure to reapply even if the product is water-resistant.

While all sunscreens provide some level of protection against UVB rays, no product screens out all UVA rays. Some may advertise UVA protection, but there's no system yet for rating UVA protection. Even when you use a sunscreen with a high SPF number, there's no way to know how much UVA protection you're getting.

Regulation

The Food and Drug Administration (FDA) and the Federal Trade Commission (FTC) share responsibilities in the regulation of sunlamps and tanning devices. The FDA enforces regulations that deal with labels on the devices; the FTC investigates false, mis-

117

leading, and deceptive advertising claims about the devices. When these agencies determine that device labels don't comply with the regulations or that advertisements are not truthful, they may take corrective action. The FDA also can remove products from the marketplace.

Words and Expressions

tanning ['tæniŋ]　*n*. 硝皮，制革法，晒成褐色

side effect　副作用

beware of　对……小心

emit [i'mit]　*v*. 发出，放射，吐露，[计算机] 发射

overexposure ['əuvəriks'pəuʒə]　*n*. 感光过度

premature [ˌpremə'tjuə]　*a*. 早熟的，过早的，不按时的；*n*. 早产儿，早发

salon ['sælɔːŋ]　*n*. 大会客室（美术展览馆）

clamshell ['klæmʃəl]　*n*. 蛤壳（抓斗，蛤壳式挖泥机）

plexiglas ['pleksiglɑːs]　*n*. 胶质玻璃

malignant [mə'lignənt]　*a*. 有恶意的，恶性的，有害的；*n*. 怀恶意的人，保王党员

melanoma [ˌmelə'nəumə]　*n*. [医]（恶性）黑素瘤，（良性）胎记瘤

shortwave ['ʃɔːt'weiv]　*n*. 短波；*v*. 做短波广播

artificial [ˌaːti'fiʃəl]　*a*. 人造的，虚伪的，武断的

glare [glɛə]　*n*. 闪耀光，刺眼；*v*. 发眩光，瞪视

goggle ['gɔgl]　*n*. 眼睛睁视，护目镜；*vi*. 瞪视，瞪大眼睛看

retina ['retinə]　*n*. 网膜

cornea ['kɔːniə]　*n*. 角膜

lens [lenz]　*n*. 镜头，透镜

cloud [klaud]　*n*. 云，忧色，云状的烟；*v*. 以云遮蔽，笼罩

cataract ['kætərækt]　*n*. 大瀑布，奔流，洪水

eyelid ['ailid]　*n*. 眼皮，眼睑

118

undesirable [ˌʌndi'zaiərəbl]   a. 不受欢迎的，不良的

leathery ['leðəri]   a. 皮似的，皮质的，皮般强韧的

birth control pill   避孕丸

timer ['taimə]   n. 计时员（计时器，跑表，定时器，延时调节器）

snugly ['snʌgli]   ad. 紧紧地，紧密地

sterilize ['sterilaiz]   v. 使成不毛，断种，杀菌

lupus ['lu:pəs]   n. 狼疮，天狼座

diabetes [ˌdaiə'bi:ti:z, -ti:s]   n. 糖尿病

susceptible [sə'septəbl]   n. 易受影响者，易受感染者；a. 易受影响的，易感动的，容许

cold sore   n. 感冒疮，（伤风发热时的）唇疱疹

sunlamp ['sʌn'læmp]   n. 太阳灯

antihistamine [ˌænti'histəmi:n]   n. 抗组织胺

tranquilizer ['træŋkwilaizə]   n. 镇静剂（增稳装置）

enforce [in'fɔ:s]   v. 厉行，强迫，执行

After-Reading Task

1. According to the passage，why the ads that claim indoor tanning devices are a safe alternative to outdoor tanning may be false ?

   A. indoor tanning devices emit ultraviolet rays.

   B. indoor tanning devices absorb ultraviolet rays

   C. indoor tanning will not cause skin cancer.

   D. indoor tanning will not cause skin aging.

2. Which following one is not true about the "Tanning Devices"?

   A. many older tanning devices used light sources that emitted shortwave ultraviolet rays (UVB) that actually caused burning.

   B. the tanning beds emit mostly longwave (UVA) light sources.

   C. UVA rays are more likely to cause burning than UVB rays.

   D. UVA rays are suspected to have links to malignant melanoma and immune system damage.

3. There are some claims commonly made about indoor tanning and the facts，which one is wrong?

A. Ultraviolet light is divided into two wavelength bands.

B. Shortwave ultraviolet rays can burn the outer layer of skin.

C. Longwave ultraviolet rays penetrate less deeply.

D. Longwave ultraviolet rays can weaken the skin's inner connective tissue.

4. Overexposure to the sun can damage the body except _____.

   A. damaging the retina

   B. burning the cornea

   C. changing the structure of the lens

   D. developing skin tan

5. According to the passage, which parlance is right?

   A. Unprotected exposure to utltraviolet rays results in premature skin aging.

   B. Tan year round without the harmful side effects often associated with natural sunlight

   C. You can achieve a deep year-round tan with gentle, comfortable, and safe UVA light.

   D. Unlike the sun, indoor tanning will not cause skin cancer or skin aging.

6. How can we protect ourself from the indoor tanning except?

   A. Unlimit our exposure time with a tanning device.

   B. Use goggles to protect our eyes.

   C. Consider our medical history.

   D. Limit our children to avoid sunburn.

7. Which of the following is not right about sunscreens?

   A. Using sunscreens with sun protection factor (SPF) numbers of 15 or more could benefit us.

   B. Swimming and perspiration reduce the actual SPF value for many sunscreens, but not to reapply if the product is water-resistant.

   C. You can achieve a deep year-round tan with gentle, comfortable, and safe UVA light.

   D. Tan year round without the harmful side effects often associated with natural sunlight.

8. What's the author's attitude towards the indoor tanning?

   A. Critical   B. Approved   C. Objective   D. Indifferent

9. According to FDA and FTC's duty, which statement is ture?

   A. Only FDA exert the responsibility in the regulation of sunlamps and tanning devices.

B. FDA enforces regulations that deal with labels on the devices.

C. FTA investigates false, misleading, and deceptive advertising claims about the devices.

D. FTC can remove products from the marketplace.

Further Reading

Tanning Lotion

Prevent the need for treatment of sun burns with, sunscreen, sun tan lotions, products and sun care tips, absolutely vital for your skin's health. Tanning lotions can enhance your tan and make your skin look golden brown. Tanning lotions usually contain sun screens and most tanning lotions act as a moisturizer while providing UVB, & UVA protection. It is necessary to wear sunscreen products, even in the dead of winter you should never leave the house without some kind of sun protection. In fact applying sunscreen is so important when using sun tan lotions, that it should be a step in your beauty routine.

Tanning lotions with a high UV protection is extremely important. Ultraviolet light, even at low-level exposures erodes the skin's support structure. It breaks down collagen, causes wrinkles and sagging. Ninety percent of your wrinkles are caused by the sun's ultraviolet light. If you are concerned about your appearance then using sun care products will reduce the signs of premature aging.

A good sunscreen in a tanning lotion to prevent sun burn should have a minimum SPF (sun protection factor) rating of 15 to prevent nasty sun burns. If possible apply sunscreen at least 20 minutes before going outside to give the active ingredients a chance to be absorbed.

Sun damage is cumulative and irreversible, protect your skin

121

from the sun. Safe tanning products and supplies are available for purchase online of sun burn prevention and remedys for sun burn treatment relief. If you start using sun care products now you can prevent further damage to your skin.

UNIT FOUR MATERIAL

Lesson 13 Cosmetic Ingredients:
Understanding the Puffery

The lotion contained bovine albumin and the label claimed it would give a "face lift without surgery." The Food and Drug Administration said the claims caused the product to be a misbranded drug. In 1968, the court said no. "If lifting and firming products are deemed intended to affect the structure of the body, girdles and brassieres must be devices within the meaning of the law."

In 1969 an appellate court overturned this decision, but the issues persist today. "Most cosmetics contain ingredients that are promoted with exaggerated claims of beauty or long-lasting effects to create an image," says John E. Bailey, Ph. D. , director of FDA's division of color and cosmetics. "Image is what the cosmetic industry sells through its products, and it's up to the consumer to believe it or not," Bailey says.

In the past, cosmetic manufacturers have depended upon mysterious "gimmick" additives, such as turtle oil to promote skin rejuvenation or tighten chin muscles, shark oil, queen bee royal jelly, chick embryo extract, horse blood serum, and pigskin extracts.

Promotion of these "gimmick" additives, combined with today's more sophisticated cosmetic ingredients, is what Bailey and the cosmetic industry call "puffery."

"The argument is sometimes made that while Congress intended

123

to safeguard the health and economic interests of consumers with the Federal Food, Drug, and Cosmetic Act, it also meant to protect a manufacturer's right to market a product free of excessive government regulation. And, in an industry that sells personal image, especially images of beauty and sex appeal, not allowing the puffery claims would certainly hurt the marketing," says Bailey.

But there's hope for credibility in claims for cosmetic ingredients. Some of the more responsible cosmetic firms are rethinking their claims that push believability to its outside edge. Linda Allen Schoen of Neutrogena says that today's more knowledgeable consumer wants "facts versus puffery—products based on skin care realities, promises banked on achievable benefits. "Besides", says Schoen, "limited recession dollars tend to be spent on products consumers can trust."

Still, with the exception of colors and certain prohibited ingredients, a cosmetic manufacturer may use essentially any raw material in a product and market it without prior FDA approval. The prohibited ingredients are biothionol, hexachlorophene, mercury compounds (except as preservatives in eye cosmetics), vinyl chloride and zirconium salts in aerosol products, halogenated salicylanilides, chloroform, and methylene chloride.

Federal regulations require ingredients to be listed on product labels in descending order by quantity, but often the list is not user-friendly. Because cosmetic ingredients are often complex chemical substances, the list may be incomprehensible to the product's average user. However, if the same name is used by all manufacturers, consumers can compare different products and make reasonable value judgments.

Although cosmetic claims, even those considered "puffery," are allowed without scientific substantiation, if a cosmetic makes a medical claim, such as removing dandruff, the product is regulated as an over-the-counter drug for which scientific studies demonstrating safety and effectiveness must be submitted to FDA.

Baffling Names

Because of the unusual and sometimes bewildering nature of some ingredients in cosmetics, consumers often ask FDA for explanations. "My night cream contains liposomes—what is that?" "Why is placenta used in cosmetics—is it human placenta, and could I get a disease from it?" "What are cerebrosides and ceremides?"

FDA cosmetic scientists can explain the nature of an ingredient when it is identified by its chemical name. But when an ingredient is listed by its trade name, FDA usually must consult the manufacturer's trade literature or the International Cosmetic Ingredient Dictionary, published by the Cosmetic, Toiletry, and Fragrance Association, Inc. , the industry's major trade association. The dictionary, now in its fourth edition, provides a uniform system for assigning ingredient names. FDA currently recognizes the second edition as a primary reference.

Here is what FDA knows about some currently marketed ingredients:

Liposomes are microscopic sacs, or spheres, manufactured from a variety of fatty substances, including phospholipids. While phospholipids are natural components of cell membranes, the material actually used in cosmetics may be obtained either from natural or synthetic sources. When properly mixed with water, phospholipids form liposome spheres, which can "trap" any substance that will dissolve in water or oil.

Manufacturers say that liposomes act like a delivery system. They claim that, when present in a cream or lotion, liposomes can more easily penetrate the surface skin to underlying layers, "melt," and deposit other ingredients of the product.

Nayad is a trade name for yeast extract. The manufacturer's literature describes Nayad as a "new system that takes yeast cells and refines them hundreds of times... What results is a highly concentrated, odor-free, unusually potent yeast extract ..." The same literature reports that "no one really knows how Nayad is working in the skin; all we know for certain is the way it makes the skin look and feel. Test subjects report a noticeable smoothing of lines and wrinkles. " FDA has no data to either substantiate or refute these claims.

Vitamins are added to cosmetics by manufacturers because foods containing vitamins A, D, E, K, and some of the B complex group are necessary in diets to maintain healthy skin and hair. Using these vitamins in cosmetics that are applied to the skin surface implies that skin will be nourished by them.

But Stanley R. Milstein, Ph. D. , associate director for FDA's cosmetics division, says the notion that skin can be nourished by a vitamin applied to its surface has not been proven clinically. For that reason, says Milstein, a vitamin added to a cosmetic product must be listed in the ingredient label by its chemical name so that it doesn't convey a misleading message. However, FDA does not prohibit listing vitamins by their common names on the principal display panel of a cosmetic as long as the consumer is not misled and no therapeutic claims are made.

Some leaders in the cosmetic industry, such as Neutrogena's Schoen, agree with the FDA position on vitamins in skin care products. Others, such as Chris Vaughn of Sun Pharmaceuticals, Ltd. , cite clinical studies done by Hoffmann-La Roche and others that show that vitamins can penetrate layers of skin and have beneficial

126

effects. This, however, would make it a drug use, and manufacturers who use vitamins in their products don't usually make claims that would cause their products to be classified as drugs. Vaughn says that getting a drug classification is time-consuming and expensive, and in his opinion not justifiable because the informed consumer understands the beneficial properties of vitamins.

Although the debate about the value of vitamins in skin care products continues, it is generally accepted that a sufficient quantity of vitamin E (shown on ingredient lists as tocopherol), an antioxidant, preserves the fatty components in cosmetic creams and lotions to prevent off-color and off odors.

Aloe vera is a plant from the lily family whose anti-irritant properties have been recognized since before the days of Cleopatra. It is listed as an ingredient in many skin lotions, but it would take much more aloe vera than most products contain for the anti-irritant properties to work.

Milstein explains that aloe vera, as a cosmetic ingredient, is expensive because it requires delicate processing and handling. A product that contains the 5 to 10 percent aloe vera necessary for the anti-irritant properties to be effective would send the price out of range for many consumers.

What About Biological Ingredients?

A number of biological products in cosmetics have raised consumer concern:

Human placenta is the nourishing lining of the womb (uterus), which is expelled after birth. When placental materials were first used as cosmetic ingredients in the 1940s, manufacturers promoted the products as providing beneficial hormonal effects such as stimulating tissue growth and removing wrinkles. (Although newborn infants emerge from the womb with wrinkled skin!) The hormone content and the tissue-growth and wrinkle-removing claims classified the placenta-containing products as drugs, and FDA declared them to be ineffective and therefore misbranded.

FDA's challenge caused placenta suppliers to change marketing strategies by claiming that hormones in their placenta ingredients had been extracted and were no longer in the product. They then offered placental raw materials without medical claims—only as a source of protein.

Can you get a disease from placental cosmetic ingredients? Bailey says no. Placenta used in cosmetics is washed and processed many times to destroy any harmful bacteria or viruses. Besides that, says Bailey, the cosmetic matrix (components that bind the ingredients in products) is made from a wide variety of substances, such as alcohol and preservatives, that would present a hostile environment to any viruses or bacteria the placenta might have carried.

Amniotic liquid (from cow or ox) is the fluid that surrounds the developing fetus and protects it from physical injury. It is promoted for benefits similar to those of human placenta and has limited use in moisturizers, hair lotions, scalp treatments, and shampoos.

Collagen (from young cows) is the protein substance found in connective tissue. (Connective tissue binds together and supports organs and other body structures.) A great deal of research has been done on the different types and uses for collagen. In cosmetics, collagen has a moisturizing effect. It is not water soluble, but it holds water. FDA says there is no convincing evidence that collagen can penetrate the skin and have an effect below the surface.

Cerebrosides (from animals or plants) are a type of glycolipid (a chemically combined form of fatty substance and carbohydrate) produced naturally in basal epidermal cells—the deepest layer of

128

skin. After cerebrosides are formed, they are secreted to the outside of the cells and serve as a protective coating. As new cells form in lower layers of skin, the older skin cells move closer to surface layers and start to dry out. During this process, the cerebrosides are chemically changed and form ceramides, part of a network of membranes between cells. Skin moisture and suppleness comes from this network.

The raw material for cerebrosides in cosmetics comes from cattle, oxen or swine brain cells or other nervous system tissues. Alternatively, the raw material may be isolated from plant sources. Industry cosmetic scientists claim that the use of cerebrosides in skin products results in a smoother skin surface and better moisture retention, effects that translate into marketing claims such as luminosity and ever-improving hydration. FDA has not evaluated the studies on which these claims are based.

Industry Self-Regulation

"The cosmetic industry is sensitive to the image of an uncontrolled market where anything goes," says Bailey. "They counter this image with well-established self-regulation programs. Part of the incentive for such industry policy is to avoid increased regulatory authority."

The most well-known of industry-sponsored self-regulation is the Cosmetic Ingredient Review (CIR), sponsored by the Cosmetic Toiletry and Fragrance Association. The CIR is accomplished by a panel of scientific and medical experts who evaluate cosmetic ingredients for safety and publish detailed reviews of available safety data. "A finding of safety by the CIR provides a degree of confidence that the ingredient can safely be used in cosmetics," Bailey says. "In the absence of the CIR program, there would be no systematic examination of the safety of individual cosmetic ingredients." FDA has no statutory authority to require that the data be submitted to the agency.

FDA encourages industry cooperation through its cosmetic voluntary reporting program. Cosmetic firms registered in the program voluntarily report manufacturing and formulation information, along with product experience data, to FDA. Adverse reactions such as skin irritations are also reported. Using this information, FDA can determine a baseline reaction rate for specific product categories such as hair coloring or eye makeup preparations. The agency gives participating companies this baseline information so they can compare their own adverse reaction rates to the FDA-established baseline.

Words and Expressions

puffery ['pʌfəri]   *n.* 极力称赞，夸大广告

albumin ['æl'bjumin]   *n.* 蛋白质，蛋白素

claim [kleim]   *n.* 要求，要求权；*v.* 要求，请求，主张，声称，说明，断言

The Food and Drug Administration (FDA)   食品和药品管理局（美国）

deem [di:m]   *v.* 认为，相信

girdle ['gɔ:dl]   *n.* 腰带，围绕物；*v.* 以腰带束缚，在…周围绕

brassiere ['bræsiə]   *n.* 奶罩，乳罩

appellate [ə'pelit]   受理上诉的

overturn [,əuvə'tə:n]   *n.* 倾覆，破减，革命；*v.* 推翻，颠倒

promote [prə'məut]   *v.* 促进，提升，升迁，促销

exaggerate [ig'zædʒəreit]   *v.* 夸大，夸张

gimmick ['gimik]   *n.* 骗局（骗人的玩意）；*vt.* 搞骗人的玩意

turtle oil   海龟油

rejuvenation   *n.* 复原（再生，更新，嫩化，恢复）

130

shark oil　　鲨鱼肝油

queen bee royal jelly　　蜂王王浆

chick embryo extract　　小鸡胚胎提取物

serum ['siərəm] *n.* 浆液，血清，乳浆

pigskin ['pigskin] *n.* 猪皮，猪皮革，鞍

sophisticated [sə'fistikeitid] *a.* 诡辩的，久经世故的

argument ['ɑːgjumənt] *n.* 辩论，争论，论据，理由

safeguard ['seif,gɑːd] *n.* 保卫，保护措施或条款；*v.* 保卫，保护

Federal Food，Drug，and Cosmetic Act　《联邦食品、药品和化妆品法》

excessive [ik'sesiv] *a.* 过多的，过分的

credibility [,kredi'biliti] *n.* 可信用，确实性，可靠

responsible [ris'pɒnsəbl] *a.* 有责任的，负责的，责任重大的，应负责的

rethink [ri'θiŋk] *v.* 再想，重想

bank on *vt.* 指望（依赖，依靠）

recession [ri'seʃən] *n.* 后退，凹入的地方，不景气

prohibit [prə'hibit] *v.* 禁止，阻止；*vt.* 禁止

biothionol　　*n.* 硫双二氯酚

hexachlorophene [,heksə'klɔːfəfiːn] *n.* [化] 六氯酚

mercury ['məːkjuri] *n.* 水银

zirconium [zəː'kəuniəm] *n.* 锆

halogenated ['hælədʒəneit] *vt.* 卤化（加卤）

salicylanilide [,sælisil'ænilaid, -lid] *n.* [化] N-水杨酰苯胺

chloroform ['klɔ(ː)rəfəːm] *n.* *n.* 氯仿

methylene chloride　　*n.* 二氯甲烷

in descending order by quantity　　按量由高到低排列

incomprehensible [,inkɔmpri'hensəbl] *a.* 不能理解，费解的，无限的

dandruff ['dændrʌf] *n.* 头皮屑

over-the-counter（OTC）drug　　非处方药

baffling *a.* 令人困惑的

bewildering [bi'wildəriŋ]　*a.* 令人困惑的，使人混乱的

liposome ['lipəusəum，'lai-]　*n.* [生] 脂质体

placenta [plə'sentə]　*n.* 胎盘

cerebroside ['seribrəusaid]　*n.* [生化] 脑苷脂

ceramide ['serəmaid]　*n.* [生化] 神经酰胺

identify [ai'dentifai]　*v.* 识别，认明，鉴定

trade name　　商品名

the International Cosmetic Ingredient Dictionary　　化妆品成分辞典

Cosmetic Toiletry and Fragrance Association（CTFA）　化妆品盥洗
　　用品香味用品协会

sac [sæk]　*n.* 囊，液囊

microscopic [maikrə'skɔpik]　*a.* 显微镜的

sphere [sfiə]　*a.* 球体的；*n.* 范围，领域，球，球体

phospholipid [ˌfɔsfəu'lipid]　*n.* 磷脂

cell membrane　*n.* 细胞膜

underlying [ˌʌndə'laiiŋ]　*a.* 在下面的

yeast extract　　酵母抽提物，酵母膏

nourish ['nʌriʃ]　*v.* 滋养，使…健壮，怀有

division [di'viʒən]　*n.* 区分，分开，除法，公司，部门

convey [kən'vei]　*v.* 传达，运输，转移，[计算机] 输送

therapeutic [θerə'pjuːtik]　*a.* 治疗的，治疗学的；*n.* 治疗剂，治疗学家

justifiable ['dʒʌstifaiəbl]　*a.* 有理的，可辩解的，可证明的

aloe vera　*n.* 真芦荟，羊角掌：

delicate ['delikit]　*a.* 细致优雅的，微妙的，美味的

biological [ˌbaiə'lɔdʒikəl]　*a.* 生物学的

lining ['lainiŋ]　*n.* 衬里，内层

womb [wuːm]　*n.* 子宫

expel [iks'pel]　*v.* 驱逐，逐出，开除

hormone ['hɔːməun]　*n.* 荷尔蒙，激素

ineffective [ˌini'fektiv]　*a.* 无效的

132

bacteria [bæk'tiəriə]　*n.* 细菌

virus ['vaiərəs]　*n.* 病毒

hostile ['hɔstail]　*a.* 怀敌意的，敌对的

amniotic liquid　羊水

fetus ['fiːtəs]　*n.* 胎，胎儿

collagen ['kɔlə,dʒən]　*n.* 胶原

connective tissue　*n.* 结缔组织

convincing evidence　*n.* 令人信服的证据

glycolipid [,glaikə'lipid]　*n.* [生化] 糖脂类

fatty substance　脂肪物质

carbohydrate ['kɑːbəu'haidreit]　*n.* 碳水化合物，糖

basal epidermal cell　基底层细胞

a protective coating　保护涂层

swine [swain]　*n.* 猪

alternatively [ɔ:l'təːnətivli]　*ad.* 二者择一地，作为选择

luminosity [,ljuːmi'nɔsiti]　*n.* 光明，光辉，光度，[计算机] 光度

hydration [hai'dreiʃən]　*n.* 水合

incentive [in'sentiv]　*a.* 刺激的，鼓励的　*n.* 刺激，鼓励，动机

sponsor ['spɔnsə]　*n.* 保证人，赞助者　*v.* 发起，赞助

Cosmetic Ingredient Review（CIR）　化妆品成分评估

systematic [,sisti'mætik]　*a.* 有系统的，分类的，体系的

individual [,indi'vidjuəl]　*a.* 个别的；*n.* 个人，个体

adverse ['ædvəːs]　*a.* 不利的

hair coloring　染发

endorse [in'dɔːs]　*v.* 支持，赞同，背书于

eligible ['elidʒəbl]　*a.* 可以选的，有资格的，合格的；*n.* 有资格者，合格者，适任者

submission [səb'miʃən]　*n.* 服从，柔和

accumulate [ə'kjuːmjuleit]　*v.* 积聚，堆积

sustain [səs'tein]　*v.* 承受，支持，经受，维持

133

小　知　识

一、什么是 INCI?

化妆品是一类与人体健康密切相关的日用化学产品,化妆品原料的理化性质和毒理对化妆品的品质和卫生安全起着决定性的作用。为此,世界各国的健康卫生管理部门,化妆品行业协会和消费者协会都非常关注化妆品的组成原料。

在化妆品容器包装上标注成分名称,既有利于卫生监督管理,又有利于消费者合理选用。

鉴于上述情况的需要,国际上为此制订了 INCI (International Nomenclatrue Cosmetic Ingredient 国际专业命名化妆品原料) 名称,已为美国、欧盟成员国、日本、加拿大、巴西、韩国、泰国、菲律宾、沙特阿拉伯等许多国家承认、引用或使用。我国卫生部对进口化妆品配方中原料的申报名称也以 INCI 名称为准,但一直缺少一本成册的 INCI 英汉对照名称,为了与国际接轨,我们编译了这本 INCI 英汉对照名称,目的是促进我国对化妆品原料 INCI 名称译名规范化,有利于卫生部对化妆品安全性的管理和指导,也可满足我国消费者对进口化妆品标签上原料名称的了解。并为我国将来规范化妆品标注原料名称作为参考。

本名单的 INCI 名称,是根据 CTFA (The Cosmetic, Toiletry, and Fragrance Association) 1997 年出版的第七版 INCD (International Cosmetic Ingredient Dictionary) 所编译。随着时间推移,化妆品原料将不断增加,INCI 名称会随之增补和修改,本名单也将随之增补和修改,以适应社会需要。

本名单难免存在欠妥之处,祈盼各界提出宝贵建议,以便今后不断修改完善。

本名单所收集的化妆品原料,仅作为它们的 INCI 英汉名称对照。绝不意味它们全是我国允许使用的化妆品原料。

二、国际专业命名化妆品原料 (INCI) 名称的汉文译名通则

1	每个 INCI 名称只译成一个汉文名。力求和 INCI 名称对应。
	INCI 名称凡与中华人民共和国药典和中国药品通用名称药品名称相同的原料,除个别药用辅料名称外,译名皆按这两个法典中的汉文名称订名。 例如:Fluorosalan 氟沙仑 　　　 Etocrylene 依托立林 　　　 Alcloxa 铝克洛沙 　　　 Lapyrium Chloride 拉匹氯铵 　　　 Carbomer 卡波姆

2		植物性原料的汉文名后面括附林奈(Linne)系统命名的植物拉丁文属名或种名。 例如:Eleuthero Ginseng(Acanthopanax senticosus)Extract 刺五加(Acanthopanax senticosus)提取物
3		色料如果有 CI 号的话,则汉文名称后面就括附它的 CI(色料索引)号。 例如:FD&C Yellow No. 5 FD&C 黄 5 号(CI 19140) Pigment red No. 48 颜料红 No. 48(CI 15865)
4		为了避免译成汉文名称过于冗长起见,对于某些 INCI 名称中的缩写词不再译出,而是直接引用于汉文名称中。在缩写词附录中列出了它们的英文原词和汉文译名。
5		INCI 名称同时附有它的 CAS 号和 Einecs/Elincs 号供读者参考使用。
6		多元醇,碳原子数目比较大的链烷醇,环链烷醇,含芳香核的醇,某些结构复杂的醇及酚类同酸类结合成的酯类名词,统一将醇名或酚名置于词前。 例如:Glyceryl Disterate 甘油二硬脂酸酯 Cetyl Lactate 鲸蜡醇乳酸酯
7		原则上,碳原子数目不大的链烷醇与酸结合成的酯类,统一将醇名置于"酸"后"酯"前,并略去"醇"字。 例如:Ethyl Isostearate 异硬脂酸乙酯 Decyl Oleate 油酸癸酯
8		INCI 名称中一些专业命名规则规定的词意,词干,词根,后缀和它们的汉文订名如下
	(1)	INCI 名称的专业命名规则将烷基二甲基胺氧化物中的"Dimethyl"一词省略, 例如:Stearamine Oxide 代表 Stearyl Dimethylamine Oxide。汉文名亦从简对应,订名为"硬脂胺氧化物",而不订名为"硬脂基二甲基氧化(叔)胺"
	(2)	INCI 名称的专业命名规则,通常将单替代衍生物前缀"mono"缺省。例如"Glyeryl Stearate"代表"Glyeryl mono-Stearate"。汉文名亦从简对应,订名为"甘油硬脂酸酯"而不订名为"甘油单硬脂酸酯"
	(3)	INCI 名称有些合成词干 例如:Cetearyl 代表 Cetyl 和 Stearyl 的合成词干,Cetearyl Alcohol 汉文订名为鲸蜡硬脂醇 Ceteareth 代表 Ceteth 和 Steareth 的合成词干 Ceteareth-10 汉文订名为鲸蜡硬脂醇醚-10 Cetoleth 代表 Ceteth 和 Oleth 的合成词干 中 Cetoleth-8 汉文订名为鲸蜡醇油醇醚-8

	(4)	羊毛脂衍生物的名称中通常含词根'lan',译为羊毛脂。 例如:Laneth-10 Acetate 羊毛脂醇醚-10 乙酸酯
	(5)	两性表面活性剂的 INCI 名称中的组合词根"ampho",译为两性基。 例如 Sodium Cocoamphoacetate 椰油酰两性基乙酸钠
	(6)	Copolyol 代表某聚合物分子中带有 Polyoxyethylene 和/或 Polyoxypropylene 侧链。译为共聚醇
	(7)	线形非交联共聚物中的词干"Acrylates"译为丙烯酸(酯)类;词干"Crotonates"译为巴豆酸(酯)类。 例如:Acrylates copolymer 丙烯酸(酯)类共聚物 VA/Vinyl butyl benzoate/crotonates copolymer VA/丁苯甲酸乙烯酯/巴豆酸(酯)类共聚物
	(8)	词干"Glyceride"译为甘油酯,表示含意为甘油单酯 "Glycerides"译为甘油酯类,表示含意为甘油单酯,双酯和三酯的混合酯
8	(9)	含有后缀"eth"的乙氧基化烷醇,将"eth"译为"聚醚"置于词干之后,在后缀其后附加的数字代表氧乙基数目的平均值。 例如:Ceteareth-12 鲸蜡硬脂醇聚醚-12 Oleth-5 油醇聚醚-5 Cetoleth-22 鲸蜡醇油醇聚醚-22 但在"eth"后缀附加数字方面,有与上述通则不尽相同的情况。 例如:在"eth"后缀没有附加数字则代表氧乙基数目在 1—4 之间。 Sodium Laureth Sulfate 月桂醇聚醚-(1—4)硫酸酯钠盐
		Nonoxynol-n, Nonyl Nonoxynol-n,和 Octoxynol-n 都属于乙氧基化的烷基酚,"-n"代表化学式里的氧乙基数目。 例如:Nonoxynol-23, 壬基酚聚醚-23 Nonyl Nonoxynol-150, 二壬基酚聚醚-150 Octoxynol-n 辛基酚聚醚-70
	(10)	含有词干"monium","dimonium""trimonium"译为甲基…铵,二甲基…铵和三甲基…铵,它们的氯化物、溴化物季铵类,译为汉文名时将氯化、溴化置于铵字前。 例如:Dihydrogenated tallowamidoethyl hydroxyethylmonium chloride 二氢化牛脂酰胺乙基羟乙基甲基氯化铵 Stearyl octyldimonium Chloride 硬脂基辛基二甲基氯化铵 Laurtrimonium bromide 月桂基三甲基溴化铵 Dihydrogenated tallowamidoethyl hydroxyethylmonium Chloride 二牛脂酰胺乙基羟乙基甲基氯化铵

8	(11)	INCI 名称中,某些由动物油脂或植物油脂衍生的混合性脂肪酸,脂肪醇,脂肪胺,甘油酯的名称,及酰基,烃基等词干名,其汉文名冠以相应的动物油脂名或植物油脂名译出。 例如:Coceth-75 椰油醇聚醚-75 　　　Coconut Acid 椰油酸 　　　Coconut Alcohol 椰油醇 　　　Cocamide 椰油酰胺 　　　Cocamine 椰油胺 　　　Coco-Caprylate/Caprate 椰油醇辛酸酯/癸酸酯 　　　Coco-Betaine 椰油基-甜菜碱 　　　Cocotrimonium Chloride 椰油基三甲基氯化铵 　　　Cocoyl Sarcosine 椰油酰基肌氨酸 　　　Glyceryl Cocoate 甘油椰油酸酯 　　　Palm Acide 棕榈油酸 　　　Palm Alcohol 棕榈油醇 　　　Palmamide MEA 棕榈油酰胺 MEA 　　　Palm Glyceride 棕榈油酸甘油酯 　　　Palm Kernelamidopropyl Betaine 棕榈仁油酰胺丙基甜菜碱 　　　Dipalmoylethyl Hydroxyethylmonium methosulfate 二棕榈油酰氧乙基羟乙基甲基铵甲基硫酸盐 　　　Sodium Cocoamphopropyloate 椰油酰两性基丙酸钠 　　　Sodium Wheat germamphoacetate 小麦胚油酰两性基乙酸钠 　　　Tallow Acide 牛脂酸 　　　Sodium Tallowate 牛脂酸钠 　　　Sodium Tallow Sulfate 牛脂醇硫酸酯钠 　　　Minkamidoproprylamine Oxide 貂油酰胺丙基胺氧化物 　　　PEG-13 mink glycerides　PEG -13 貂油甘油酯类 　　　Dimethicone Copolyol Cocoa Butterate 聚二甲基硅氧烷共聚醇可可脂酸酯

After-Reading Task

1. Which of the following, the Food and Drug Administration think, can affect the structure of the body?

   A. bovine albumin　　B. girdles　　C. brassieres　　D. all of the above

2. In the sentence "They *counter* this image with well-established self-regulation programs" the italicized word can be replaced by _____ .

A. meet   B. offer in response   C. oppose   D. none of the above

3. Which of the following is a not biological ingredient?

   A. collagen   B. placenta   C. carbohydrate   D. cerebrosides

4. Which of the following is different from the others?

   A. cattle   B. ox   C. swine   D. cow

5. Which statement of the terms is false?

   A. Some cosmetic firms are beginning to adjust their claims.

   B. The exaggerated claims made the cosmetics almost unbelievable.

   C. All consumers want facts instead of puffery—products.

   D. The purchase of cosmetics is affected the income of consumers.

6. What of the following may be used in a product by a cosmetic manufacturer and market it without prior FDA approval.

   A. color additive   B. chloroform   C. hexachlorophene   D. sodium chloride

7. Which statement of the terms is true?

   A. Some vitamins are necessary in diets to maintain healthy skin and hair, so that a vitamin applied to its surface can nourish skin.

   B. Vitamin E can make some Ingredients in cosmetic creams hard to deteriorate.

   C. Consumer cannot understand the beneficial properties of vitamins.

   D. The manufacturer would like to make their product classified as drugs.

8. About Aloe vera, which one is untrue?

   A. It can be used in many skin lotions.

   B. It cannot be used in cosmetics directly.

   C. It is plant that can mitigate the irritant.

   D. It's too expensive for many consumers.

9. Which of the following is true?

   A. There are hormones in their placenta.

   B. Human placenta can remove wrinkles.

   C. There is no any virus or bacteria in human placenta.

   D. The cosmetic matrix is not beneficial to survival of viruses or bacteria.

10. About industry self-regulation, which one is true?

    A. FDA approves the safety of the ingredients from the firm registered in the voluntary program.

    B. The cosmetic industries welcome regulatory authority.

    C. The information a firm submits to FDA maybe wrong.

    D. FDA endorses all the safety data of cosmetic ingredients evaluated by CIR.

138

Further Reading

Vitamins: Introduction and Index

Vitamins are organic molecules that are necessary for normal metabolism in animals, but they are not synthesized in the body or are synthesized in inadequate quantities. Consequently, vitamins must be obtained from the diet. Most vitamins function as coenzymes or cofactors. Deficiency states are recognized for all vitamins, and in many cases, excessive intake also leads to disease. Fat-Soluble Vitamins is listed in Table 5 and Water-Soluble Vitamis is listed in Table 6.

Table 5 Fat-Soluble Vitamins

Names	Major Sources	Comments
Vitamin A (retinol)	Present in many animal tissues, especially fish and liver. Carotinoids in green plants serve can be converted to vitamin A following ingestion	Necessary for a broad range of bodily function, including production of vision pigments, resistance to infectious agents and maintenance of health in many epithelial cells. Disease results from both deficiency and excess
Vitamin D (cholecalciferol)	Synthesized in the skin when exposed to sunlight (and thus not a true vitamin). Also present at low concentration in some natural foods, and in many artificially-fortified food products.	A steroid hormone. Major effect is to facilitate absorption of calcium from the intestine, and thereby assist in maintaining calcium homeostasis. Receptors are present in most cells and it likely has many additional effects
Vitamin E (tocopherol)	Vegetable oils, leafy green vegetables and whole grains	A family of molecules that function as antioxidants, particularly to prevent oxidation of unsaturated fatty acids and maintain the integrity of cell membranes. Deficiency can lead to reproductive function, leading to the nickname of "antisterility vitamin"

Table 6 Water-Soluble Vitamins

Names	Major Sources	Comments
Vitamin C (Ascorbic acid)	Present in fruits and vegetables. Rich sources include citrus fruits, strawberries, tomatoes and leafy green vegetables. Most animals can synthesize ascorbic acid; those that cannot include primates (including humans), guinea pigs and (I'm not making this up) Mongolian fruit bats	A major function is synthesis of hydroxyproline, an important component of collagen and, thereby, all connective tissues. Essential for growth of cartilage, bone and teeth, and for wound healing. Deficiency results in the disease scurvy
Riboflavin (Vitamin B2)	Present in wide variety of foods, including milk, meats and grains	Precursor to the coenzymes flavin adenine dinucleotide (FAD) and flavin mononucleotide (FMN), which serve as hydrogen carriers in a number of important oxidation-reduction (respiration) reactions within mitochondria
Niacin (Nicotinamide)	Present in meats, leafy green vegatables, potatoes and peanuts. Can be synthesized in small amounts within the body from tryptophan	Precursor to the coenzymes nicotinamide adenine dinucleotide (NAD) and nicotinamide adenine dinucleotide phosphate (NADPH), which serve as hydrogen carriers in such important processes as glycolysis, Kreb's cycle and oxidative phosphorylation
Pyridoxine (Vitamin B6)	Present in meat from mammals, fish and poultry. Also present in a number of vegetables, including potatoes and tomatoes	The precursor to pyridoxal phosphate, a coenzyme for several important reactions involving protein metabolism, including the transamination reactions necessary for synthesis of amino acids
Pantothenic Acid	Present in a broad variety of foods, including grain, legumes, egg yolk, and meat. Also synthesized by intestinal bacteria	The precursor to coenzyme A, which is an enzyme critical to the oxidation and/or synthesis of carbohydrates and fatty acids

Names	Major Sources	Comments
Cobalamin (Vitamin B12)	Microbial synthesis is the sole source of this vitamin in nature. It is obtained almost exclusively from ingestion of animal products, and is essentially absent from plant products	A cobalt-containing coenzyme involved in numerous metabolic pathways. Deficiency usually results from failure to absorb the molecule due to inadequate quantities of intrinsic factor, and is typically manifest as a defect in red blood cell formation (pernicious anemia)
Folic Acid	Present in many natural foods, including dark-green vegetables (spinich!), beef, eggs, whole grains. Also synthesized by intestinal bacteria	Serves as a coenzyme in the synthesis of several amino acids, as well as purines and thymine, and therefore DNA. Deficiency is typically manifest as growth failure and anemia

Lesson 14　Emulsion and its Stability

Paints, polishes, pesticides, metal cutting oils, margarine, ice cream, cosmetics, metal cleaners and textile processing oils etc. are all emulsions or are used in emulsified form.

An emulsion is a significantly stable suspension of particles of a liquid of a certain size within a second, immiscible liquid. The term "significantly stable" means relative to the intended use and may range from a few minutes to a few years. Two types of emulsions are recognized: a) macroemulsions, this is the usual type of emulsions in which the particles range from 0.2 to 50 μm in size being easily visible under the microscope; h) microemulsions, this type of emulsions has particles from 0.01 to 0.2 μm (10 to 200nm) in size.

The size of the particles dispersed in an emulsion determines its appearance to the naked eye. If the diameter of the dispersed

141

particles is about $1\mu m$, the emulsion is milky white; 1 to $0.1\mu m$, blue white; 0.1 to 0.05 μm, gray and semitransparent; less than $0.05\mu m$, transparent. Thus macroemulsions are opaque and micro emulsions are either transparent or semitransparent to visible light.

Two immisible, pure liquids can not form an emulsion because the tremendously large interface created. In order to obtain a stable emulsion, a third component, called the emulsifying agent, must be present in the system. The emulsifying agent is usually a surfactant. The most effective emulsifying agents are usually mixture of two or more substances.

Based on the nature of the dispersed phase, emulsions can also be classified into two types: a) oil-in-water (o/w), and b) water-in-oil (w/o). The o/w type is a dispersion of a water-immisible liquid (called the oil) in an aqueous phase, and the oil is called the discontinuous phase (the inner phase). On the other hand, the w/o type is a dispersion of water or aqueous solution in a water-immisible liquid, and in this case the water is called the discontinuous phase (the inner phase), the oil (the water-immisible liquid) is called the continuous (outer) phase. The type of emulsion formed by the water and the oil depends primarily on the nature of the emulsifier used and to a minor extent, on the process used in preparing the emulsion and the relative proportions of the "oil" and "water" present. In general, o/w emulsions are formed by emulsifying agents more soluble in water than in the "oil" phase, whereas w/o emulsions are formed by the emulsifiers that are more soluble in the "oil" than in water. This is known as the Bancroft rule. One type can be converted to the other when the conditions are changed.

Distinguishment of the emulsions: a) Dilution—an emulsion can be diluted by the outer phase. Thus, o/w emulsions can easily be diluted by water whereas w/o emulsions can easily be diluted by "oil"; b) Conductivity measurement—o/w emulsions have electrical conductivties similar to that of the water whereas w/o emulsions do not conduct current; c) Colouration—w/o emulsions can be colored by oil-soluble dyes, whereas o/w ones will be colored by water-soluble dyes; d) Refractive index method—if the two phases have different refractive indices, a droplet under a microscope will appear brighter, when focussing upward, if the inner phase's refractive index is larger than that of the continuous phase; and will darker if its refractive index is smaller than that of the continuous phase; e) Filter paper test—a drop of an o/w emulsion produces an immediate wide, moist area; a drop of w/o does not. If the paper is first impregnated with a 20% cobaltous chloride solution and then dried before test, the area around the drop of o/w emulsion turns pink immediately, whereas the area around the drop of w/o emulsion remains blue (no color change).

In the formation of emulsions the fine dispersion of the inner phases (the discontinuous phase) produces a tremendous increase in the area of the interface between the two phases, these results in turn in a correspondingly large increase in the interfacial free energy of the system. Thus the emulsion produced is highly unstable thermodynamically. The function of the emulsifier is to stabilize this unstable system for a sufficient time so that the emulsion can perform its function.

The stabilization the emulsifier does is as follow: the emulsifier molecules adsorb at the L/L interface as an oriented interfacial film; reduces the interfacial tension markedly; decreases the rate of coalescence of the dispersed liquid particles by forming mechanical and/or electrical barriers around them.

The steric and electrical barriers inhibit the close approach of one particle to another. In the formation of macroemulsions, the reduction

143

of interfacial tension reduces the amount of mechanical work needed to break the inner phase into dispersed particles; in this case, the interfacial tension should be reduced to a value of zero, at least temporarily, so as to get a microemulsion spontaneously.

Factors that determine the stability of an emulsion include physical nature of the interfacial film resulting from the adsorbed surfactants, existence of an electrical or steric barrier to coalescence on the dispersed droplets, size distribution of droplets, phase volume ratio, temperature, and so on. Anything that disturbs the interface decreases the stability of the emulsion, the increased vapor pressure resulting from the increase in temperature causes an increased flow of molecules through the interface an decreased the stability of the emulsion. Furthermore, an increase in temperature increases the rate of diffusion of the dispersed particles and the probability of collision and also the coalesence rate of the dispersed particles.

Emulsions may be converted from w/o into o/w and vice versa by varying some of the conditions.

The order of addition of the phases: by adding the water to the oil plus emulsifier, a w/o emulsion may be obtained, whereas the addition of oil to the same emulsifier and water, an o/w emulsion will be obtained;

The nature of the emulsifier: an emulsifier that is more oil-soluble tends to produce a w/o emulsion, whereas a more water-soluble one tends to produce an o/w emulsion;

The phase volume ratio: greater ratio of oil to water tends to give a w/o emulsion and vice versa;

The temperature: as the temperature is increased, an o/w emulsion with a PEO (polyethlene Oxide) non-ionic may invert to w/o, because the PEO non-ionic surfactant becomes more hydrophobic when the temperature is increased. On the other hand, some emulsions with ionics may invert to w/o from o/w ones on cooling;

Other additives: an addition of strong electrolyte to o/w emulsions stabilized by ionics may invert them to w/o ones by decreasing the electrical potential on the dispersed particles, and increasing the interaction between the surfactant and counter ions; whereas the addition of long-chain alcohols or fatty acids may invert an o/w to w/o one by make the emulsifiers more hydrophobic.

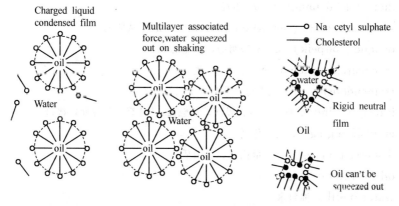

Figure 5 Process of converting an o/w emulsion to w/o

The process of converting an o/w emulsion to w/o one is illustrated diagrammatically in Figure 5. It can be seen from this figure that the charged film in the o/w emulsion is neutralized and the oil droplets tend to coagulate to form the continuous phase. The trapped water is surrounded by an interfacial film forming irregularly shaped droplets of water.

Words and Expressions

paint [peint]　*n.* 油漆，颜料，绘画作品；*v.* 油漆，绘画

polish ['pɔliʃ]　*n.* 光泽，优雅，精良；*v.* 擦亮，磨光，推敲

pesticide ['pestisaid]　*n.* 杀虫剂

metal cutting oil　金属切削油

margarine [mɑːdʒəˈriːn, ˈmɑːgərin] n. 人造黄油

emulsion [iˈmʌlʃən] 感光乳剂，乳状液

Surfactant [səːˈfæktənt] n. 表面活化剂

suspension [səsˈpenʃən] n. 悬挂，未决，中止

immiscible [iˈmisəbl] a. 不能混合的，不融洽的

microscope [ˈmaikrəskəup] n. 显微镜

diameter [daiˈæmitə] n. 直径

semitransparent [ˈsemitrænsˈpɛərənt] a. 半透明的

opaque [əuˈpeik] a. 不透明的，难懂的

transparent [trænsˈpɛərənt] a. 透明的

tremendously ad. 惊人地（非常，十二分）

interface [ˈintə(ː)ˌfeis] n. 界面，接触面；[计算机] 界面，接口

emulsifying agent　乳化剂

dispersed phase n. 分散内相，分散质

oil-in-water　水包油

water-in-oil　油包水

discontinuous phase/inner phase　非连续相

continuous（outer）phase　连续相

distinguishment　区别

dilution [daiˈljuːʃən,diˈl-] n. 稀释，渗水

dilute [daiˈljuːt,diˈl-] v. 冲淡，稀释

conductivity [ˈkɔndʌkˈtiviti] n. 传导性，传导率

colouration [ˌkʌləˈreiʃən] n. 着色

refractive [riˈfræktiv] a. 折射的，有折射力的，曲折的

impregnate [ˈimpregneit] vt. 注入（灌注，浸渍，充满，饱和，包含）；
　　a. 浸透的（饱和的）

cobaltous chloride　氯化亚钴

oriented interfacial film　定向界面膜

coalescence [ˌkəuəˈlesns] n. 接合，结合，合并

spontaneously　*ad*. 自发地（自生地，自然产生地，自然地，天然地）

non-ionic surfactant　　非离子表面活性剂

hydrophobic [ˌhaidrəuˈfəubik]　*a*. 恐水病的，狂犬病的，患恐水病的

electrolyte [iˈlektrəulait]　*n*. 电解物，电解质，电解液

electrical potential　　电势，电位

counter ion　　抗衡离子；相反离子

diagrammatically　*ad*. 用图解法

coagulate [kəuˈægjuleit]　*v*. 凝结，使凝结

Glossary

Surfactants in common use
常用表面活性剂

英　文　名	缩　写	中文名
surface active agent	SAA	表面活性剂
Anionic surface active agent	a-SAA	阴离子表面活性剂
Nonionic surface active agent	n-SAA	非离子表面活性剂
Cationic surface active agent	c-SAA	阳离子表面活性剂
alKyl poly glycoside	APG	烷基糖苷
llnear alkyl benzene sulphonate	LAS	直链烷基苯磺酸盐
alkyl sulfate	AS	烷基硫酸盐
secondary alkyl sulphate	SAS	仲烷基硫酸盐
Fatty alcohol polyethyleneglycol ether sulfate	AES	脂肪醇聚氧乙烯醚硫酸盐
alkenyl sulphonate	AOS	烯基磺酸盐
fatty acid methyl ester sulphonate	MES	脂肪酸甲酯磺酸盐
Alkyl Epoxy ethylene Carboxy acid	AEC	脂肪醇聚氧乙烯醚羧酸盐
Disodium Laureth(3) Sulfosuccinate	AESS	脂肪醇聚氧乙烯醚(3)磺基琥珀酸单酯二钠
fatty alcohol-polyoxyethylene ether	AE	脂肪醇聚氧乙烯醚
mono alkyl phosphoric acid ester	MAP	单烷基磷酸酯
Cocofatty aid monoethanol amide	CMEA	椰油酸单乙醇酰胺
Coconut fatty aid diethanolamide	6501	椰油酸二乙醇酰胺
laurie acid diethanolamide	LDEA	月桂酸二乙醇酰胺
Fatty acid monoethanol amide	FMEA	脂肪酸单乙醇酰胺
Lauroamide propyl betaine	LAPB	月桂酰胺丙基甜菜碱
Sodium fatty alcohol sulfate	K12	脂肪醇硫酸盐
Cocoanut amide propyl betaine	CAPB	椰油酰胺丙基甜菜碱
Cocoanut amide betaine	CAB	椰油酰胺甜菜碱
Lauroamide amine oxide	LAPO	月桂酰胺氧化胺
Cocoamide propyl amine oxide	CAPO	椰油酰胺丙基氧化胺

After-Reading Task

1. According to the text of the definition of emulsion, the emulsion may not include ____?

    A. Paints   B. Polishes   C. Pesticides   D. alcohol

2. What is the difference between macroemulsions and microemulsions?

    A. Macroemulsion is more stable than microemulsions.

    B. Macroemulsion and microemulsion are two types of emulsions.

    C. Macroemulsion is the usual type of emulsions in which the particles range from 0. 2 to 50 μm in size.

    D. Microemulsion is easily visible under the microscope.

3. Which of the following statement is unture about the apperance of emulsion to the naked eyes?

    A. The color of the particles dispersed in an emulsion determines its appearance to the naked eye.

    B. If the diameter of the dispersed particles is about 1μm , the emulsion is milky white.

    C. The macroemulsions are opaque to visible light.

    D. The microemulsions are either transparent or semitransparent to visible light.

4. Emulsions can also be classified into two types, which statement is wrong about the o/w type emulsions?

    A. The o/w type is a dispersion of a water-immisible liquid in an aqueous phase.

    B. The water-immisible liquid is called the water.

    C. The oil is called the discontinuous phase.

    D. The oil is also called the inner phase.

5. The type of emulsion formed by the water and the oil depends primarily.

    A. on the nature of the emulsifier used and to a minor extent

    B. on the process used in preparing the emulsion

    C. on the relative proportions of the "oil" and "water" present

    D. all of the above

6. Which of the following measurement can distinguish the emulsions?

    A. Dilution   B. Conductivity measurement

    C. Colouration   D. All of the above

148

7. The stabilization the emulsifier does is as follow.

   A. The emulsifier molecules adsorb at the L/L interface as an oriented interfacial film.

   B. Increases the rate of coalescence of the dispersed liquid particles by forming mechanical and/or electrical barriers around them.

   C. Induces the interfacial tension markedly.

   D. The emulsifier molecules adsorb at the G/L interface as an oriented interfacial film.

8. Factors that determine the stability of an emulsion include _____ .

   A. physical nature of the interfacial film resulting from the adsorbed surfactants

   B. existence of an electrical or steric barrier to coalescence on the dispersed droplets

   C. size distribution of droplets, phase volume ratio, temperature

   D. all of the above

9. How can emulsions be converted from o/w into w/o?

   A. By adding the water to emulsifier

   B. By adding an emulsifier that is more oil-soluble

   C. Greater ratio of water to oil

   D. By adding strong electrolyte to the emulsions

10. According to the text of the definition of emulsion, the emulsion may not include _____ ?

   A. Paints   B. Polishes   C. Pesticides   D. alcohol

11. What is the difference between macroemulsions and microemulsions?

   A. Macroemulsion is more stable than microemulsions.

   B. Macroemulsion and microemulsion are two types of emulsions.

   C. Macroemulsion is the usual type of emulsions in which the particles range from 0.2 to 50 μm in size.

   D. Microemulsion is easily visible under the microscope.

12. Which of the following statement is unture about the apperance of emulsion to the naked eyes?

   A. The color of the particles dispersed in an emulsion determines its appearance to the naked eye.

   B. If the diameter of the dispersed particles is about 1μm , the emulsion is milky white.

C. The macroemulsions are opaque to visible light.

D. The microemulsions are either transparent or semitransparent to visible light.

13. Emulsions can also be classified into two types, which statement is wrong about the o/w type emulsions?

A. The o/w type is a dispersion of a water-immisible liquid in an aqueous phase.

B. The water-immisible liquid is called the water.

C. The oil is called the discontinuous phase.

D. The oil is also called the inner phase.

14. The type of emulsion formed by the water and the oil depends primarily _____ .

A. on the nature of the emulsifier used and to a minor extent

B. on the process used in preparing the emulsion

C. on the relative proportions of the "oil" and "water" present

D. all of the above

15. Which of the following measurement can distinguish the emulsions?

A. Dilution   B. Conductivity measurement

C. Colouration   D. All of the above

16. The stabilization the emulsifier does is as follow.

A. The emulsifier molecules adsorb at the L/L interface as an oriented interfacial film.

B. Increases the rate of coalescence of the dispersed liquid particles by forming mechanical and/or electrical barriers around them.

C. Induces the interfacial tension markedly.

D. The emulsifier molecules adsorb at the G/L interface as an oriented interfacial film.

17. Factors that determine the stability of an emulsion include _____ .

A. physical nature of the interfacial film resulting from the adsorbed surfactants

B. existence of an electrical or steric barrier to coalescence on the dispersed droplets

C. size distribution of droplets, phase volume ratio, temperature

D. all of the above

18. How can emulsions be converted from o/w into w/o?

A. By adding the water to emulsifier

B. By adding an emulsifier that is more oil-soluble

C. Greater ratio of water to oil

D. By adding strong electrolyte to the emulsions

Further Reading

Cosmetic sunscreen preparation

The present invention relates to a sunscreen cosmetic exhibiting a satisfactory dispersion of a micro particle zinc oxide as well as excellent stability and ultraviolet rays protection effect. Namely, a micro particle zinc oxide is readily and highly dispersed by means of a surface treatment with a silicic anhydride and a silicone and by an incorporation of a polyoxyalkylene-modified polysiloxane. The present invention is relates to a sunscreen cosmetic obtained by the technical approach described above, which has an excellent ultraviolet rays protection effect and a satisfactory stability with no reaction with a free fatty acid being allowed to occur.

Also, a micro particle zinc oxide treated with a silicic anhydride and a silicone is highly dispersed using a media-agitating mill or a high pressure dispersing machine. The present invention relates to a sunscreen cosmetic obtained by the technical approach described above, which has an excellent ultraviolet rays protection effect and a satisfactory stability with no reaction with a free fatty acid being allowed to occur.

Especially by combining a composite powder obtained by coating a micro particle zinc oxide whose particle size is 0. 1nm or less with a silicic anhydride at a coating rate of 5% to 30% (wt) followed by a further surface treatment with a silicone with a polyoxyalkylene-modified polysiloxane, the micro particle zinc oxide can be brought into a highly dispersed condition which can not be achieved so far. Accordingly, the ultraviolet rays protection effect of a sun-screen cosmetic can be improved. Also in the present invention, by dispersing a silicone-treated composite powder by a strong mechanical force using a media-agitating mill or a high pressure dispersing machine, a micro particle zinc oxide can be brought into a finely dispersed condition which can not be achieved so far, and the ultraviolet rays protection effect of a sunscreen cosmetic can be improved.

In a silicone-treated composite powder described above, a micro particle zinc oxide is coated uniformly with a silicic anhydride. Accordingly, the elution of a zinc ion into the system is suppressed to prevent the formation of a metallic soap as a result of the reaction with a free fatty acid. Moreover, even when a strong mechanical force is exerted by a media-agitating mill or a high pressure dispersing machine, there is no inconvenience that a surface treatment coating is peeled off to expose a non-treated hydrophilic surface. As a result, no reaction with water takes place. Since no gelation due to a time period or a temperature occurs, the viscosity of the system can continuously be kept stably, thus providing a sunscreen cosmetic exhibiting a sustained favorable use feeling.

What is a color additive

Technically, a color additive is any dye, pigment or substance that can impart color when added or applied to a food, drug, cosmetic or to the human body.

The Food and Drug Administration (FDA) is responsible for regulating all color additives used in the United States. All color additives permitted for use in foods are classified as "certifiable" or "exempt from certification" .

Certifiable color additives are man-made, with each batch being tested by manufacturer and FDA. This "approval" process,

152

known as color additive certification, assures the safety, quality, consistency and strength of the color additive prior to its use in foods.

There are nine certified colors approved for use in food in the United States. One example is FD&C Yellow No. 6, which is used in cereals, bakery goods, snack foods and other foods.

Color additives that are exempt from certification include pigments derived from natural sources such as vegetables, minerals or animals, and man-made counterparts of natural derivatives.

For example, caramel color is produced commercially by heating sugar and other carbohydrates under strictly controlled conditions for use in sauces, gravies, soft drinks, baked goods and other foods.

Whether a color additive is certifiable or exempt from certification has no bearing on its overall safety. Both types of color additives are subject to rigorous standards of safety prior to their approval for use in foods.

Certifiable color additives are used widely because their coloring ability is more intense than most colors derived from natural products; thus, they are often added to foods in smaller quantities. In addition, certifiable color additives are more stable, provide better color uniformity and blend together easily to provide a wide range of hues. Certifiable color additives generally do not impart undesirable flavors to foods, while color derived from foods such as beets and cranberries can produce such unintended effects.

Of nine certifiable colors approved for use in the United States, seven color additives are used in food manufacturing. Regulations known as Good Manufacturing Practices limit the amount of color added to foods. Too much color would make foods unattractive to consumers, in addition to increasing costs.

153

Lesson 15　Essential Oils

They are subtle, therapeutic-grade oils distilled from plants, shrubs, flowers, trees, roots, bushes and seeds. They are oxygenating and help transport nutrients to the cells of our body. Without oxygen, nutrients cannot be assimilated; therefore, the oxygenating essential oils can help us maintain our health.

Benefits of Essential Oils

One of the most popular applications for essential oils is in the field of aromatherapy. This highly skilled art uses essential oils to assist in the healing of physical, psychological and aesthetic ailments. It is the only therapy that utilizes the most neglected of the senses, smell.

There are many ways to incorporate the benefits of aromatherapy into our daily lives. They may used to stimulate and invigorate us in the morning, and then to calm and restore our peace of mind at the end of the day. Essential oils may soothe inflammation, act as an antiseptic, help dull pain and stimulate digestion. We encourage you to experiment with our full line of essential oil products so that you may discover which uses and fragrances work best for you in any given situation or state of mind. Once you've learned a little about the uses and benefits of essential oils, you'll be amazed at how you can take control of your health, the air you breathe and the food you eat-all in a safe, chemical free manner.

Essential oils have cytophylactic (cell regeneration), antiseptic, and wound healing effects as well as anti-fungal and anti-inflammative properties making them the ultimate active principles for holistic natural skin-care.

How do Essential Oils work?

154

Essential oils are composed of tiny molecules which are easily dissolved in alcohol, emulsifiers and fats. This allows them to penetrate the skin easily and work into the body by mixing with the fatty tissue.

As these highly volatile essences evaporate they are also inhaled, thus entering the body via the millions of sensitive cells that line the nasal passages. These send messages straight to the brain, and affect the emotions by working on the limbic system, which also controls the major functions of the body. Thus in an aromatherapy treatment the essential oils are able to enhance both your physical and psychological well-being at the same time.

Each oil has a distinct chemical composition which determines its fragrance, color, volatility and the ways in which it affects the system, giving each oil its unique set of beneficial properties.

What are the effects of using Essential Oils?

Oils can directly or indirectly affect the body's physiological systems. For instance, a couple of drops of peppermint taken orally can aid digestion and inhalations of mucolytic oils can relieve respiratory symptoms. Used topically for their antiseptic and soothing effects, essential oils can successfully treat minor skin conditions. It has been demonstrated that the application of certain essential oils to the skin can produce vasodilation which in turn causes warming of underlying muscles, however this is an indirect effect of the oil acting on the superficial tissues, it is not a pharmacological effect produced as a result of the oil entering the systemic circulation via the skin. In addition, because of the effect of relaxation on the brain and the subsequent sedating or stimulating of the nervous system, essential oils can also indirectly raise and lower blood pressure and possibly aid in normalization of hormonal secretion.

Because of olfaction's direct connection to the brain, sending electrical messages directly into the limbic system, essential oils can have effects on emotions and mental states. Perception of odors can have a major impact on memory, learning, emotions, thinking and feeling. As therapeutic agents, essential oils work similarly to tranquilizers but in a subtle organic way. Most scents uplift spirits and calm the nervous system. For example, lavender is calming and sedative; basil, rosemary and peppermint are uplifting and stimulating; and jasmine and ylang-ylang are exciting or euphoric.

Now you have understood what are essential oils, lets move on to different ways of using essential oils. Or get more information on aromatherapy.

Words and Expressions

subtle ['sʌtl]   *a.* 狡猾的，敏感的，微妙的，精细的，稀薄的

distill [di'stil]   *v.* 蒸馏，滴下

shrub [ʃrʌb]   *n.* 灌木

bush [buʃ]   *n.* 灌木，灌木丛

seed [si:d]   *n.* 种子；*vi.* （植物）结实，播种；*vt.* 播种

oxygenate ['ɔksidʒineit]   *v.* ［化］以氧处理，氧化

nutrient ['nju:triənt]   *a.* 营养的，滋养的；*n.* 营养物，营养品

assimilate [ə'simileit]   *v.* 使……同化，比较，比拟

psychological [,saikə'lɔdʒikəl]   *a.* 心理（学）的

ailment ['eilmənt]   *n.* 小病，疾病

stimulate ['stimjuleit]   *vt.* 刺激，激励，鼓舞

invigorate [in'vigəreit]   *v.* 鼓舞，激励；*vt.* 增添活力

inflammation [,inflə'meiʃən]   *n.* 发炎，红肿，炎症

antiseptic [,ænti'septik]   *n.* 杀菌剂，防腐剂；*a.* 杀菌的，防腐的

dull [dʌl]   *a.* 感觉或理解迟钝的，无趣的，呆滞的，阴暗的；*vt.* 使迟钝，

156

使阴暗，缓和；vi. 变迟钝，减少

cytophylactic [ˌsaitəfiˈlæktik] a. 细胞防御的

fungal [ˈfʌŋgəl] a. 真菌的

holistic [həuˈlistik] a. 整体的，全盘的

tiny [ˈtaini] a. 极小的，微小的

nasal [ˈneizəl] a. 鼻的，鼻声的，护鼻的；n. 鼻音，鼻音字

limbic [ˈlimbik] a. 边的，缘的

volatility [ˌvɔləˈtiliti] n. 挥发性

peppermint [ˈpepəmint] n. 薄荷，薄荷糖，薄荷味

orally [ˈɔːrəli] ad. 口头地，口述地

aid [eid] n. 帮助，有帮助的事物；v. 援助，帮助

inhalation [ˌinhəˈleiʃən] n. 吸入，吸入药剂

mucolytic [ˌmjukəuˈlitik] a. [生化] 黏液溶解的

respiratory [ˈrespərətɔriː] a. 呼吸的

vasodilation [ˌveizəudaiˈleiʃən] n. [生理] 血管舒张

superficial [ˌsjuːpəˈfiʃəl] a. 表面的，肤浅的

sedate [siˈdeit] a. 安静的，镇静的

normalization [ˌnɔːməlaiˈzeiʃən] n. 常态化，正常化，正规化

secretion [siˈkriːʃən] n. 分泌，分泌物，分泌液

olfaction [ɔlˈfækʃən] n. 嗅觉

perception [pəˈsepʃən] n. 感觉，知觉

organic [ɔːˈgænik] a. 器官的，有机的，根本的，接近自然的

uplift [ʌpˈlift] n. 高扬，道德的向上，精神昂扬；v. 提高，抬起

sedative [ˈsedətiv] a. 使安静的，使镇静的；n. 镇静剂，能使安静的东西

basil [ˈbæzi] n. 罗勒

rosemary [ˈrəuzməri] n. 迷迭香

jasmine [ˈdʒæsmin] n. 茉莉

ylang-ylang [iːˈlɑːŋiːˈlɑːŋ] n. [植] （菲律宾，马来西亚产的）依兰树 （所产的依兰油用于做香水）

euphoric [juːˈfɔrik] a. 欣快症的，欣快的

Essential oil
精油

洋茴香精油	Aniseed	柠檬精油	Lemon
八角茴香精油	Anise-star	菩提花精油	Linden Blossom
山金车精油	Arnica	山鸡椒精油	Litsea Cubeba
月桂精油	Bay	桔精油	Mandarin
安息香精油	Benzoin	松红梅精油	Manuka
佛手柑精油	Bergamot	金盏菊精油	Marigold
桦木精油	Birch	马郁兰精油	Marjoram
桦木芽精油	Birch Bud	金合欢精油	Mimosa
黑胡椒精油	Black Pepper	艾草精油	Mugwort
樟树精油	Camphor	没药精油	Myrrh
藏茴香精油	Caraway	香桃木精油	Myrtle
豆蔻精油	Cardamom	橙花精油	Neroli
胡萝卜种子油	Carrot Seed	肉豆蔻精油	Nutmeg
雪松精油	Cedarwood	橙精油	Orange
芹菜精油	Celery	橙花纯露精油	Orange-Flower Water
洋甘菊精油	Chamomile	野马郁兰精油	Oregano
肉桂精油	Cinnamon	玫瑰草精油	Palmarosa
香茅精油	Citronella	欧芹精油	Parsley
丁香精油	Clove	广藿香精油	Patchouli
芫荽精油	Coriander	薄荷精油	Peppermint
小茴香精油	Cumin	苦橙叶精油	Petitgrain
丝柏精油	Cypress	松树精油	Pine
紫锥花精油	Echinacea	玫瑰精油	Rose
榄香脂精油	Elemi	玫瑰籽油精油	Rosehip
月见草油	Evening Primose Oil	迷迭香精油	Rosemary
茴香精油	Fennel	玫瑰纯露精油	Rose Water
乳香精油	Frankincense	花梨木精油	Rosewood
白松香精油	Galbanum	檀香精油	Sandalwood
大蒜精油	Garlic	绿薄荷精油	Spearmint
天竺葵精油	Geraium	甘松精油	Spikenard
姜精油	Ginger	万寿菊精油	Tagetes
葡萄柚精油	Grapefruit	龙艾精油	Tarragon
愈创木精油	Guaiacwood	松脂精油	Terebinth
永久花精油	Helichrysum	侧柏精油	Thyja
芳樟精油	Ho-leaf/Ho-wood	百里香精油	Thyme
土木香精油	Inula	茶树精油	Ti-tree
茉莉精油	Jasmine	柠檬马鞭草精油	Verbena
杜松精油	Juniper	岩兰草精油	Vetivert
熏衣草精油	Lavender	紫罗兰精油	Violet

158

After-Reading Task

1. Which of the folowing statement is not ture about the essential oils?
   A. Essential oils are subtle, therapeutic-grade oils distilled from plants, shrubs, flowers, trees, roots, bushes and seeds.
   B. Essential oils are hydrogenating.
   C. The oxygenating essential oils can help us maintain our health.
   D. Essential oils help transport nutrients to the cells of our body.
2. According to the passage, one of the most popular applications for essential oils is _____.
   A. in the field of aromatherapy
   B. in the healing of physical ailments
   C. maintaining our health
   D. in the healing of psychological ailments
3. There are many ways to incorporate the benefits of aromatherapy into our daily lives. Essential oils may _____.
   A. soothe inflammation
   B. act as an antiseptic
   C. help dull pain and stimulate digestion
   D. all of the above
4. Essential oils are easily dissolved in some resolvents except _____.
   A. alcohol   B. fats   C. water   D. emulsifiers
5. Which of the folowing statement is not ture about how the essential oils work?
   A. The essential oils can penetrate the skin easily and work into the body by mixing with the fatty tissue.
   B. The essential oils have highly volatile essences.
   C. The essential oils are inhaled and entered the body via the millions of sensitive cells.
   D. The essential oils are able to enhance both your physical and psychological well-being.
6. According to the passage, what are the effects of using Essential Oils?
   A. affecting the body's physiological systems
   B. the antiseptic and soothing effects
   C. the effect of relaxation on the brain
   D. All of the above

7. Why essential oils can have effects on emotions and mental states?

    A. Perception of odors can't have a major impact on memory, learning, emotions, thinking and feeling.

    B. Because of olfaction's direct connection to the brain, sending electrical messages directly into the limbic system.

    C. Essential oils work similarly to tranquilizers but in a subtle organic way.

    D. Essential oils are easily dissolved in some resolvents.

Further Reading

What is Aromatherapy?

Aromatherapy is the practice of using volatile plant oils, including essential oils, for psychological and physical well-being.

A selection of aromatherapy products.

Essential oils which are the pure "essence" of a plant, have been found to provide both psychological and physical benefits when used correctly and safely. There are many essential oils. The Essential Oil Profiles area details over 90 essential oils. Absolutes, CO_2 s and hydrosols are also commonly utilized in aromatherapy. Click on the links to learn more about them. The term "essential oil" is often used as a blanket term to also include CO_2 s and absolutes.

It is important to note that perfume oils also known as fragrance oils or "fragrances" **are not the same** as essential oils. Perfume oils and fragrances contain unnatural chemicals and do not provide the therapeutic benefits of essential oils. Unfortunately, many companies improperly use the term aromatherapy on products that contain unnatural and perfume oils, so it's important to look at the ingredient label when seeking true aromatherapy products.

The Benefit of an "Aroma"

Essential oils that are inhaled into the lungs are believed to offer both psychological and physical benefits; not only does the aroma of the natural essential oil stimulate the brain to trigger a reaction, but the natural constituents (naturally occurring chemicals) of the essential oil are drawn into the lungs and can also supply physical benefit. If not done correctly and safely, however, the use of essential oils can also have severe consequences.

The Benefit of Physical Application

Oils that are applied to the skin are believed to be absorbed into the bloodstream. The components of the various oils are believed to aid in a variety of health, beauty and hygiene conditions. Since essential oils are so powerful and concentrated, they should never be applied to the skin in their undiluted form. To apply essential oils to the skin, "carrier oils" which are pure vegetable oils are used to dilute the essential oils and "carry" them to the skin. Common carrier oils include sweet almond oil, apricot kernel oil and grapeseed oil. A more detailed definition of Carrier Oils is found on the What are Carrier Oils page. A detailed list of carrier oils and their properties can be found on the Carrier Oils Used in Aromatherapy properties page.

Other Benefits

Essential Oils can supply other benefits as well. Some oils, for instance, act as a natural repellent and pesticide. You may recall using "citronella" candles during the summer to keep mosquitoes away. Citronella essential oil is the ingredient in the candles that provides this benefit. Visit the Essential Oil Uses page for more information on the variety of ways that you can use essential oils.

Essential Oil Blends

Essential oils may be blended together to provide an especially pleasing aroma. Oils can be blended together to also provide a specific therapeutic action. A synergistic essential oil blend of the correct oils in proper proportions is considered to be greater in total benefit than each oil working independently. AromaWeb's Recipes area offers a variety of recipes and synergies.

About Aromatherapy Products

Not all ready-made aromatherapy products labeled with the word "aromatherapy" are pure and natural. Products that contain artificial ingredients do not provide true aromatherapy benefits. At worst, they provide no benefit. At best, they provide only a fraction of the benefit that natural products supply. Buyers seeking true aromatherapy products must look at the ingredients within a product to ensure that the product does not contain fragrance oils or unpure (chemical) components. A general rule-of-thumb is to be wary of products that do not list their ingredients and those that do not boast of having pure essential oils (look for products that contain pure essential oils on their ingredient list and avoid those that have words like fragrance). A note, however, is that some sellers of good-quality aromatherapy blends do not list their ingredients because they are worried that others may copy their creation. By asking the seller more about the blend, and listening to how they respond, you should have a better idea about the quality of the blend being sold. Good suppliers really should be happy to tell you the ingredients when asked as some people should avoid particular oils due to health problems.

Lesson 16　Preservatives

Formulating with preservatives can sometimes be very difficult. More and more products coming on the market contain ingredients which make cosmetic systems very difficult to preserve. Preservation is mandated by the United States Food and Drug Administration. The government states that products sold to the general public must be safe for use when it is applied to the body and it must be free of contamination. Cosmetics are a self-regulated industry. The government leaves it up to us, the formulators, to protect the products we sell from microbial contamination so they are safe to use by the consumer.

We may have a product that is free of contaminants, but the product must be preserved adequately to kill the microorganisms that are introduced by the consumers themselves. One also must be careful as to avoid over-preserving a product. Too much preservative in a product is no good either. In this particular case, more isn't better. A microbiology challenge test will show the minimum amount of preservative needed to provide a kill in a product over time. Support your local microbiologist.

As a formulator, one must do much more research to find the right combination of preservatives to kill any contaminants that may find their way into our products. More research is required simply because many preservatives that worked very well in the past are not being used any longer by the formulator. This could be due to bad press, or there are new things being brought to light by these standards every day preservatives such as safety issues or irritation potential.

With the popularity of all natural cosmetic products, it becomes even more difficult as many of the current preservatives on the market today are synthetic. So how do we preserve a natural product? There are some natural preservative available today but most are not what we consider "broad spectrum", meant to kill a wide variety of microorganisms (bacteria, mold, yeast, fungus, etc.). They are, however, very active at pH 5 to 9 and at 45 to 50℃ temperatures, the range where microbes like to grow. They are usually used in conjunction with other preservatives to kill off the microorganisms that may commonly find their way into cosmetic products. This does make the formulator's job quite challenging (no pun intended).

The major issue is that with decorative cosmetics, there is the extra phase—the color phase—which must be taken into consideration when preserving the product. Different ingredients must be used in conjunction with the colorants to stabilize the system. These new systems now become more difficult to preserve, and conventional preservation systems may not be sufficient. Then the package that is to be used the deliver the color has to be taken into consideration. Will it be a source of contamination itself?

We are very lucky though; many common, natural ingredients today have their own anti-microbial activity. They are very easy to obtain and work very well in various cosmetic applications. And they look good on the ingredient label as well. In a future technical article, we will list some of these natural "preservative" ingredients and how much you can use to effectively obtain a sufficient kill in your product. When used in combination with other ingredients this effect is even more substantial. Yet there are still some preservatives that we use today, that we just cannot live without. They work so well in so many different cosmetic applications. You will find them in almost every cosmetic product on the market. Sometimes it can be more difficult to find the right preservative combination and levels, than to stabilize a product itself. A significant amount of trial and error may be necessary.

Words and Expressions

---

mandate ['mændeit]　　*n.* 命令，指令，要求；*v.* 委任统治

Contamination [kənˌtæmiˈneiʃən]　n. 污染
microbiology challenge test　微生物挑战实验
broad spectrum　广谱
mold [məuld]　n. 模子，雏型，霉；v. 形成，塑造，发霉
microbe [ˈmaikrəub]　n. 微生物
conjunction [kənˈdʒʌŋkʃən]　n. 连接词，连合，关连
extra [ˈekstrə]　a. 额外的；ad. 特别地；n. 额外的事物
colorant [ˈkʌlərənt]　n. 着色剂
trial and error [ˈkʌlərənt]　反复实验

Glossary

Relevant words of microorganism
微生物相关术语

antibiotic	抗生素	broad spectrum	广谱
antibody	抗体	narrow spectrum	窄谱
antigen	抗原	pathogenidty	致病性
disinfection	消毒	differential stain	鉴别染色
asepsis	无菌	inoculation	接种
thermal death point	致死温度	growth factor	生长因子
antiseptic	防腐剂	contaminant	污染物
enriched medium	加富培养基	nutrient	营养物质
sporangium	孢子囊	spirochete	螺旋体
gram-stain	革兰氏染色	strain	菌株
gram-negative bacteria	革兰氏阴性菌	gram-positive bacteria	革兰氏阳性菌
burkholderia cepacia	洋葱假单胞菌	*pseudomonas* aeruginosa	绿脓杆菌
candia albicans	白色念珠菌	*salmonella* spp	沙门氏菌
escherichia coli	大肠杆菌	*staphylococcus aureus*	金黄色葡萄球菌

After-Reading Task

1. Which one mandate the Preservation in the United States?
　　A. food and Drug Administration　　B. government
　　C. the general public　　D. cosmetics industry

2. Which of the following is true from the passage?

   A. We can't have a product that is free of contaminants.

   B. Too much preservative in a product is very good.

   C. The product must be preserved adequately to kill the contaminants.

   D. One also must be careful as to avoid over-preserving a product.

3. As a formulator, one must _____ .

   A. not to find the right combination of preservatives

   B. do much more research to find the right combination of preservatives

   C. to kill any contaminants

   D. find contaminants in our products

4. Why does the natural preservative available today make the formulator's job quite challenging?

   A. They are, very active at pH 5 to 9 and at 45 to 50℃ temperatures, the range where microbes like to grow.

   B. They can kill off the microorganisms that may commonly find their way into cosmetic products by themselves.

   C. They are what we consider "broad spectrum", meant to kill a wide variety of microorganisms.

   D. We can preserve a natural product by the natural preservative available today.

5. Which must be taken into consideration when conventional preservation systems may not be sufficient ?

   A. the extra phase   B. the color phase

   C. the package   D. all of the above

6. Which of the following is wrong from the passage?

   A. Natural ingredients today have their own anti-microbial activity.

   B. Natural ingredients today are very easy to obtain and work very well in various cosmetic applications.

   C. Natural ingredients today look good on the ingredient label as well.

   D. We have list some of the natural "preservative" ingredients and how much you can use to effectively obtain a sufficient kill in your product.

Further Reading

Preservatives in cosmetics

Much is said about preservatives used in cosmetics, and when

166

surfing around on the web, you will be supplied with literally thousands of pages of information dealing with it, but with such a variety of conflicting ideas and data that people simply do not know who and what to believe.

To start placing this in perspective:

The most important thing is that any cosmetic products must be safe for use.

Any product manufactured without an ingredient to prevent and control microbial growth, will start to go off and may even start growing potentially pathogenic organisms.

To control microbial growth and to stabilize any cosmetic product, some form of preservative needs to be used.

The downside of preservatives also has some compelling arguments. Some ingredients can cause allergies in susceptible people, including dermatitis and other side effects.

The most important word to keep in mind when discussing preservatives, is the word "balance" . You need to include enough preservative to control microbial growth, yet not too much so as to cause allergies, dermatitis or any side effects.

When you wish to achieve this balance it takes both time and money, as you need to do microbial and stability tests on your products.

Should a manufacturer decide not to spend the time or money on testing and refining a formula, a stable product can still be made, by including high amounts of preservatives. This will stop microbial growth, but can cause all the negative effects - dermatitis, allergies and other side effects.

We prefer to spend the money on developing a product, and

167

tracking its entire manufacturing process, by batch, to ensure that our products are stable, yet not over-filled with preservatives.

Parabens and all their cousins are the most widely used preservatives in cosmetics, and if included and used correctly by the formulating manufacturer, are safe to use.

Various allegations are made against parabens, and these claims range from their being a cause of breast cancer and liver problems, etc.

Most of these claims are not applicable to cosmetics, as parabens are only used topically and not systemically, with due reference to our comments above regarding the quantities in the formulations.

It must also be noted that the European Cosmetic Toiletry and Perfumery Association (COLIPA) affirm that parabens are hydrolyzed in the skin and that they do not enter the bloodstream. Parabens are not officially identified or listed as an endocrine disrupting chemical by any government or regulatory organization.

UNIT FIVE MAKEUP

Lesson 17 How to Apply Eye Make Up Tips to Look Stunning

Learning how to apply eye make up tips may seem more complicated than for other types of make-up because there is such a variety of colors, tools, and techniques to use. Yet, it is the most important because your eyes are the most expressive facial feature you have.

Keep Your Eyes in Focus Applying Eye Make Up Tips

After all, when you look into someone's face, what is the first feature you focus on?

Their eyes! Yes, the eyes have it! We communicate through our eyes and convey our emotions through them. That's why eye make up (eye shadow) should enhance your eyes (as far as eye color and shape) and not be just excessive (that actually looks nasty and it definitely gets attention but not the kind you want!).

You can have lots of fun while learning to apply eye make up tips. If you have never taken an art class, this is your chance to learn to paint on a living canvas. You can call up a few girl friends and play around while learning how to apply eye make up tips. The techniques you will learn here should give you the courage to give it a try.

Applying Eye Make Up Tips to Create the Illusion of Depth

Eye shadows come in in several textures, powders (compacts),

pencils, and creams:

Powder can be used either dry or wet and it's really easy to control. Make sure you look for a powder that feels moist.

Pencils are fairly easy to use, but you need to remember to smear the line as you go or you'll have lines all over your face.

Creams tend to be hard to control. They can look beautiful and stay that way if you use a good quality eye foundation (eye primer), otherwise they can slip and slide into the creases on your eyes and eyelids.

As you already know, eye make up come in a wide range of beautiful colors. But don't think that just because you have blue eyes you have to wear blue eye make up!

Experiment with Eye Make Up Tips to Find the Balance...

You really need to experiment and play with new colors and have fun learning to apply eye shadow that is within the same shade and that complement each other (you can soften and blend similar colors easier). That's why matte, neutral eye make up is a favorite. When applied properly it draws people's gazes "into" your beautiful eyes, not "at" your eyes.

The ideal behind eye make up tips application is to create illusions that minimize "faults" and increase the perception of picture perfect expressive eyes. Eye makeup should enhance your eye's shape and color. To outline the contour of the eye, you can use eyeliners or pencils.

Eye make up tips can be used for shading and shaping the eye, and mascara to give eyelashes the illusion of length and thickness.

When it comes to creating the illusion of light and shadow, eye makeup does a wonderful job, once you can apply eye make up tips appropriately.

Here's the general rule to apply eye make up tips. You need to use four different-colored shadows as follows: a neutral-toned base, a main color, a lighter shade for highlighting, a darker shade for emphasizing.

It is also important that you have access to a magnifying mirror, and to have a set of variety-sized brushes, and/or cosmetic sponges handy to blend the eye make up.

Should Your Eye Shadow Match Your Eye Color? | ...

As mentioned earlier, excess color detracts from your eyes and becomes counter productive, especially when you try to match it to your eye color. Many times, in trying to match the eye make up to your eye color you end up distracting away from your eyes because the matching color (mismatching in some cases!)  becomes the attraction (this is especially true with non-neutral colors).

So, in following eye make up tips, you'll find that neutral eye shadows are the smart choice because they are easy to work with and complement your skin tone. Of course, neutral doesn't have to mean every shade of brown. Any of the following colors can be considered neutral in the appropriate shade. gray, gold, blue, vanilla, olive, brown, pale purple, mauve, beige.

Applying Eye Make Up Tips to Shade and Highlight...

The techniques of shading and highlighting are used to enhance the natural shape of the eye. Of course, the colors that work the best using these techniques are neutral shades (matte), especially light colored high lighter such as white or cream, and shading color.

You must always remember that: light colors advance (make an area seem larger or closer) while dark colors recede (make an area seem smaller or further away). To create the desired illusion, it is essential to apply eye make up in a way that works with light and dark together and keeps your eyelid shape in mind.

Words and Expressions

stun [stʌn] *v.* 使目瞪口呆，使晕倒，使惊吓

nasty ['næsti] *a.* 污秽的，下流的，险恶的

gaze [geiz] *n.* 凝视，注视

perception [pə'sepʃən] *n.* 感觉，知觉

shading ['ʃeidiŋ] *n.* 底纹，留下阴影

eyelash ['ai,læʃ] *n.* 睫毛

highlight ['hailait] *n.* 加亮区；*v.* 加亮，强调

complement ['kɔmplimənt] *n.* 补足物，补语，余角；*v.* 补助

olive ['ɔliv] *n.* 橄榄，橄榄树，橄榄色；*a.* 黄绿色的，黄褐色的，橄榄色的

vanilla [və'nilə] *n.* 香草

mauve [məuv] *n.* 淡紫色

beige [beiʒ] *a.* 米黄色的；*n.* 米黄色

matte [mæt] *n.* 暗区，不光滑的

After-Reading Task

1. Why the author says your eyes are the most expressive facial feature you have?

   A. Because how to apply eye make up tips may seem more complicated than for other types of make-up.

   B. Because there is such a variety of colors, tools, and techniques to use.

C. Because when you look into someone's face, eye is the first feature you focus on.

D. Because you can have lots of fun while learning to apply eye make up tips.

2. How can you apply the right eye make up for you?

A. If you have blue eyes you have to wear blue eye make up.

B. Powder can be used neither dry nor wet.

C. Pencils are fairly difficult to use.

D. Creams tend to be hard to control.

3. Which of the following statement is not ture about the experiment with eye make up?

A. You really needn't to experiment and play with new colors.

B. Eye makeup should enhance your eye's shape and color.

C. To outline the contour of the eye, you can use eyeliners or pencils.

D. Eye make up tips can be used for shading and shaping the eye.

4. It is also important that you have_____to blend the eye make up.

A. access to a magnifying mirror   B. a set of variety-sized brushes

C. cosmetic sponges handy   D. all of the above

5. Which one is wrong about your eye shadow matching your eye color?

A. Excess color detracts from your eyes and becomes counter productive, especially when you try to match it to your eye color.

B. When the eye make up to your eye color you end up distracting away from your eyes.

C. You'll find that neutral eye shadows are the smart choice because they are easy to work with and complement your skin tone.

D. None of the following colors can be considered neutral in the appropriate shade: blue, vanilla, olive, brown, pale purple, beige.

Further Reading

Tips for Makeup Application

This article basically gives a step-by-step guide on how to apply makeup and the basic tools that are needed.

Applying make-up should not be difficult. It should be a regime that accents your beauty internally, by making you feel good about yourself and externally, by making you look terrific.

First of all, start with a clean face. You will need several tools to make your make-up look it's best. Brushes are very important so be sure to invest in some good quality tools.

Apply Foundation, Concealer and Powders

This is the base for your make-up application. Apply the foundation with your fingers or a Q-tip in dots in areas of your face. With a cosmetic sponge, spread the foundation until it is well-blended into the skin. Be sure to check and make sure that you do not have any lines showing underneath the chin area.

Next, you will need to apply concealer to any blemishes or under-eye circles that you may have. You can use a shade lighter than you skin-tone. When applying concealer to the undereye area, pat gently into the skin and do not rub. Using your finger, pat the concealer into the skin on the blemish areas also until you can no longer see the concealer.

Now it is time to set the previous applications by applying translucent face powder. Get out a big, fluffy powder brush and dip it into some loose facial powder. You can then apply the powder over your entire face.

A few extra tips in this area include apply foundation and powder to your eyelids and lips. This will help your make-up stay on longer.

Start with the Lips

Use a lip pencil to outline the lips and make them stand out. The next step will be to apply lipstick with a lip brush. A lip brush makes the lipstick look professionally applied. If you put the lipstick on first, it will set the scene for applying your other make up.

Brighten Up Your Eyes

Apply a neutral color eye shadow over the lid and up to the eyebrow. Next put a lighter shade on the brow bone and blend it in. Use a blending brush to sweep softly over the lid to blend the shadow in well.

174

Next, apply the eye liner. The best way to line the eye be to use an eye pencil and draw a line underneath the lashes. Take a Q-tip or a liner pencil and blend the liner to get a smoky affect. Last of all, pay special attention to your eyelashes. Use an eyelash curler and curl the lashes for a few seconds. This will open up your eyes and make them look more beautiful than ever. At this point, apply a coat of mascara to the upper lashes and then the lower lashes. A second coat may be used but let the first coat dry first.

Blush

Smile, take a blush brush and apply a shade of blush to your cheeks. After this part, sweep the brush back into the hairline. This will make your face glow.

This is the basics of make-up application. There are many colors and tools to experiment. Find your look and remember, applying make-up is an art which makes you look your best.

Color Your Hair At Home

There are a great number of women who change their own hair color themselves. There are a lot of different tools that are available to help change the hair color and these tools have made things pretty easy. The hair color adds texture, volume and gives shine to the hair. You do not have to make any appointments with your hairstylist to get your hair done and you can do that at home pretty easily.

1. How To Last Your Hair Color Longer: We must take note that the dry air and the sunlight takes out the hair color that we apply and the color fades away at a very fast rate. It must be noted that after applying the hair color, you must not apply shampoo for at least one day so as to extend the hair color longer. There are hair colors in the market that ensure that they last longer and have specific chemicals inside them that ensures that. So you must remember that you do not shampoo much so as to extend the dura-

tion of your hair color.

2. How To Get The Same Shade As The Package: It seems almost impossible to match the shade of hair that you see on the box. You must do a test on a strand of hair that are not on the surface and then you will know as to what color you are going to get. By testing the color before you would be able to see as to what outcome will be there and it would prevent you from having a look that you never wanted or thought of. So you must stay within two shades of your natural hair color.

3. How Can I Color My Hair That Are Gray: It must be noted that the gray hair do not take on the dye as they do not contain melanin, which is the binder of the dye. The gray hair are coarser. The only option that the person has is that they opt for a permanent hair dye and leave it on their hair for the complete amount of time that is specified on the hair color box. You must also apply the warm towel after you have placed it in a dryer and wrap it around the hair as it will let the hair color develop.

4. How To Color The Roots: You must use the head color with the special Root Touch Up Kit, which allows you to target the roots more effectively.

Lesson 18   Perfumes For Women

The scent that you wear is a reflection of your personality. There are a lot of perfumes that are out there in the market and, but the problem that arises is that which are the ones that would suit you the best.

There can be an easy way that you are able to find out the right perfume for you by knowing as to which category you like the best and you think would be the best expression of your personality.

We will discuss about the different categories that are there from which you can pick up the perfume, which includes floral, fruity, woody, greens and oriental. We will be discussing on them one by one in the coming paragraphs.

Floral: The floral perfumes have the fragrance of flowers. These include jasmine, lavender, etc. Floral perfumes have been liked by many people throughout the world and are mostly chosen by women because it gives a wonderful fragrance. These perfumes are best for all ages and can be worn for all occasions. One can even call them evergreen fragrances. Just to name a few of the floral fragrances that are there by the world's renowned brand labels include, Anais Anais by Cacharel, Escape by Calvin Klein, and Sunflowers by Elizabeth Arden.

Fruity: The fruity fragrances are spicy and fresh. These fragrances can be used in both the warm and cool weather months. These fragrances can go really well with any occasion and will cause the heads to turn. They are pretty light and pretty cool to wear. Just to name a few of the fruity fragrances, they are, Champagne by Yves Saint Laurent, Cheap and Chic by Moschino and DKNY's Be Delicious.

Woody: These perfumes have the natural fragrance of wood. It just feels that you are surrounded by wood and there is a smooth fragrance of the wood all around you. The types that are there in this category are cedar, patchouli and sandalwood and are really amazing to wear. These are really good for women who are mature and these perfumes would give them a true sophisticated match. These perfumes can also be worn during the warm and cooler months as well. In order to name some of the few woody fragrances include, Givenchy Organza, Chanel No. 19 and Lovely by Sarah Jessica Parker.

Greens: The green perfumes give the essence of the cut grass and crunchy spring buds. They are very light and go pretty well with the casual wear. These perfumes are very much favorable for the young ones and can be pretty easily worn at all occasions. The examples of these fragrances include Diorissimo by Christian Dior, Metal Jeans Women by Versace and Charlie by Revlon.

Oriental: Oriental perfumes are strong and are supplemented with the different sweet scents such as vanilla, musk, flowers and resins. The oriental perfumes do usually go in a mix of different blends as mentioned above and are just excellent. They can be worn by anyone regardless the age and on any given occasion. These include Fendi by Fendi, Chance by Chanel.

You must also know that when you are on your hunt to buy the perfume, you must also ask the sales person to tell you about the different cross breeds that are there of different perfumes so you have a wide option as to what other options are there for you to select from and you can make the best choice possible.

Words and Expressions

reflection [reˈflekʃən] *n*. 反射，映象，倒影，反省，沉思，反映
pick up 捡起，拾起
floral [ˈflɔːrəl] *a*. 花似的，花的，植物的
fruity [ˈfruːti] *a*. 水果的，有水果香味的，圆润的
oriental [ˌɔ(ː)riˈentl] *a*. 东方人的
jasmine [ˈdʒæsmin] *n*. 茉莉
lavender [ˈlævində] *n*. 淡紫色，熏衣草
occasion [əˈkeiʒən] *n*. 场合，机会，理由；*v*. 致使，惹起，引起
evergreen [ˈevəgriːn] *n*. 常绿树，常绿植物；*a*. 常绿的
sunflower [ˈsʌnflauə] *n*. 向日葵

spicy ['spaisi] *a*. 芳香的（辛辣的）

cedar ['si:də] *n*. 西洋杉，香柏

patchouli ['pætʃuli(:)] *n*. [植] 广藿香，天竺薄荷，广藿香油（制香料用）

sandalwood ['sændlwud] *n*. 檀香木

sophisticate [sə'fistikeit] *n*. 久经世故的人，老油条；*v*. 玩弄诡辩，掺合，弄复杂

crunchy ['krʌntʃi] *a*. 发嘎吱嘎吱声的，易碎的

bud [bʌd] *n*. 芽，花蕾；*v*. 发芽，萌芽

supplement ['sʌplimənt] *n*. 补充物，增刊；*v*. 补充，增补

vanilla [və'nilə] *n*. 香草

musk [mʌsk] *n*. 麝香鹿，能发出麝香的各种各样的植物

breed *n*. 品种，族类；*v*. 养育，繁殖，引起

Glossary

Flowers
鲜花

azalea	杜鹃花	lily	百合
begonia	秋海棠	mangnolia	木兰花
Brazil	巴西木	mangnolia	玉兰花
cactus	仙人掌	morning glory	牵牛（喇叭花）
camellia	山茶花	narcissus	水仙花
carnation	麝香石竹（康乃馨）	oleander	夹竹桃
Chinese enkianthus	灯笼花	orchid	兰花
Chinese flowering	海棠花	pansy	三色堇
crab-apple	（野生）酸苹果	peony	牡丹
chrysanthemum	菊花	peony	芍药
dahlia	大丽花	phalaenopsis	蝶兰
daisy	雏菊	rose	玫瑰
datura	曼陀罗	lilac	丁香
epiphyllum	昙花	setose asparagus	文竹
fringed iris	蝴蝶花	touch-me-not(balsam)	凤仙花
fuchsia	倒挂金钟	tulip	郁金香
gardenia	栀子	Violet stock violet	紫罗兰
India canna	美人蕉	water hyacinth	凤眼兰
jasmine	茉莉		

After-Reading Task

1. How can you find out the right perfume for you?
   A. You can pick up the perfume from the different categories that are there.
   B. The scent that you wear is a reflection of your personality.
   C. There are a lot of perfumes that are out there in the market.
   D. by knowing as to which category you like the best and you think would be the best expression of your personality.

2. The floral perfumes have the fragrance of_____?
   A. flowers   B. spicy   C. wood   D. grass

3. Why most women chose the floral perfumes?
   A. Floral perfumes have been liked by many people.
   B. Because it gives a wonderful fragrance.
   C. Because these fragrances can be used in both the warm and cool weather months.
   D. Because these fragrances can go really well with any occasion and will cause the heads to turn.

4. The world's renowned brand labels of the floral fragrances include_____.
   A. Escape by Calvin Klein
   B. Champagne by Yves Saint Laurent
   C. Lovely by Sarah Jessica Parker
   D. Chance by Chanel

5. Which of the following statement is ture about the fruity fragrances?
   A. These fragrances can be used in neither the warm nor cool weather months.
   B. The fruity fragrances are spicy and fresh.
   C. These fragrances cann't go really well with any occasion.
   D. They are the best for all ages and can be worn for all occasions.

6. The woody fragrance are really good for women_____.
   A. for all ages and can be worn for all occasions
   B. used in both the warm and cool weather months
   C. who are the young ones and can be pretty easily worn at all occasions
   D. who are mature and these perfumes would give them a true sophisticated match

7. Which of the following statement is not ture about the green fragrances?

180

A. The green perfumes give the essence of the cut grass and crunchy spring buds.

B. They are very light and go pretty well with the casual wear.

C. These perfumes are very much favorable for all women and can be pretty easily worn at all occasions.

D. The examples of these fragrances include Diorissimo by Christian Dior, Metal Jeans Women by Versace and Charlie by Revlon.

8. Which of the following statement is not ture about the oriental fragrances?

A. Oriental perfumes are strong and are supplemented with the different sweet scents such as vanilla, musk, flowers and resins.

B. The oriental perfumes do usually go in a mix of different blends as mentioned above and are just excellent.

C. They can be worn by anyone regardless the age and on any given occasion.

D. The examples of the oriental fragrances include Diorissimo by Christian Dior, Metal Jeans Women by Versace and Charlie by Revlon.

Further Reading

A Brief History of Perfumery

The human use of scents, aromas and fragrances has its origins lost in ancient times. Why and when people started to prepare them will never be known. However, archeological findings, early written texts and oral tradition, show that the history of aromas goes deep back in time. Early civiliza-tions offered scent flowers, herbs and resins in worship of their Gods. When burned, some plants released stronger aromas and scented smoke fires became part of religious rituals, a mystical mean of communication between the heaven and earth, a tradition followed by many religions until the present days.

The Assyrian and the Egyptians, who started their civilizations in the fourth millennium B. C. , knew how to use medicinal plants to make

181

 remedies as well as scented oils, unguents and balms. The demand for the raw materials needed in fragrances and remedies led to the discovery of new methods of extracting scents. A large number of new techniques were mastered and craftsman developed processes like pressing, decoction, pulverization and maceration, and made the initial attempts to produce essential oils by distillation.

Alexandria became the most important trade center of the region, receiving goods from the Eastern trade, processing Arabian drugs and Indian perfumes. The raw materials arrived from Arabia, Persia, India and China. The use  of perfumes spread to Greece where they started to be used not only in religious practices but also for personal purposes, a fundamental change in the direction of the modern employment of perfumes and cosmetics and their present industrial production. Following the trend, the Romans used fragrances lavishly. Their manuscripts describe and illustrate herbs brought from all over the world.

 A decline in the use of aromas for personal purposes occurred with the fall of the Roman Empire and during the Middle Ages in Europe, when perfume was again only used in church rituals and for cover the stench of disease. Fortunately exotic flowers, herbs and spices became once again available in Europe when trade to the Orient was reestablished in the beginning of the 13th century A. C.. From the Arabs came the knowledge of alchemy and distillation of essential oils. Venice became the center of the perfume trade and soon perfumery spread to other European countries. The perfume trade

developed rapidly as the Crusaders reintroduced
the personal use of perfume upon their return to
Europe.

It is interesting to note that until then, i. e. for
more than 4000 years, the raw materials employed
in the manufacturing of aromas, perfumes, remedies
and cosmetics came exclusively from natural vegetal or animal sources.
It was only in the late 18th century A. C. that the first synthetic fragrance material was produced. This was the beginning of the modern
age of perfumery. With the event of synthetics, perfumery would no
longer be exclusively used by the wealthy.

The large scale industrial production of per
fumes increased after the appearance of larger numbers of new synthetics. Naturals were used to soften
synthetics. However, the synthetics were often
harsh and lacked the softness proper of naturals.

So naturals remained an important part of modern
formulations. On the other hand, some synthetic raw materials
may induce allergic reactions and other skin problems in some
users.

The return to non-industrial techniques of manufacture and the
use of natural products can be achieved by making your own perfumes, cosmetics, balms, remedies, soaps, perfumed oils and
so forth. It may sound a pretentious and absurd proposition to
most people but, as you will see, making your own perfumes is
not only easy but also a source of great pleasure and fun.

Lesson 19　Applicaion of Foundation

Applying foundation is the most sensitive thing, as if it is not done appropriately, then it would give you a pretty bad look. Therefore you need to understand as to how you are going to apply the foundation that would suit you the best. The right way to apply a foundation is that your skin looks natural and does not look any odd. If you are applying the foundation the right way then you are able to hide the roughness, spots, blemishes of your skin.

So when you are to apply a foundation, you must see as to what is your skin type and color, as this will help you to select the right foundation for you.

Now in the coming paragraphs, we are going to discuss different foundations one by one.

Liquid Foundations are suitable for all skin types. These foundations, they usually cover the entire area pretty easily and gives you a more natural look. They are pretty easy to apply as well. You can get the liquid foundations that are prepared in both the water based and the oil based formulas.

Cream Foundations are not a good choice because they dry up pretty quickly and it makes the blending of the makeup pretty difficult. They give a pretty extensive coverage and are known for their moisturizing properties and hence it is ideal for the normal and dry skin.

Compact Foundations are the best choice for oily and normal skin. They give lighter coverage when they are applied with a dry sponge and they give a heavy coverage when they are applied with a wet sponge.

Dual Active Powder Foundations are best for women who have less time for makeup and are in the working class and have to meet their deadlines. This provides the foundation and the powder in one application and gives excellent coverage.

The tinted moisturizer is best for all skin types and it gives a nice glow to your skin and helps moisturize the dry skin that gets more dry with the exposure to the sun. These moisturizers commonly are available with an SPF protection.

When you are selecting the foundation for you, you must know that the color of the foundation must be identical to your skin tone. So, you must go for a foundation that is yellow based foundation and must avoid the pink or orange tones. When you are selecting the color, you must select it in the natural light, which will give you the right idea as to what is best for you.

When you are applying the foundation, you must apply the foundation dots carefully on one side of the face first and then blend them well with the makeup sponge from top of your face to down, which would create a smooth and even finish. Now you need to repeat the same procedure to the opposite side. You must blend the foundation correctly and you must make sure that you have blended the foundation under the jawline, under the hair line and the ear lobes, corners of the nose, corners of the eyes and under the eyes. After applying the foundation, you must apply the powder by gently dusting it on the skin and this will set your foundation.

Words and Expressions

apply [əˈplai]   v. 应用，申请，涂
odd [ɔd]   a. 奇数的，古怪的，剩余的；n. 奇数
roughness [ˈrʌfnis]   n. 粗糙，凹凸面，蓬乱的毛发
paragraph [ˈpærəɡrɑːf]   n. （文章）段，节，段落；vt. 将…分段
Liquid Foundation   液体粉底
oil based formula   油基配方
cream foundation   粉底霜
compact foundation   粉饼

sponge [spʌndʒ] n. 海绵，海绵状的东西；v. 用海绵擦拭，吸收掉，抹掉
dual Active Powder Foundations   双效粉底
working class   工人阶级的
deadline ['dedlain] n. 最后期限
tinted a. 带色彩的
glow [gləu] n. 赤热，光辉，热情；v. 发红光，红光焕发
identical (to) a. 相同于（和…一致）
go for v. 去找，努力获取，被认为，主张，拥护
pink [piŋk] a. 粉红色的；n. 粉红色
make sure that vt. 查明，确信
jawline ['dʒɔːˌlain] n. 下颌的轮廓，下巴的外形
lobe [ləub] n. 圆形突出部，耳朵，裂片
dusting ['dʌstiŋ] n. 打扫，殴打，暴风雨的

After-Reading Task

1. According to the passage, applying foundation is the most sensitive thing, you should do the right thing except _____ .
   A. need to understand how to apply the foundation
   B. must see what is your skin color
   C. must see what is your skin type
   D. select the oundation optionally

2. Which following one is not true about the "Liquid Foundations"?
   A. Liquid Foundations are suitable for all skin types.
   B. Liquid Foundations usually cover the entire area pretty easily and gives you a more natural look.
   C. Liquid Foundations are pretty easy to apply as well.
   D. The liquid foundations can't be prepared in the oil based formulas.

3. Cream Foundations are knowing for _____ .
   A. Being idle for the normal and dry skin
   B. Being ideal for the normal and dry skin
   C. the blending of the makeup pretty easy
   D. their drying up properties

4. The best choice for oily and normal skin is to use _____?

   A. Liquid Foundations

   B. Cream Foundations.

   C. Compact Foundations.

   D. Dual Active Powder Foundations

5. When you are selecting the foundation for you, you must know that _____.

   A. the color of the foundation must be identical to your skin tone

   B. you must go for a pink based foundation

   C. you must select a foundation in the dark light

   D. You have to meet their deadlines

6. When you are applying the foundation, you must _____.

   A. blend the foundation well with the makeup sponge from top of your face to down first

   B. apply the foundation dots carefully on one side of the face second

   C. blend the foundation correctly

   D. must make sure that you have blended the foundation up the jawline

Further Reading

Tips For Applying Makeup

There are a lot of techniques that you can use while applying makeup, which will change your look and appearance and would make you look a whole lot beautiful. There are some things that you can consider such as what is the right color for your skin tone, how to apply the makeup, etc. In this article we are going to discuss these things to give you a general idea as to what is right for you.

1. You must not apply shadows to your eyes that are white or black and if you think you need to apply a light color you can select light beige. If you prefer to apply dark color and like it more, you can apply brown or gray.

2. Just remember that if you have an olive complexion, then

you must avoid the gray shades.

3. You must not use the vibrant colors if you have a pale complexion.

4. If you are a blonde, then you must use pink shades for blush and lipstick, brunettes must use peach, and for redheads, they must use the shades that are bronze. You can also check the different shades with your skin to see as to what are the colors that suit you the best.

5. If you want to have a natural look, you can use brown mascara.

6. If you have small eyes and you want your eyes to pop, you can curl your eyelashes with a curler and apply mascara.

7. For eyelids, you must apply a light color on the lid and a darker shade on the upper outer lid. You must another shade around your eyelid crease that is darkest and you must blend it well too.

8. You must use a round tip blush brush and blend it well.

9. You can place foundation in dots on your forehead, cheeks, nose and chin and rub it well with your fingers.

10. You can apply a lip liner on your lips and then apply a lipstick for longer lasting effect.

11. Apply eye shadows with the makeup brushes and not use the tiny brushes that come with your cosmetic kits.

12. If you have acne, you must apply Neutrogena Foundation, which covers the acne spots really well and is tested and proven.

13. You must pat an eye cream underneath the eyes and then use a concealer, which has the yellowish tone and then apply the foundation according to your skin tone.

14. You can use an eyebrow pencil, which is sharp so that

you can make thin eyebrow lines.

15. If you have a wide nose, then you must use a dark foundation and just apply it to the sides of your nose and then highlight the center of your nose by a light colored powder.

What Is A Facial

A facial cleans, exfoliates and nourishes the skin to promote clear, well-hydrated skin. A facial is the second most popular spa service after massage.

The Basic Steps of a Facial

A facial involves a few basic steps:

cleansing

skin analysis, where the esthetician puts eyepads over your eyes and looks at your skin through a brightly lit magnifying lamp

exfoliation, usually while a steam vapor is directed at your face.

extraction of blackheads if you want it and it's suitable for your skin type. (It can cause broken capillaries.)

facial massage to relax you and stimulate your skin and facial muscles

a mask targeted to your skin type (dry, oily, combination, sensitive, mature.)

application of toners and protective creams

advice on home skin care

Who Gives A Facial?

A facial is given by a licensed esthetician with special training in skin care.

How Much Does a Facial Cost?

A facial usually starts around $75 at a day spa in a smaller city. Prices will be higher at destination spas, resort and hotel spas. Special masks and serums also make the price go higher.

How Often Should I Get A Facial?

Ideally, get a facial every four to six weeks because that's how long it takes the skin to regenerate. Try to have a facial at least four times a year, as the season changes. You may need it more frequently if you are trying to clear up a case of acne, especially at the beginning.

Variations on the Classic European Facial

Variations on the classic European facial include the "mini-facial" (cleansing without extractions) and specialty facials. Add vitamin C, and you have an "age defense" facial. It's an "oxygen facial" when a mist of pure oxygen is part of the treatment, and a "collagen facial" when special collagen sheets are placed on the skin. An acne facial will pay special attention to extractions.

Lesson 20　Tattoos and Permanent Makeup

FDA considers the inks used in intradermal tattoos, including permanent makeup, to be cosmetics and considers the pigments used in the inks to be color additives requiring premarket approval under the Federal Food, Drug, and Cosmetic Act. However, because of other public health priorities and a previous lack of evidence of safety concerns, FDA has not traditionally regulated tattoo inks or the pigments used in them. The actual practice of tattooing is regulated by local jurisdictions. FDA is aware of more than 150 reports of adverse reactions in consumers to certain permanent make-up ink shades, and it is possible that the actual number of women affected was greater. In addition, concerns raised by the scientific community regarding the pigments used in these inks have prompted FDA to investigate the safe use of tattoo inks. FDA continues to evaluate the extent and severity of adverse events associated with tattooing and is conducting research on inks. As new information is assessed, the agency will consider whether additional actions are necessary to protect public health.

In addition to the reported adverse reactions, areas of concern include tattoo removal, infections that result from tattooing, and the increasing variety of pigments and diluents being used in tattooing. More than fifty different pigments and shades are in use, and the list continues to grow. Although a number of color additives are approved for use in cosmetics, none is approved for injection into the skin. Using an unapproved color additive in a tattoo ink makes the ink adulterated. Many pigments used in tattoo inks are not approved for skin contact at all. Some are industrial grade colors that are suitable for printers' ink or automobile paint.

Nevertheless, many individuals choose to undergo tattooing in its various forms. For some, it is an aesthetic choice or an initiation rite. Some choose permanent makeup as a time saver or because they have physical difficulty applying regular, temporary makeup. For others, tattooing is an adjunct to reconstructive surgery, particularly of the face or breast, to simulate natural pigmentation. People who have lost their eyebrows due to alopecia (a form of hair loss) may choose to have "eyebrows" tattooed on, while people with vitiligo (a lack of pigmentation in areas of the skin) may try tattooing to help camouflage the condition.

Whatever their reason, consumers should be aware of the risks involved in order to make an informed decision.

What Risks Are Involved in Tattooing?

The following are the primary complications that can result from tattooing:

Infection. Unsterile tattooing equipment and needles can transmit infectious diseases, such as hepatitis and skin infections

191

caused by Staphylococcus aureus ("staph") bacteria Tattoos received at facilities not regulated by your state or at facilities that use unsterile equipment (or re-use ink) may prevent you from being accepted as a blood or plasma donor for twelve months.

Removal problems. Despite advances in laser technology, removing a tattoo is a painstaking process, usually involving several treatments and considerable expense. Complete removal without scarring may be impossible.

Allergic reactions. Although FDA has received reports of numerous adverse ractions associated with certain shades of ink in permanent makeup, marketed by a particular manufacturer, reports of allergic reactions to tattoo pigments have been rare. However, when they happen they may be particularly troublesome because the pigments can be hard to remove. Occasionally, people may develop an allergic reaction to tattoos they have had for years.

Granulomas. These are nodules that may form around material that the body perceives as foreign, such as particles of tattoo pigment.

Keloid formation. If you are prone to developing keloids—scars that grow beyond normal boundaries—you are at risk of keloid formation from a tattoo. Keloids may form any time you injure or traumatize your skin. Micropigmentation: State of the Art, a book written by Charles Zwerling, M. D. , Annette Walker, R. N. , and Norman Goldstein, M. D. , states that keloids occur more frequently as a consequence of tattoo removal.

MRI complications. There have been reports of people with tattoos or permanent makeup who experienced swelling or burning in the affected areas when they underwent magnetic resonance imaging (MRI). This seems to occur only rarely and apparently without lasting effects.

192

There also have been reports of tattoo pigments interfering with the quality of the image. This seems to occur mainly when a person with permanent eyeliner undergoes MRI of the eyes. Mascara may produce a similar effect. The difference is that mascara is easily removable.

The cause of these complications is uncertain. Some have theorized that they result from an interaction with the metallic components of some pigments.

However, the risks of avoiding an MRI when your doctor has recommended one are likely to be much greater than the risks of complications from an interaction between the MRI and tattoo or permanent makeup. Instead of avoiding an MRI, individuals who have tattoos or permanent makeup should inform the radiologist or technician of this fact in order to take appropriate precautions and avoid complications.

A Common Problem: Dissatisfaction

A common problem that may develop with tattoos is the desire to remove them. Removing tattoos and permanent makeup can be very difficult.

Although tattoos may be satisfactory at first, they sometimes fade. Also, if the tattooist injects the pigments too deeply into the skin, the pigments may migrate beyond the original sites, resulting in a blurred appearance.

Another cause of dissatisfaction is that the human body changes over time, and styles change with the season. The permanent makeup that may have looked flattering when first injected may later clash with changing skin tones and facial or body contours. People who plan to have facial cosmetic surgery are advised that the appearance of their permanent makeup may become distorted. The tattoo that seemed stylish at first may become dated

193

and embarrassing. And changing tattoos or permanent makeup is not as easy as changing your mind.

Consult your healthcare provider about the best removal techniques for you.

What About Temporary Tattoos?

Temporary tattoos, such as those applied to the skin with a moistened wad of cotton, fade several days after application. Most contain color additives approved for cosmetic use on the skin. However, the agency has issued an import alert for certain foreign-made temporary tattoos.

The temporary tattoos subject to the import alert are not allowed into the United States because they don't carry the FDA-mandated ingredient labels or they contain colors not permitted by FDA for use in cosmetics applied to the skin. FDA has received reports of allergic reactions to temporary tattoos.

In a similar action, FDA has issued an import alert for henna intended for use on the skin. Henna is approved only for use as a hair dye, not for direct application to the skin. Also, henna typically produces a reddish brown tint, raising questions about what ingredients are added to produce the varieties of colors labeled as "henna", such as "black henna" and "blue henna." FDA has also received reports of allergic reactions to products applied to the skin that contain henna.

Words and Expressions

tattoo [təˈtuː, tæˈtuː] n. &vt. (在皮肤上) 刺图案，文身
intradermal [ˌintrəˈdəːml] a. 皮内的，皮层内的
jurisdictions [ˌdʒuərisˈdikʃən] n. 司法权，审判权，管辖权
severity [siˈveriti] n. 严格，严重，激烈

diluent ['diljuənt]　*a.* 冲淡，稀释；*n.* 稀释液，稀释药

injection [in'dʒekʃən]　*n.* 注射

unapproved ['ʌnə'pruːvd]　*a.* 未经同意的（未准的）

adulterate [ə'dʌltəreit]　*v.* 搀……使品质变劣

pigment ['pigmənt]　*n.* 色素，颜料；*v.* 把……加颜色，变色

printer ['printə]　*n.* 打印机，印刷工

automobile ['ɔːtəməbiːl]　*n.* 汽车

aesthetic [iːs'θetik]　*a.* 美学的，审美的，有美感

rite [rait]　*n.* 仪式，典礼

adjunct ['ædʒʌŋkt]　*n.* 附属物，附件，修饰语

reconstructive [.riːkən'strʌktiv]　*a.* 重建的，改造的，有益于再建的

alopecia [.ælə'piːsiə]　*n.* 秃头症

vitiligo [.viti'laigəu]　*n.* 白癜风

camouflage ['kæmuflɑːʒ]　*v.* 伪装，欺瞒

unsterile　*a.* 未杀菌的

infectious [in'fekʃəs]　*a.* 传染的

hepatitis [.hepə'taitis]　*n.* 肝炎

staphylococcus [.stæfiləu'kɔkəs]　*n.* 葡萄状球菌

plasma ['plæzmə]　*n.* 等离子体（血浆，深绿玉髓）

painstaking ['peinsteikiŋ]　*n.* 辛苦，苦心，工夫；*a.* 辛苦的，勤勉的，小心的

scar [skɑː]　*n.* 疤痕，伤痕，断崖；*v.* 结疤，使……有伤痕，痊愈

granulomas [.grænju'ləumə]　*n.* ［医］肉芽肿，肉芽瘤

nodule ['nɔdjuːl]　*n.* 小节，小瘤，小结节

keloid ['kiːlɔid]　*n.* ［医］瘢痕疙瘩，瘢痕瘤

prone [prəun]　*a.* 俯卧的，易于……的，有……倾向的

boundary ['baundəri]　*n.* 分界线，边界

traumatize ['trɔːmətaiz]　*v.* 使受损伤，使受精神上创伤

magnetic resonance imaging（MRI）　磁共振成像

complication [.kɔmpli'keiʃ(ə)n]　*n.* 复杂化，使……复杂的因素

eyeliner ['ailainə(r)] *n.* 眼线膏

radiologist [ˌreidi'ɔlədʒist] *n.* 放射线学者

technician [tek'niʃ(ə)n] *n.* 技术员，技师

precaution [pri'kɔːʃən] *n.* 预防，留心，警戒

dissatisfaction ['disˌsætis'fækʃən] *n.* 不满

fade [feid] *v.* 褪色，消失，凋谢

blur [bləː] *v.* 使……模糊

clash [klæʃ] *n.* 冲突，撞击声，抵触；*v.* 冲突，抵触，使……发出撞击声

contour ['kɔntuə] *n.* 轮廓（等高线，周线，电路，概要）；*vt.* 画轮廓（画等高线）

stylish ['stailiʃ] *a.* 现代风格的，流行的，潇洒的

moisten ['mɔisn] *v.* 弄湿

wad [wɔd] *v.* 使……成一团

henna ['henə] *n.* 指甲花，指甲花染料，红褐色

reddish ['rediʃ] *a.* 带红色的，微红的；*n.* 色彩，浅色；痕迹

Glossary

护肤	skin care	晚霜	night cream
洗面奶	facial cleanser/face wash	眼部 GEL	eye gel
爽肤水	toner/astringent	面膜	facial mask/masque
紧肤水	firming lotion	眼膜	eye mask
柔肤水	toner/smoothing toner(facial mist/facial spray/complexion mist)	护唇用	Lip care
		口红护膜	Lip coat
		磨砂膏	facial scrub
护肤霜	moisturizers and creams	去黑头	pore cleanser/striper pore refining
保湿	moisturizer		
隔离霜,防晒	sun screen/sun block	去死皮	Exfoliating Scrub
美白	whitening	润肤露(身体)	bodylotion/moisturizer
露	lotion	护手霜	hand lotion/moisturizer
霜	cream	沐浴露	body wash
日霜	day cream		

After-Reading Task

1. Which of the following is ture about tattoos from the first paragraph？

196

A. FDA has traditionally regulated tattoo inks or the pigments.

B. FDA doesn't consider the inks used in intradermal tattoos to be cosmetics.

C. FDA continues to evaluate the extent and severity of adverse events associated with tattooing.

D. FDA hasn't conducted research on tattoo inks.

2. Why has FDA not traditionally regulated tattoo inks or the pigments used in intradermal tattoos?

A. because of other public health priorities and a previous lack of evidence of safety concerns.

B. because of the inks used in intradermal tattoosto be cosmetic.

C. because of the pigments used in the inks to be color additives.

D. because of concerns raised by the scientific community regarding the pigments used in these inks.

3. According to the passage which following is true about tattoo ink?

A. There are less than 150 reports of adverse reactions in consumers to certain permanent make-up ink shades.

B. A number of color additives are approved for injection into the skin.

C. Many pigments used in tattoo inks are not approved for skin contact at all.

D. Using an approved color additive in a tattoo ink makes the ink adulterated.

4. People may choose to have "eyebrows" tattooed on, the reason maybe _____.

A. they have lost their eyebrows due to alopecia

B. they have physical difficulty applying regular

C. it is an aesthetic choice or an initiation rite

D. they choose permanent makeup as a time saver

5. Which of the following isn't the primary complications that can result from tattooing?

A. Infection   B. Removal problems

C. Allergic reactions   D. cataract

6. Which of the following is not true about MRI?

A. When people underwent magnetic resonance imaging they would experience swelling or burning in the affected areas.

197

B. When a person with permanent eyeliner undergoes MRI of the eyes the tattoo pigments maybe interfered with the quality of the image.

C. Mascara may produce a similar effect as MRI. There aren't difference in the effect made by mascara and MRI.

D. The risks of avoiding an MRI are likely to be much greater than the risks of complications from an interaction between the MRI and tattoo or permanent makeup.

7. Which of the following is wrong about the Dissatisfaction of tattoos?

A. Removing the dissatisfacted tattoos and permanent makeup can be very easy.

B. Tattoos sometimes fade or results in a blurred appearance.

C. One cause of dissatisfaction is that the human body changes over time, and styles change with the season.

D. The tattoo that seemed stylish at first may become dated and embarrassing.

8. According to the passage, which of the following statement about the temporary tattoos is likely true?

A. Temporary tattoos applied to the skin with a moistened wad of cotton, fade several days after application.

B. Temporary tattoos contain color additives approved for drug use on the skin .

C. The temporary tattoos subject to the import alert are allowed into the United States.

D. FDA hasn't received reports of allergic reactions to temporary tattoos.

Further Reading

Getting a Tattoo

If you're thinking about getting a tattoo, there is one very important thing you have to keep in mind—getting it done safely. Although it might look a whole lot cooler than a big scab, a new tattoo is also a wound. Like any other slice, scrape, puncture, cut, or penetration to your skin, a tattoo is at risk for infections and disease.

First, make sure you're up to date with your immunizations (especially hepatitis and tetanus shots) and plan where you'll get medical care if your tattoo becomes infected (signs of infection include excessive redness or tenderness around the tattoo, prolonged bleeding, pus, or changes in your skin color around the tattoo).

If you have a medical problem such as heart disease, allergies, diabetes, skin disorders, a condition that affects your immune system, or infections—or if you are pregnant—ask your doctor if there are any special concerns you should have or precautions you should take beforehand. Also, if you're prone to getting keloids (an overgrowth of scar tissue in the area of the wound), it's probably best to avoid getting a tattoo altogether.

It's very important to make sure the tattoo studio is clean and safe, and that all equipment used is disposable (in the case of needles, gloves, masks, etc.) and sterilized (everything else). Some states, cities, and communities set up standards for tattoo studios, but others don't. You can call your state, county, or local health department to find out about the laws in your community, ask for recommendations on licensed tattoo shops, or check for any complaints about a particular studio.

Professional studios usually take pride in their cleanliness. Here are some things to check for:

Make sure the tattoo studio has an autoclave (a device that uses steam, pressure, and heat for sterilization). You should be allowed to watch as equipment is sterilized in the autoclave.

Check that the tattoo artist is a licensed practitioner. If so, the tattoo artist should be able to provide you with references.

Be sure that the tattoo studio follows the Occupational Safety and Health Administration's Universal Precautions. These are regulations that outline procedures to be followed when dealing with bodily fluids (in this case, blood).

If the studio looks unclean, if anything looks out of the ordinary, or if you feel in any way uncomfortable, find a better place to get your tattoo.

APPENDIX

APPENDIX Ⅰ Vocabulary

a protective coating 保护涂层

according to 根据

account for *v.* 说明，占，解决，得分

accumulate [əˈkjuːmjuleit] *v.* 积聚，堆积

acne [ˈækni] *n.* 粉刺

active Ingredient 活性组分，有效成分

address [əˈdres] *n.* 住址，致词，讲话；*vt.* 发表演说，写地址，（图书、文章等）讨论（某主题）

adher to 坚持，依附

adjunct [ˈædʒʌŋkt] *n.* 附属物，附件，修饰语

adolescence [ˌædəuˈlesəns] *n.* 青春期

adulterate [əˈdʌltəreit] *v.* 搀……使品质变劣

adverse [ˈædvəːs] *a.* 不利的

adverse reaction 有害反应，逆反应

aerosol [ˈɛərəsɔl] *n.* 气溶胶，气雾剂，喷雾器

aesthetic [iːsˈθetik] *a.* 美学的，审美的，有美感

affiliation [əˌfiliˈeiʃən] *n.* 加入，联盟，友好关系

affluence [ˈæfluəns] *n.* 富裕

affluent [ˈæfluənt] *a.* 富裕的；*n.* 支流

aftermath [ˈɑːftəmæθ] *n.* 不幸事件之后果，余波

airbrush [ˈɛəbrʌʃ] *n.* & *v.* 喷枪

albumin [ˈælˈbjumin] *n.* 蛋白质，蛋白素

alkali salt of fatty acids　*n.* 脂肪酸碱盐

all the time　一直

allergic [ə'lə:dʒik]　*a.* 过敏的

allocate ['æləukeit]　*v.* 分派，分配，分配额

aloe vera　*n.* 真芦荟，羊角掌：

alopecia [æləˈpiːsiə]　*n.* 秃头症

alpha hydroxy acid（AHA）　a-羟基酸

alphabetically　*adv.* 按字母表顺序地

alter　*v.* 改变

alternatively [ɔːlˈtəːnətivli]　*ad.* 二者择一地，作为选择

altruism ['æltruizəm]　*n.* 利他主义，利他

amniotic liquid　羊水

among others　除了别的以外，其中

annum ['ænəm]　*n.* 年

antidandruff　*a.* 去头屑的

antihistamine [ˌæntiˈhistəmiːn]　*n.* 抗组织胺

antiperspirant　*n.* 止汗药

appeal（to）[əˈpiːl]　*n.* 恳求，上诉，吸引力；*v.* 求助，诉请，呼吁

appellate [əˈpelit]　受理上诉的

applicator ['æplikeitə]　*n.* 敷贴器（撒药机，扣环起子，高频发热电极）

apply [əˈplai]　*v.* 应用，申请，涂

argument ['ɑːgjumənt]　*n.* 辩论，争论，论据，理由

aromatherapy　用香料按摩

artificial [ˌɑːtiˈfiʃəl]　*a.* 人造的，虚伪的，武断的

associate [əˈsəuʃieit]　*n.* 同伴，伙伴；*v.* 联合，联想；*a.* 副的

assurance ['əʃuərəns]　*n.* 保证，确信，保险

astringent [əsˈtrindʒənt]　*n.* 收敛剂；*a.* 收敛性的，严酷的

authority [ɔːˈθɔriti]　*n.* 权力，权威，当局，职权

automobile ['ɔːtəməbiːl]　*n.* 汽车

awareness [əˈwæənis]　*n.* 认识（了解，知道）

202

bacteria [bæk'tiəriə] *n.* 细菌

baffling *a.* 令人困惑的

ban [bæn] *n.* 禁令；*v.* 禁止；*vt.* 禁止，取缔

bank on *vt.* 指望（依赖，依靠）

basal epidermal cell 基底层细胞

beach [bi:tʃ] *n.* 海滩；*v.* 拖（船）上岸；*vt.* 使船冲上滩

beautician [bju:'tiʃən] *n.* 美容师

beige [beiʒ] *a.* 米黄色的；*n.* 米黄色

beware of 对……小心

bewildering [bi'wildəriŋ] *a.* 令人困惑的，使人混乱的

bifocals [bai'fəukəlz] 远近视两用眼镜

billion ['biljən] *num. &n.* 十亿

biological [ˌbaiə'lɔdʒikəl] *a.* 生物学的

biothionol 硫双二氯酚

birth control pill 避孕丸

bleach [bli:tʃ] *n.* 漂白剂；*v.* 变白，漂白

blemish ['blemiʃ] *n* 污点，缺点，*v.* 弄脏，污损，损害

blistering ['blistəriŋ] 起凸，形成气孔，爆皮，起泡

blocking [blɔk] *n.* 街区，木块，石块；*v.* 阻塞

blur [blə:] *v.* 使……模糊

blush [blrf] *v.* 脸红，羞愧，呈现红色，使成红色；*n.* 脸红，红色，
红光

boom [bu:m] *n.* 繁荣，隆隆声；*v.* 急速发展

boost [bu:st] *n.* 推进，支援；*v.* 推进，提高

boundary ['baundəri] *n.* 分界线，边界

brassiere ['bræsiə] *n.* 奶罩，乳罩

break from 决裂

breed [bri:d] *n.* 品种，族类；*v.* 养育，繁殖，引起

brim [brim] *n.* 边，边缘，（河）边；*v.* 满，使……盈

bud [bʌd] *n.* 芽，花蕾；*v.* 发芽，萌芽

buoy [bɔi]   *n*. 浮标，浮筒，救生圈；*v*. 使……浮，支撑

camouflage ['kæmuflɑːʒ]   *v*. 伪装，欺瞒

camp [kæmp]   *n*. 露营，帐篷；*v*. 露营，扎营

candle ['kændl]   *n*. 蜡烛

capped [kæp]   *n*. 帽子，盖子；*v*. 给戴帽，覆盖于……顶端

carbohydrate ['kɑːbəu'haidreit]   *n*. 碳水化合物，糖

cataract ['kætərækt]   *n*. 大瀑布，奔流，洪水

category ['kætigəri]   *n*. 种类，类别

cater（to）['keitə]   *v*. 备办食物，投合，迎合

cedar ['siːdə]   *n*. 西洋杉，香柏

cell membrane   *n*. 细胞膜

cellulite ['seljəlait]   *n*.（胖女人臀腿部的）脂肪团

ceramide ['serəmaid]   *n*.［生化］神经酰胺

cerebroside ['seribrəusaid]   *n*.［生化］脑苷脂

certification [ˌsəːtifi'keiʃən]   *n*. 证明，保证，鉴定

ceruse ['siəruːs]   *n*. 铅白

chafing   *n*.［医］皮肤发炎

challenge ['tʃælindʒ]   *n*. 挑战；*v*. 向……挑战

channel ['tʃænl]   *n*. 通道，频道，海峡；*v*. 引导，开导，形成河道

characteristics   *n*. 特性，特征

chick embryo extract   小鸡胚胎提取物

chlorofluorocarbon   *n*. 氟氯碳

chloroform ['klɔ(ː)rəfɔːm]   *n*. 氯仿

circulation [ˌsəːkju'leiʃən]   *n*. 流通，循环，发行量

claim [kleim]   *n*. 要求，要求权；*v*. 要求，请求，主张，声称，说明，断言

clamshell ['klæmʃəl]   *n*. 蛤壳（抓斗，蛤壳式挖泥机）

clash [klæʃ]   *n*. 冲突，撞击声，抵触；*v*. 冲突，抵触，使……发出撞击声

clear up   整顿，清理，收拾说明，澄清，（天气）转晴，除，解除（疑虑等）

clog [klɔg]   *n*. 阻塞（止轮器）；*vt*. 阻塞（粘住，塞满）

204

clogging ['klɔgiŋ] n. 结渣（阻塞，闭合）

cloud [klaud] n. 云，忧色，云状的烟；v. 以云遮蔽，笼罩

clue [kluː] n. 线索；v. 提示

clusters ['klʌstə] n. 串，丛，群；v. 聚合，成串，丛生，使……聚集

coarse [kɔːs] a. 粗糙的，下等的，粗俗的

cognitive ['kɔgnitiv] a. 认知的，认识的，有认识力的

cold sore n. 感冒疮；（伤风发热时的）唇疱疹

collagen ['kɔlə,dʒən] n. 胶原

combination skin type 复合皮肤类型

combine [kəm'bain] n. 集团，联合收割机；v. 化合，结合，联合

comedogenic [,kɔmidə'dʒenik] a. 趋于使痤疮产生或恶化

commitment [kə'mitmənt] n. 委托，实行，承诺，保证（律）拘禁令；奉献，献身

common sense 常识（尤指判断力）

compact foundation 粉饼

compendium [kəm'pendiəm] n. 简要，概略，提纲

competition [kɔmpi'tiʃən] n. 比赛，竞争

complement ['kɔmplimənt] n. 补足物，补语，余角；v. 补助

complexion [kəm'plekʃən] n. 外观（状态，形势，开色，配容）；vt. 染（上色）

complicate ['kɔmplikeit] v. 弄复杂，使错综，使起纠纷

complication [,kɔmpli'keiʃ(ə)n] n. 复杂化，使……复杂的因素

comply with 应允，同意；遵照，根据

conducive to microbial growth 有益于细菌生长的

conduct ['kɔndʌkt, -dəkt] n. 行为，举动，品行；vt. 引导，管理；导电，传热

connective tissue n. 结缔组织

conscious (of) ['kɔnʃəs] a. 神志清醒的，意识到的，自觉的，有意的

consequence ['kɔnsikwəns] ad. 因而，所以；n. 结果，后果

contaminate [kən'tæmineit] v. 弄脏，污染

205

contour [ˈkɔntuə] n. 轮廓（等高线，周线，电路，概要）；vt. 画轮廓（画等高线）

convene [kənˈviːn] v. 集合，召集，召唤，聚集，集合

convey [kənˈvei] v. 传达，运输，转移，[计算机] 输送

convincing evidence n. 令人信服的证据

core [kɔː] n. 果心，核心，要点；vt. 挖去（水果的）果心

cornea [ˈkɔːniə] n. 角膜

cosmetic [kɔzˈmetik] n. 化妆品；a. 化妆用的

counselor [ˈkaunsələ] n. 顾问，参事，法律顾问

counterfeit [ˈkauntəfit] n. 膺品，伪造品；a. 假冒的，假装的；v. 仿造，伪装，假装

coverage [ˈkʌvəridʒ] n. 涉及范围

cream foundation 粉底霜

credibility [ˌkrediˈbiliti] n. 可信用，确实性，可靠

criteria [kraiˈtiəriə] n. 标准

crunchy [ˈkrʌntʃi] a. 发嘎吱嘎吱声的，易碎的

curiosity [ˌkjuəriˈɔsiti] n. 好奇，好奇心

customary shelf life [ˈkʌstəməri] a. 习惯的，惯例的

damp [dæmp] n. 湿气；a. 潮湿的

dandruff [ˈdændrʌf] n. 头皮屑

deadline [ˈdedlain] n. 最后期限

deadliness [ˈdedlinis] n. 致命的

decay [diˈkei] n. 衰退，腐败；v. 衰退，腐败

deceptive [diˈseptiv] a. 迷惑的，虚伪的，诈欺的

decode [ˌdiːˈkəud] vt. 解码，译解

deem [diːm] v. 认为，相信

defective [diˈfektiv] a. 有缺陷的，欠缺，不完全变化动词；n. 有缺陷的人，不完全变化动词

deleterious [ˌdeliˈtiəriəs] a. 有害于，有毒的

delicate [ˈdelikit] a. 细致优雅的，微妙的，美味的

206

demonstrate ['demənstreit] v. 示范，演示，证明，示威

dental ['dentl] a. 牙齿的，牙科的

deodorant [di:'əudərənt] n. 除臭剂

dermatitis [,də:mə'taitis] n. [医] 皮炎

dermatology [,də:mə'tɔlədʒi] n. 皮肤（病）学

descend [di'send] v. 下来，下降，遗传，突击

designate ['dezigneit] v. 指定，标示

deteriorate [di'tiəriəreit] v. 恶化

devastation [,devəs'teiʃən] n. 破坏，劫掠

diabetes [,daiə'bi:ti:z, -ti:s] n. 糖尿病

diagnosis [,daiəg'nəusis] n. 诊断

diaper ['daiəpə] n. 尿布；vt. 换尿布

dilemma [di'lemə,dai-] n. 困境，进退两难

diluent ['diljuənt] a. 冲淡，稀释；n. 稀释液，稀释药

discard [dis'kɑ:d] n. 丢弃，扔掉；v. 丢弃，抛弃

discourage [dis'kʌridʒ] v. 使气馁，阻碍

disposable income   可支配收入

dissatisfaction ['dis,sætis'fækʃən] n. 不满

dissemination [di,semi'neiʃən] 传播，宣传，传染（病毒）

distorted [dis'tɔ:tid] a. 扭歪的，受到曲解的

diversify [dai'və:sifai] v. 使成形形色色，使多样化，使变化

diversity [dai'və:siti] n. 差异，多样性

division [di'viʒən] n. 区分，分开，除法，公司，部门

dominate ['dɔmineit] v. 支配，占优势

Draize test   兔眼刺激性试验

dual Active Powder Foundations   双效粉底

duplicative a. 加倍的，二重的，复制的

dusting ['dʌstiŋ] n. 打扫，殴打，暴风雨

dynamic [dai'næmik] a. 动态的，有动力的，有力的

eligible ['elidʒəbl] a. 可以选的，有资格的，合格的；n. 有资格者，合

格者，适任者

eliminate [i'limineit] v. 除去，排除，剔除，[计算机] 消除

emergence [i'mə:dʒəns] n. 出现

emit [i'mit] v. 发出，放射，吐露，[计算机] 发射

endorse [in'dɔ:s] v. 支持，赞同，背书于

endurance [in'djurəns] n. 忍耐，忍耐力，耐性

enforce [in'fɔ:s] v. 厉行，强迫，执行

enormous [i'nɔ:məs] a. 巨大的，庞大的

entry ['entri] n. 进入，入口，登记

essential oil n. 香精油

establish the brand image 建立品牌形象

establishment [is'tæbliʃmənt] n. 公司，确立，制定，设施

evergreen ['evəgri:n] n. 常绿树，常绿植物；a. 常绿的

evolve into vt. 发展成（进化成）

exaggerate [ig'zædʒəreit] v. 夸大，夸张

excessive [ik'sesiv] a. 过多的，过分的

executive [ig'zekjutiv] a. 行政的；n. 执行者，主管

expatriate [eks'pætrieit] n. 亡命国外者；v. 逐出国外，脱离国籍，放逐

expel [iks'pel] v. 驱逐，逐出，开除

expiration date 产品有效期

explore [iks'plɔ:] v. 探险，探测，探究，[计算机] 探讨

extender [iks'tendə] n. 扩充器（延长器，增充剂）

eye shadow 眼影

eye-area cosmetic 眼部化妆品

eyelash ['ai,læʃ] n. 睫毛

eyelid ['ailid] n. 眼皮，眼睑

eyeliner ['ailainə(r)] n. 眼线膏

fabric ['fæbrik] n. 织物，布，结构

facial mask n. 美容面具

fade [feid] v. 褪色，消失，凋谢

faithfully ['feiθfuli] ad. 忠实，诚心诚意，深信着

fashionable ['fæʃənəbl] a. 时髦地，按照流行地

fatally ['feitəli] ad. 致命地，不幸地，宿命地

fatty substance 脂肪物质

female population （全体）女居民，妇女人口

fetus ['fi:təs] n. 胎，胎儿

find out vt. 找出（查明，发现，想出，认识到，揭发出来）

fingernail ['fiŋgəneil] n. 手指甲

fingernail polish n. 指甲油

flaky ['fleiki] a. 薄片的，成片的薄而易剥落的

flawless ['flɔ:lis] a. 完美的，无瑕疵的

flexible ['fleksəbl] a. 灵活的，易弯曲的，柔韧的

floral ['flɔ:rəl] a. 花似的，花的，植物的

fluoride ['flu(:)əraid] n. （护齿的）氟化物

focus on vt. 集中在

follow-up n. 追踪调查，追踪报道，后续产品；a. 继续的，作为重复的

foodstuff ['fu:dstʌf] n. 食品，食料

forward ['fɔ:wəd] vt. 转寄，促进，运送；a. 早的，前进的；ad. 向前地，向将来

foundation [faun'deiʃən] n. 粉底，基础，根据，建立

fragrance ['freigrəns] n. 芬芳，香气，香味

fruity ['fru:ti] a. 水果的，有水果香味的，圆润的

fuel demand 拉动需求

fuel growth 拉动增长

fungi ['fʌndʒai，'fʌŋgai] n. 菌类，蘑菇

gaze [geiz] n. 凝视，注视

gear [giə] n. 齿轮，传动装置；v. 调整，（使）适合，换挡

giants ['dʒaiənts] n. [希神] 一个巨人种族（常与天上诸神作战并取胜，后来雅典娜和宙斯在海格立斯帮助下才将他们战败）

gimmick ['gimik]　*n.* 骗局（骗人的玩意）；*vt.* 搞骗人的玩意

girdle ['gə:dl]　*n.* 腰带，围绕物；*v.* 以腰带束缚，在……周围绕

glare [glɛə]　*n.* 闪耀光，刺眼；*v.* 发眩光，瞪视

glow [gləu]　*n.* 赤热，光辉，热情；*v.* 发红光，红光焕发

glycolipid [ˌglaikə'lipid]　*n.* [生化] 糖脂类

go for　*v.* 去找，努力获取，被认为，主张，拥护

goggle ['gɔgl]　*n.* 眼睛睁视，护目镜；*vi.* 瞪视，瞪大眼睛看

grant [grɑ:nt]　*n.* 拨款；*vt.* 授予，同意，承认

granulomas [ˌgrænju'ləumə]　*n.* [医] 肉芽肿，肉芽瘤

greasy ['gri:si，'gri:zi]　*a.* 油腻的，滑溜溜的，泥泞的

grooming　*n.* 修饰

guarantee [ˌgærən'ti:]　*v. & n.* 保证，担保

guide [gaid]　*n.* 引导者，指南，路标

guideline ['gaidˌlain]　*n.* 指引

hairspray　*n.* 头发定型剂

halocarbon [ˌhæləu'kɑ:bən]　*n.* 卤代烃（卤化碳）

halogenated ['hælədʒəneit]　*vt.* 卤化（加卤）

halter ['hɔ:ltə]　*n.* 缰绳，绞索，女性三角背心的颈部系带

hamper ['hæmpə]　*n.* 食盒，食篮；*v.* 阻碍，使……困累，困累

harsh [hɑ:ʃ]　*a.* 粗糙的，刺耳的，严厉的

headquarter [ˌhed'kwɔ:tə]　*n.* 总部，总局

henna ['henə]　*n.* 指甲花，指甲花染料，红褐色

hepatitis [ˌhepə'taitis]　*n.* 肝炎

hexachlorophene [ˌheksə'klɔ:rəfi:n]　*n.* [化] 六氯酚

high-end cosmetic market　化妆品高端市场

highlight ['hailait]　*n.* 加亮区；*v.* 加亮，强调

hormone ['hɔ:məun]　*n.* 荷尔蒙，激素

hostile ['hɔstail]　*a.* 怀敌意的，敌对的

hue [hju:]　*n.* 色，色彩，叫声，[计算机] 色调

hurricane ['hʌrikən，-kin]　*n.* 飓风，快速强烈的事物

hydration [hai'dreiʃən] *n.* 水合

hygiene ['haidʒiːn] *n.* 卫生，卫生学

hypermarket [ˌhaipə'maːkit] *n.* 特大百货商场，特大超级商场

hypermarket [ˌhaipə'maːkit] *n.* 特大百货商场，特大超级商场

hypoallergenic [ˌhipəuælə'dʒenik] *a.* [医] 低变应原的

identical（to） *a.* 相同于（和……一致）

identify [ai'dentifai] *v.* 识别，认明，鉴定

immediate [i'miːdjət] *a.* 直接的，紧接的，紧靠的，立即的，知觉的

immune [i'mjuːm] *a.* 免除的，免疫的；*n.* 免疫者

impart [im'paːt] *vt.* 给予，传授，告知

implement ['implimənt] *n.* 工具，器具；*vt.* 实现，执行，使……生效

implementation [ˌimplimen'teiʃən] *n.* 安装启用，实行，履行

impossibility [imˌpɔsə'biləti] *n.* 不可能之事，不可能

improperly [im'prɔpəli] *ad.* 不正确地，不适当地

In addition *ad.* 另外

In addition to 除……之外（还）

in descending order by quantity 按量由高到低排列

in order of predominance 静脉曲张

in pure form 以纯净的形态

in vitro tests 体外试验

inadequacy [in'ædikwəsi] *n.* 不适当，不十分，不完全

inadequate [in'ædikwit] *a.* 不充分的，不适当的

incentive [in'sentiv] *a.* 刺激的，鼓励的；*n.* 刺激，鼓励，动机

incinerate [in'sinəreit] *v.* 焚化，毁弃

incomprehensible [ˌinkɔmpri'hensəbl] *a.* 不能理解，费解的，无限的

individual [ˌindi'vidjuəl] *a.* 个别的；*n.* 个人，个体

ineffective [ˌini'fektiv] *a.* 无效的

inevitably [in'evitəbli] *ad.* 不可避免地

infection [in'fekʃən] *n.* 传染，影响，传染病

infectious [in'fekʃəs] *a.* 传染的

ingredient [in'gri:diənt] *n*. 成分，因素

inhale [in'heil] *v*. 吸入

injection [in'dʒekʃən] *n*. 注射

injunction [in'dʒʌŋkʃən] *n*. 命令，指令，劝告

injurious [in'dʒuəriəs] *a*. 有害的

injury ['indʒəri] *n*. 受伤处，损害，伤害

innovation [,inəu'veiʃən] *n*. 创新，革新

inspection [in'spekʃən] *n*. 检查，视察

inspirational [,inspə'reiʃənəl] *a*. 带有灵感的，给予灵感的，灵感的

integrity [in'tegriti] *n*. 诚实，正直，完整，完善

intensive [in'tensiv] *a*. 集中的，强化的，精细的，深入的

intentionally [in'tenʃənəli] *ad*. 企图地，策划地，故意地

interchangeable [intə'tʃeindʒəb(ə)l] *a*. 可互换的

interstate [,intə(:)'steit] *a*. 洲际的

intradermal [,intrə'də:ml] *a*. 皮内的，皮层内的

invalid [in'vælid] *a*. 无效的，伤残的；*n*. 病人，残疾者

invisible [in'vizəbl] *a*. 看不见的，无形的

it could better if   如果……，那就更好

itching ['itʃiŋ] *a*. 渴望的，贪得的，痒的

jasmine ['dʒæsmin] *n*. 茉莉

jawline ['dʒɔ:lain] *n*. 下颌的轮廓，下巴的外形

jurisdictions [,dʒuəris'dikʃən] *n*. 司法权，审判权，管辖权

justifiable ['dʒʌstifaiəbl] *a*. 有理的，可辩解的，可证明的

keen [ki:n] *a*. 锋利的，敏锐的，强烈的

keep abreast of   了解……的最新情况，与……齐头并进

keloid ['ki:lɔid] *n*. [医] 瘢痕疙瘩，瘢痕瘤

kill off   消灭光，除去

lash [læʃ] *n*. 鞭子，鞭打，睫毛；*v*. 鞭打，摆动，扎捆

launch [lɔ:ntʃ, lɑ:ntʃ] *n*. & *v*. 下水，发射，开始，升天，汽艇

lavender ['lævində] *n*. 淡紫色，熏衣草

leaflet ['li:flit] *n.* 小叶，传单

leak [li:k] *n.* 漏洞；*v.* 漏，泄漏

leathery ['leðəri] *a.* 皮似的，皮质的，皮般强韧的

lengthy ['leŋθi] *a.* 冗长的，漫长的

lens [lenz] *n.* 镜头，透镜

liberally ['libərəli] *ad.* 不受限制地，公平地，大方地

license ['laisəns] *n.* 执照，许可证，特许；*v.* 许可，特许

lifeguard ['laifgɑ:d] *n.* 救生员

lining ['lainiŋ] *n.* 衬里，内层

liposome ['lipəusəum，'lai-] *n.* [生] 脂质体

lipstick ['lipstik] *n.* 口红

Liquid Foundation 液体粉底

lobe [ləub] *n.* 圆形突出部，耳朵，裂片

logistics [lə'dʒistiks] *n.* 后勤，后勤学

long-term *a.* 长期的

look after *vt.* 目送（寻求，照料，看管）

lucrative ['lu:krətiv，lju-] *a.* 有利益的，获利的，合算的

luminosity [,lju:mi'nɔsiti] *n.* 光明，光辉，光度，[计算机] 光度

lupus ['lu:pəs] *n.* 狼疮，天狼座

lure [ljuə] *n.* 饵，诱惑；*v.* 引诱，诱惑

macro ['mækrəu] *n.* 宏，巨；*a.* 巨大的，大量使用的

magnetic resonance imaging（MRI） 磁共振成像

make money 挣钱

make sure that *vt.* 查明，确信

malignant [mə'lignənt] *a.* 有恶意的，恶性的，有害的；*n.* 怀恶意的人，保
王党员

mandatory ['mændətəri] *a.* 命令的，强制性的

market access 市场准入

mascara [mæs'kɑ:rə] *n.* 染眉毛；*v.* 涂染眉毛剂

massaging ['mæsɑ:ʒ] *n.* 按摩，揉；*v.* 按摩，揉

matte [mæt] *a.* 暗区，不光滑的

mauve [məuv] *n.* 淡紫色

media ['miːdjə] *n.* 媒体，新闻媒介，传播媒介

melanoma [ˌmeləˈnəumə] *n.* [医]（恶性）黑素瘤，（良性）胎记瘤

mercury ['məːkjuri] *n.* 水银

methyl methacrylate *n.* 异丁烯酸甲酯

methylene chloride 二氯甲烷

microorganism [maikrəuˈɔːgəniz(ə)m] *n.* 微生物

microscopic [maikrəˈskɔpik] *a.* 显微镜的

midday ['middei] *n.* 正午，中午；*a.* 正午的

minimize ['minimaiz] *v.* 将……减到最少，[计算机] 最小化

misbrand ['misˈbrænd] *vt.* 贴错标签，贴假商标于

misconception ['miskənˈsepʃən] *n.* 误解，错误想法

misuse ['misˈjuːz] *vt. & n.* 误用，滥用

mitigation [ˌmitiˈgeiʃən] *n.* 缓和，减轻，镇静

moisten ['mɔisn] *v.* 弄湿

moisturizer ['mɔistʃəraizə] *n.* 润肤霜

moldy ['məuldi] *a.* 发霉的

mole [məul] *n.* [医] 胎块，痣

monitor ['mɔnitə] *v.* 监视，监听，监督，[计算机] 监视；*n.* 监督器，
    级长，监听员

monograph ['mɔnəugrɑːf] *n.* 专题论文

monomer ['mɔnəmə] *n.* 单体

mouthwash ['mauθwɔʃ] *n.* 漱口剂，洗口药

multimedia ['mʌltiˈmiːdjə] *n.* 多媒体

musk [mʌsk] *n.* 麝香鹿，能发出麝香的各种各样的植物

nasty ['næsti] *a.* 污秽的，下流的，险恶的

negligible ['neglidʒəbl] *a.* 可以忽略的，微不足道的

nodule ['nɔdjuːl] *n.* 小节，小瘤，小结节

nonetheless [ˌnʌnðəˈles] *ad.* 尽管如此（仍然）；*conj.* 尽管如此（仍然）

214

nourish [ˈnʌriʃ] v. 滋养，使……健壮，怀有

occasion [əˈkeiʒən] n. 场合，机会，理由；v. 致使，惹起，引起

occasionally [əˈkeiʒənəli] ad. 偶尔地

odd [ɔd] a. 奇数的，古怪的，剩余的；n. 奇数

offending a. 不愉快的，厌恶的

oil based formula 油基配方

oiliness [ˈɔilinis] n. 油质，油气，油腻

oldy [ˈəuldi] n. 老人，陈旧之物

oligopolistic n. 寡头垄断的

olive [ˈɔliv] n. 橄榄，橄榄树，橄榄色；a. 黄绿色的，黄褐色的，橄榄色的

omega [ˈəumiɡə] n. 希腊字母的最后一个字，终了，最后

On-site 现场

organism [ˈɔːɡənizəm] n. 生物体，有机体

oriental [ˌɔ(ː)riˈentl] a. 东方人的

osteoporosis [ˌɔstiəupɔːˈrəusis] n. 骨质疏松症

outbreak [ˈautbreik] n. 爆发

outlet [ˈautlet, -lit] n. 出口，出路，通风口，批发商店

ovarian [əuˈvɛəriən] a. 卵巢的

overexposure [ˈəuvəriksˈpəuʒə] n. 感光过度

over-the-counter（OTC）drug 非处方药

overturn [ˌəuvəˈtəːn] n. 倾覆，破减，革命；v. 推翻，颠倒

pad [pæd] n. 衬垫，填补，印色盒，信笺簿；v. 填补，徒步，夸大

painstaking [ˈpeinsteikiŋ] n. 辛苦，苦心，工夫；a. 辛苦的，勤勉的，小心的

panacea [ˌpænəˈsiə] n. 万灵药

papery [ˈpeipəri] a. 薄的，纸质的，像纸的

paraben（methyl-，propyl-，and butyl-）尼泊金脂（甲酯、丙酯和丁酯），一种防腐剂

paragraph [ˈpærəɡrɑːf] n. （文章）段，节，段落；vt. 将…分段

215

parlor ['pɑːlə] n. 客厅，会客室，店

participate in v. 参加，参与，分享

partner with v. 与……做伙伴

patch [pætʃ] n. 片，补绽，碎片；v. 补缀，掩饰，平息

patchouli ['pætʃuli(ː)] n. [植] 广藿香，天竺薄荷，广藿香油（制香料用）

pathogenic [ˌpæθəˈdʒenik] a. 致病的，病原的，发病的

pedestrian [peˈdestriən] a. 徒步的，缺乏想像的；n. 行人

peeler ['piːlə] n. 削皮器

pending ['pendiŋ] a. 未决定的，待决的；prep. 直到，当……的时候，在……期间

penetration [peniˈtreiʃən] n. 渗透，侵透，侵入

perception [pəˈsepʃən] n. 感觉，知觉

perfection [pəˈfekʃən] n. 完美，完善

perform [pəˈfɔːm] v. 执行，表演，做

performer [pəˈfɔːmə(r)] n. 表演者，执行者

perfum ['pəːfjuːm] n. 香水，香气；v. 洒香水于，薰香

permanent wave 电烫发

permanent wave product 永久定型产品

perplexing [pəˈpleksiŋ] a. 令人费解的，使人困惑的

personality [ˌpəːsəˈnæliti] n. 个性

perspiration [ˌpəːspəˈreiʃən] n. 汗，流汗，努力

perspire [pəsˈpaiə] v. 出汗，流汗

persuade [pəˈsweid] a. 空闲的，有闲的；v. 说服，劝说，说服

pertinent ['pəːtinənt] a. 相关的，中肯的，切题的

pervasive [pəːˈveisiv] a. 普遍的，蔓延的，渗透的

pet [pet] a. 宠爱的；n. 宠物，vt. 抚摸，轻抚

pharmaceutical [ˌfɑːməˈsjuːtikəl] a. 药物的（医药的）；n. 药品（成药）

phospholipid [ˌfɔsfəuˈlipid] n. 磷脂

photosensitive [ˌfəutəuˈsensitiv] a. 感光性的

216

pick up 捡起，拾起

pigment [ˈpigmənt] *n.* 色素，颜料；*v.* 把……加颜色，变色

pigskin [ˈpigskin] *n.* 猪皮，猪皮革，鞍

pink [piŋk] *a.* 粉红色的；*n.* 粉红色

pique [piːk] *n.* 生气，愤怒；*v.* 伤害……自尊心，激怒

placenta [pləˈsentə] *n.* 胎盘

plant-derived *a.* 植物来源的

plasma [ˈplæzmə] *n.* 等离子体（血浆，深绿玉髓）

plexiglas [ˈpleksiglɑːs] *n.* 胶质玻璃

poisonous [ˈpɔiznəs] *a.* 有毒的

pore [pɔː，pɔə] *n.* 毛孔，小孔；*v.* 熟读，熟视，细想

poster [ˈpəustə] *n.* 海报，招贴，脚夫

precaution [priˈkɔːʃən] *n.* 预防，留心，警戒

preliminary [priˈliminəri] *n.* 初步行动，准备，初步措施；*a.* 初步的，
开始的，预备的

premature [ˌpreməˈtjuə] *a.* 早熟的，过早的，不按时的；*n.* 早产儿，
早发

preservative [priˈzɔːvətiv] *a.* 保存的，有保存力的，防腐的；*n.* 防腐
剂，预防法，预防药

prestigious [ˌpresˈtiːdʒəs] *a.* 享有声望的，声望很高的

prey on *vt.* 捕食（掠夺，折磨）

pricing pressure *n.* 物价压力

printer [ˈprintə] *n.* 打印机，印刷工

procedure [prəˈsiːdʒə] *n.* 程序，手续，步骤

proceedings [prəˈsiːdiŋz] *n.* 公报，进程，过程，议程，诉讼（程序）

profile [ˈprəufail] *n.* 侧面，轮廓，人物素描；*v.* 描绘……轮廓，评论人
物；*n.* 概要，人物简介

prohibit [prəˈhibit] *v.* 禁止，阻止

promote [prəˈməut] *v.* 促进，提升，升迁，促销

promotion [prəˈməuʃən] *n.* 促进，提升

prone [prəun] *a.* 俯卧的，易于……的，有……倾向的

propellant [prə'pelənt] *n.* 推进剂，发射火药，推进燃料

propylene glycol 丙二醇

psoriasis [psɔ(:)'raiəsis] *n.* [医] 牛皮癣，银屑癣

Puffery ['pʌfəri] *n.* 极力称赞，夸大广告

puncture ['pʌŋktʃə] *n.* 刺穿

pursue [pə'sjuː] *v.* 追求，追捕，继续从事

quarantine ['kwɔrəntiːn] *n.* 隔离，封锁交通，检疫期间；*v.* 检疫，停止交涉

queen bee royal jelly 蜂王王浆

questionnaire [ˌkwestiə'nɛə, -tʃə-] *n.* 调查表

radiologist [ˌreidi'ɔlədʒist] *n.* 放射线学者

rank [ræŋk] *n.* 排名，等级，军衔，阶级；*a.* 繁茂的，恶臭的，讨厌的；*v.* 排列，归类于，列于

rash [ræʃ] *a.* 轻率的，匆忙的，鲁莽的；*n.* 疹子，皮疹

rating ['reitiŋ] *n.* 等级

ray [rei] *n.* 光线，射线

reach out *vt.* 伸出（伸展，招揽）

recall [ri'kɔːl] *n.* 召回，回忆，取消；*v.* 回想起，召回，恢复

recession [ri'seʃən] *n.* 后退，凹入的地方，不景气

reconstructive [ˌriːkən'strʌktiv] *a.* 重建的，改造的，有益于再建的

reddish ['rediʃ] *a.* 带红色的，微红的

reflect [ri'flekt] *v.* 反射，反映，表现，反省，细想

reflection [re'flekʃən] *n.* 反射，映象，倒影，反省，沉思，反映

refreshing [ri'freʃiŋ] *a.* 使清爽的，有精神的，爽快的

registration [ˌredʒis'treiʃən] *n.* 登记，注册

regulate ['regjuleit] *v.* 有系统的管理，规定，调节

rejuvenation *n.* 复原（再生，更新，嫩化，恢复）

renowned [ri'naund] *a.* 有名的，有声誉的

resentment [ri'zentmənt] *n.* 怨恨，愤恨

218

responsible [ris'pɔnsəbl]　*a.* 有责任的，负责的，责任重大的，应负责的

restore [ris'tɔː]　*v.* 回复，恢复，归还

rethink [ri'θiŋk]　*v.* 再想，重想

retina ['retinə]　*n.* 网膜

revenue ['revinjuː]　*n.* 财政收入，税收

revitalize [riː'vaitəlaiz]　*v.* 使复活，使重新充满活力；*vt.* 使复兴，使苏醒，使复活，使恢复

rite [rait]　*n.* 仪式，典礼

robust [rə'bʌst]　*a.* 强壮的，强健的

rosy economic outlook　光明的经济前景

roughness ['rʌfnis]　*n.* 粗糙，凹凸面，蓬乱的毛发

routinely [ru'tiːnli]　*ad.* 通常

rule of thumb　*n.* 单凭经验的方法

sac [sæk]　*n.* 囊，液囊

safeguard ['seifˌgɑːd]　*n.* 保卫，保护措施或条款；*v.* 保卫，保护

salicylanilide [ˌsælisil'ænilaid，-lid]　*n.* [化] N-水杨酰苯胺

saliva [sə'laivə]　*n.* 唾液

salon ['sælɔːŋ]　*n.* 大会客室（美术展览馆）

sandalwood ['sændlwud]　*n.* 檀香木

scaly ['skeili]　*a.* 鳞状的

scar [skɑː]　*n.* 疤痕，伤痕，断崖；*v.* 结疤，使……有伤痕，痊愈

scent [sent]　*n.* 气味，香味，痕迹；*v.* 闻出，循着遗臭追踪，发觉

scraped [skreip]　*n.* 刮掉，擦掉；*v.* 刮掉，擦掉

screen [skriːn]　*n.* 屏，幕，银幕，屏风；*v.* 选拔，掩蔽，遮蔽

seal [siːl]　*n.* 印章，封条，海豹；*v.* 盖印，封闭，猎海豹

seborrheic [ˌsebəu'trəufik]　*a.* [生理] 刺激泌脂的

segment ['segmənt]　*n.* 段，节，片断；*v.* 分割

seizure ['siːʒə]　*n.* 捕获，夺取，捕获物

serum ['siərəm]　*n.* 浆液，血清，乳浆

severity [si'veriti] *n.* 严格，严重，激烈

shading ['ʃeidiŋ] 底纹，留下阴影

shampoo [ʃæm'pu:] *n.* 洗头（洗发剂）；*vt.* 洗发

shark oil 鲨鱼肝油

sheep wool 羊毛

shelf life 货架期

shiny ['ʃaini] *a.* 有光泽的，发光的，辉煌的

shortwave ['ʃɔːt'weiv] *n.* 短波；*v.* 做短波广播

side effect 副作用

skin burn 皮肤烧伤

skirting ['skəːtiŋ] *n.* 裙料，壁脚板

slogan ['sləugən] *n.* 标语，口号

SMEs（Small and Medium Enterprises） 中小型企业

snack [snæk] *n.* 小吃，点心；*v.* 吃零食，吃点心

snugly ['snʌgli] *ad.* 紧紧地，紧密地

so much as 和……一样（甚至）

soap [səup] *n.* 肥皂

soothe [su:ð] *v.* 缓和，使……安静，安慰

sophisticate [sə'fistikeit] *n.* 久经世故的人，老油条；*v.* 玩弄诡辩，掺合，弄复杂

sophisticated [sə'fistikeitid] *a.* 诡辩的，久经世故的

specifically [spi'sifikəli] *ad.* 特定地，明确地

specify ['spesifai] *v.* 明确说明，叙述，指定，详细说明

sphere [sfiə] *a.* 球体的；*n.* 范围，领域，球，球体

spicy ['spaisi] *a.* 芳香的（辛辣的）

sponge [spʌndʒ] *n.* 海绵，海绵状的东西；*v.* 用海绵擦拭，吸收掉，抹掉

sponsor ['sponsə] *n.* 保证人，赞助者；*v.* 发起，赞助

spotlight ['spotlait] *n.* 照明灯，车头灯，公众注意中心

spray on 喷射

sprinkle ['spriŋkl] v. 洒，散置，微雨

spur [spəː] n. 马刺；v. 刺激，激励

squamous ['skweiməs] a. 有鳞的（多鳞的，鳞状的）

standard ['stændəd] a. 标准的；n. 标准

staphylococcus [ˌstæfiləuˈkɔkəs] n. 葡萄状球菌

sterilize ['sterilaiz] v. 使成不毛，断种，杀菌

stinging ['stiŋiŋ] a. 刺人的，刺一般的，激烈的

stripping ['stripiŋ] n. 拆开（脱模，剥片，洗提，轻油部分）

stun [stʌn] v. 使目瞪口呆，使晕倒，使惊吓

stylish ['stailiʃ] a. 现代风格的，流行的，潇洒的

subconscious ['sʌb'kɔnʃəs] a. 潜在意识，模糊的意识

submission [səb'miʃən] n. 服从，柔和

submit [səb'mit] vt. 呈送，递交，主张；vt. 使服从，屈服

substantially [səb'stænʃ(ə)li] ad. 实质上，本质上，大体上

substantiate [sʌbs'tænʃieit] v. 证实，实体化

substantiation [sʌbs'tænʃieitʃən] n. 实体化，证实，证明

sun protection factor（SPF） 防晒系数

sunblock n. 防晒霜，紫外线防护霜

sunburn ['sʌnbəːn] n. 日灼，晒伤；v. 晒黑

sunflower ['sʌnflauə] n. 向日葵

sunglass n. 聚集日光引火的凸透镜，太阳眼镜

sunlamp ['sʌn'læmp] n. 太阳灯

sunscreen ['sʌnskriːn] n. （防晒油中的）遮光剂

supplement ['sʌplimənt] n. 补充物，增刊；v. 补充，增补

survey [səˈvei] n. 纵览，视察，测量；v. 审视，视察，通盘考虑，调查

survive [səˈvaiv] v. 生存，生还

susceptible [səˈseptəbl] n. 易受影响者，易受感染者，a. 易受影响的，
易感动的，容许

sustain [səsˈtein] v. 承受，支持，经受，维持

swab [swɔb] n. 擦净

221

swine [swain]　n. 猪

synthetically [sin'θetikəli]　ad. 综合地，合成地

systematic [ˌsisti'mætik]　a. 有系统的，分类的，体系的

taboo [tə'buː]　n. 禁忌，禁止接近，禁止使用；a. 禁忌的；v. 禁忌，禁制，禁止

tactic ['tæktik]　n. 战略，策略

take action　采取行动（进行活动）；提起诉讼

take an active role in　发挥积极作用

take responsibility for　对……负有责任，负起对……的责任

take steps　设法，采取措施

tanning ['tæniŋ]　n. 硝皮，制革法，晒成褐色

tanning ['tæniŋ]　n. 硝皮，制革法，晒成褐色

Tartar ['tɑːtə]　n. 酒石，[医] 牙垢，鞑靼人，凶悍的人，难对付的人

tattoo [tə'tuː，tæ'tuː]　n. & vt. （在皮肤上）刺图案，文身

technician [tek'niʃ(ə)n]　n. 技术员，技师

tenant ['tenənt]　n. 房客，佃户

texture ['tekstʃə]　n. （材料等的）结构，质地

therapeutic [θerə'pjuːtik]　a. 治疗的，治疗学的；n. 治疗剂，治疗学家

therapy ['θerəpi]　n. 疗法，治疗（名词复数：therapies）

thrive [tri'mendəs]　a. 极大的，巨大的

time-consuming ['taimkənˌsjuːmiŋ]　a. 耗费时间的

timer ['taimə]　n. 计时员（计时器，跑表，定时器，延时调节器）

tint [tint]　n. 色彩；浅色；痕迹

tinted　a. 带色彩的

tissue ['tisjuː]　n. （动、植物的）组织，薄的纱织品；餐巾纸，手巾纸

tocopherol [təu'kɔfərəul]　n. [生化] 生育酚，维生素 E

toilet ['tɔilit]　n. 厕所，盥洗室

toiletry ['tɔilitri]　n. 化妆品，化妆用具

toner ['təunə]　n. 色剂．墨粉，炭粉

toning ['təuniŋ]　n. 调色（法），相片调色，调匀颜色

222

toothpaste ['tu:θpeist] *n.* 牙膏

towel ['tauəl，taul] *n.* 毛巾；*v.* 用毛巾擦；*vt.* 用毛巾擦或擦干

toweling ['tauəliŋ] *n.* 毛巾料

toweling off *v.* 擦干（……的）身子

toxicological *a.* 毒物学的

trade association 同业公会

trade name 商品名

trade secret *n.* 商业秘密，行业秘密

trade up *n.* 劝买更高价的东西

tragedy ['trædʒidi] *n.* 悲剧，惨事，灾难

tranquilizer ['træŋkwilaizə] *n.* 镇静剂（增稳装置）

traumatize ['trɔ:mətaiz] *v.* 使受损伤，使受精神上创伤

treatable ['tri:təbəl] *a.* 能处理的（好对付的）

tremendous [tri'mendəs] *a.* 巨大的，惊人的

turtle oil 海龟油

ultraviolet ['ʌltrə'aiəlit] *a.* 紫外线的

unapproved ['ʌnə'pru:vd] *a.* 未经同意的（未准的）

underarm ['ʌndərɑ:m] *a.* 于臂下的，腋下的

underlying ['ʌndə'laiiŋ] *a.* 在下面的

undesirable ['ʌndi'zaiərəbl] *a.* 不受欢迎的，不良的

undue ['ʌn'dju:] *a.* 过分的，不适当的

unique [ju'ni:k] *a.* 独一无二的，独特的，稀罕的

unsterile *a.* 未杀菌的

unveiled *pp.* 公开

upheld [ʌp'held] *v.* 支持

use condition 使用条件

valiantly ['væljəntli] *ad.* 勇敢地，英勇地

validate ['vælideit] *v.* 使……有效，确认

vanilla [və'nilə] *n.* 香草

varicose vein 静脉曲张

vehicle ['viːikl]　*n.* 传播媒介，工具，手段，交通工具，车辆

venues ['venjuː]　*n.* 犯罪地点，审判地，管辖地，发生地点，集合地点

vertebrate ['vəːtibrit]　*n.* 脊椎动物

video ['vidiəu]　*a.* 录像的；*n.* 录像（机）；*vt.* 制作……的录像

vigorous ['vigərəs]　*a.* 精力充沛的，元气旺盛的，有力的

virus ['vaiərəs]　*n.* 病毒

vitiligo [ˌvitiˈlaigəu]　*n.* 白癜风

voluptuous [vəˈlʌptuəs]　*a.* 撩人的，沉溺酒色的

vulnerability [ˌvʌlnərəˈbiləti]　*n.* 弱点，攻击

vulnerable ['vʌlnərəb(ə)l]　*a.* 易受伤害的，有弱点的

wad [wɔd]　*v.* 使……成一团

wand [wɔnd]　*n.* 棒，棍，杖

wart [wɔːt]　*n.* （皮肤上的）疣，瘊子

water-resistant ['wɔːtəriˌzistənt，'wɔ-]　*a.* 抗水的

white lead [led]　*n.* 〔化〕铅白，铅粉，〔矿〕白铅矿

wholesome ['həulsəm]　*a.* 有益健康的，合乎卫生的，健全的

with the exception of　除……之外

womb [wuːm]　*n.* 子宫

wonder about　对……好奇，对……疑惑，想知道

work out　*v.* 可以解决，设计出，作出，计算出，消耗完

working class　*a.* 工人阶级的

yeast extract　酵母抽提物，酵母膏

zirconium [zəˈkəuniəm]　*n.* 锆

APPENDIX Ⅱ　化妆品原料词典

INGREDIENTS（成分）	中 文 标 示	简　介
Acid	脱氢醋酸	防腐剂
Acyclovir	带状疱疹、水痘	药物治疗成分，需医生处方
Adapalene	维生素 A 酸衍生物	治疗痤疮有效成分,需医生处方

INGREDIENTS(成分)	中文标示	简　　介
Adenosine Triphosphate (ATP)	腺三磷酸	使皮肤代谢正常
Albumin	白蛋白	水溶性蛋白质,为中性缓冲液,是一种酵素
Alcohol	酒精	溶剂
Alfalfa Extract	紫花苜蓿萃取	含多种氨基酸及胡萝卜素,可抗老化
Algae Extract	海藻萃取液	抗氧化
Alkyl Benzoate	烃基安息香酸盐	油脂剂,作为基质
Allantoin	尿囊素	抗炎症、促进细胞修护
Almond	杏仁油	天然油脂,用作基质
Aloe Extract	芦荟萃取	镇静、保湿、滋润、抗敏、镇静、去红肿
Aloe Vera	芦荟	镇静、保湿、滋润、抗敏、镇静、去红肿
Alpha Hydroxy(AHA)	果酸	主要功效在促进皮肤新陈代谢,具有角质微剥的功效
Alpha Lipoic Acid	脂肪酸,硫辛酸	抗氧化
Alpha Tocopheryl	维生素 E	抗氧化
Aluminum Chlorohydrate	氢氯酸铝	可抑制身体出汗,常来用作止汗剂成分
Amino Acid	天然氨基酸	防止水分过度地流失,并使肌肤温和不紧绷,护肤、供给肌肤营养
Aminocaproic Acid	氨基己酸	预防肌肤敏感现象
Ammonium Glycyrrhizate	甘草酸胺	保湿、预防过敏
Amniotic Fluid	羊膜液	含丰富肌肤所需的氨基酸
Angelica	白芷	当归属,含天然维生素 C 及预防敏感作用
Angelica Sinensis Diels Extract	当归萃取	具有行气活血功效,可促进肌肤毛细微管血液循环
Angiosperm Extract	被子植物酸	具有防止发炎及抗过敏效果
Anhydroalkannin	去水紫草烯	紫草萃取精华,可抗炎、抗菌、活血、去瘀
Anthranilates		化学性防晒成分
Apple Extract	苹果萃取	含有维生素 C 等美容成分,另具有爽肤、镇静消毒作用

INGREDIENTS(成分)	中文标示	简 介
Apricot Bead	杏桃颗粒	通常加在磨砂膏中,用来去除皮肤老废角质
Apricot Kernel Oil	杏核油	富含矿物质和维生素,是天然的保湿剂,特别适合敏感性肤质
Aqua	水,溶液	基质
Arbutin	熊果素	淡化已形成的黑色素,美白成分
Arnica Extract	山金车萃取	活血散瘀
Arnica Oil	山金车油	可促使伤口愈合、消毒、消肿、防止瘀斑出现
Ascorbic Acid	维生素 C	抗氧化
Ascorbyl Glucoside(AAG)	维生素 C 甘糖	维生素 C 衍生物,为卫生署公布有效美白成分之一
Ascorbyl Pamitate	维生素 C 棕榈酸盐	一种脂溶性维生素 C,是安定的维生素 C
Ascorbyl Stearate	酯化 C	安定的维生素 C
Ascorbyl Tetraisopalmitate	脂溶性维生素 C	安定的维生素 C
Astragalus Membranaceus(Fisch) Bunge Extract	膜荚黄耆萃取	提高肌肤活力,效用比人参更佳
Avobenzone	化学性防晒成分,属 Parsol	1789 类,罕见过敏反应
Avocado Oil	骆梨油	保湿剂,含大量维生素 A、C、D、E
Azelaic Acid	壬二酸,杜鹃花酸	抑制黑色素,抗菌消炎,用来治疗痤疮的温和成分
Babassuamidopropylamine		泡沫增强剂
BaSO$_4$	硫酸钡	物理性防晒成分
Bay Extract	月桂萃取	收敛毛孔、抑制油分分泌
Bearberry Extract	熊果萃取	含食子单宁、葡萄糖甘等成分,具收敛、杀菌消毒、美白等功效
Bees Wax	蜜蜡	基质,可增强产品浓度
Bentonite	膨润土,皂土	有很好的清洁和吸附效果,亦具有抑制脸部油脂分泌的功效
Benzalkonium Chloride	氯化苯二甲烃铵	抗菌、防腐
Benzoic Acid	安息香酸,苯甲酸	防腐剂
Benzophenones(Benzophenone-3)	二苯甲酮衍生物	化学性防晒成分,可防御 UVA,属苯甲酮类

226

INGREDIENTS(成分)	中文标示	简介
Benzoyl Alcohol		产品赋型剂,作为基质
Benzoyl Peroxide	过氧化苯盐	是一种氧化剂,有抑菌的效果
Bergamot Mint Extract	佛手柑萃取	收敛毛孔、平衡油脂分泌
Betula Alba Extract	桦木芽萃取	抗菌
Betula Extract	桦木萃取	抗菌、收敛、净化作用
Bilberry Extract	覆盆子萃取	消毒、收敛、消脂、排水
Biocatalyst	酵素	促进细胞新陈代谢
Bio-Collagen	生化胶原蛋白	保湿
Bio-Enzyme	酵素,胰	促进细胞新陈代谢
Biopeptide	生化蛋白质	刺激胶原蛋白合成,预防老化,有助组织重建
Biopeptides	双性缩胺酸	促进胶原蛋白、弹力蛋白的产生,改善松弛
Biota Orientalis(L.) Endle Extract	侧柏叶萃取	镇定肌肤
Birch Tree Extract	桦树萃取	消毒、收敛,增加皮肤愈合力
Bisabolo Extract	没药萃取	收敛、消毒杀菌加快伤口愈合
Bisabolol	甜没药醇	防刺激剂,提取自洋甘菊
Bletilla Striata Reichenbach Extract	白芨萃取	含天然维生素 C,可减少黑色素沉淀
Borage Oil	琉璃苣油	天然油脂,含丰富的维生素 E、F,修补凹洞
Bromclain	菠萝酵素	代谢老旧细胞角质
Burdock	牛蒡	消毒、预防粉刺、促进细胞生长、抗发炎
Burdock Root Extract	牛蒡根萃取	调节皮脂分泌、收敛作用
Butyl Methoxydibenzoylmethane		化学性防晒成分,属 Parsol
Butyl Paraben	丁酯	防腐剂
Butyl Stearate	硬脂酸	赋型剂、基质
Butylene Glycol	丁二醇	保湿
Butylhydroxyanisol	羟基茴香二丁酯	酸化防止剂
C12-15 Alkyl Benzoate		赋型剂、基质
Calcium Pantetheine Sulfonate	维生素 B_5 衍生物	紫外线吸收剂(化学性防晒成分)
Calcium Pantothenate	泛酸钙,维生素 B_5	抗氧化、促进代谢
Calendula Extract	金盏花萃取	具舒缓、安抚敏感肌肤等功效

INGREDIENTS(成分)	中文标示	简 介
Camellia Sinensis Extract	山茶萃取,茶多酚	抗氧化
Camphor	樟树	抗痒、防过敏
Candelilla Wax	墈地里拉蜡	浓度增强剂
Caprylic/Capric Triglyceride	三甘油酯	皮肤润滑剂
Carbomer	高分子胶	浓度增强剂
Carbopol	羧乙烯聚合物	赋型剂
Carboxymethyl Chitin	几丁质衍生物	来自虾蟹外壳,为一高分子量之黏多糖体,具有保湿作用
Carnauba Wax	棕榈蜡	增加光泽感
Carrageenan	鹿角菜胶	保湿
Carrot Oil	胡萝卜油	可促使伤口愈合、镇痛、滋养、消毒、抗老化
Carthamus Tinctorius L. Extract	红花萃取	活化肌肤
Castor Oil	蓖麻油	可润滑、保湿
Centella Asiatica	老公根	紧实肌肤、增加弹性
Ceramide	神经酰胺、细胞质脂	保湿剂
Ceramide 3	分子钉	保湿剂
Ceresin	矿蜡	乳化剂
Ceteareth-12		乳化剂
Ceteareth-20		乳化剂
Cetearyl Alcohol	十六硬脂酸酯	乳化剂
Cetyl Acetate	鲸蜡醋酸盐	油脂剂
Cetyl Alcohol	鲸腊硬脂醇、十六醇	乳化剂
Cetyl Dimethicone	鲸蜡硅氧烷	油脂剂
Cetyl Palmitate	棕榈酸鲸蜡酯	乳化剂
Chamomil Oil	洋甘菊油	抗自由基、舒缓
Chamomile Extract	洋甘菊萃取	含丰富的甘菊蓝,具有防止皮肤发炎的功效,亦具有清洁、安定肌肤的效果
Chlorella Extract	绿藻萃取	滋润、保湿
Cholecalciferol	维生素 D_3,胆骨化醇	内用为增加钙质吸收,外用可治疗牛皮癣
Cholesterol	胆固醇	乳化剂
Cinnamate	桂皮酸盐类	化学性防晒成分,也是目前较安全的成分

228

INGREDIENTS(成分)	中文标示	简 介
Cinnamon Essential Oil	肉桂精油	防腐、杀菌
Cinoxate		化学性防晒成分,属桂皮酸盐类
Citric Acid	柠檬酸	防腐剂及平衡酸碱度
Citric Alcohol	柠檬醇	乳化剂
Citric Oil	柠檬油	润肤
Citron	法国香柠檬	具提神醒肤、消除肌肉疲劳以及对毛孔粗大有收敛效果等作用
Citronella Essential Oil	香茅精油	清洁、杀菌
Citrus Extract	柑橘萃取	含有维生素C,具有防菌效果,可以控制油脂分泌作用及防止雀斑、黑斑的形成
Coal Tar	煤焦油	常用来做为唇膏的染料
Cocamidopropyl Betaine	烷基酰胺类	界面活性剂,起泡剂,清洁用
Cocamidopropyl Hydroxy Sultane	烷基酰胺类	界面活性剂,起泡剂,清洁用
Cocoamide DEA		非离子界面活性剂清洁用品主要成分
Coconut Diethanolamide	烷醇酰胺	界面活性剂,起泡剂,清洁用
Coenzyme Q10	辅酶	抗氧化,可以消灭自由基,维持细胞膜的完整和稳定
Coix Seed	薏米	预防黑色素沉淀
Collagen	胶原蛋白	含有19种氨基酸,具有良好的吸水性,外用主要功能为保湿
Comfrey Extract	紫草萃取	含尿囊素,具舒缓皮肤、刺激新细胞的生长的功效
Common Licorice Extract	甘草萃取液	抗敏、镇静、去红肿
Coneflower Extract	矢车菊萃取	抗发炎,适用于敏感肤质
CO-Q10	辅酶	抗氧化,可以消灭自由基,维持细胞膜的完整和稳定
Corallina Officalis	红藻	保湿
Cress	水芹	消肿,促使伤口愈合,清洁净化、收敛肌肤
Cucumber Extract	小黄瓜萃取	含丰富维生素C,保湿、滋润、美白、活化肌肤
Cyanocobalamin	氰钴胺,维生素B12	细胞代谢
Cyclomethicone	环甲硅脂	不含油的润滑剂,能给予肌肤瞬间柔嫩肤触

INGREDIENTS(成分)	中文标示	简 介
D. N. A. （Deoxyribonucleic Acid)	脱氧核糖核酸	促进新陈代谢、保湿、预防老化 Dehydroacetic
Diazolidinyl Urea	尿素醛	防腐剂,会释放甲醛,会刺激皮肤,长期使用有致癌之虞
Dibutyl Phthalate(DBP)	磷苯甲酸二丁酯	塑化、润滑、驱虫,但是会造成新生儿天生缺陷,故已禁止使用
Dibutylhydroxytoluene	羟基甲苯二丁酯	是酸化防止剂
Dicaprylyl Ether		增加使用触感,使肌肤光滑
Dichloroacetic Acid	二氯醋酸	刺激麦拉宁色素由角质层剥落
Diisopstearate	二异硬脂酸酯	硬脂酸的衍生物,润滑剂
Diisosteary Malate		基质
Dimethicone		保湿、润泽,可在皮肤上形成一层薄膜,增加皮肤触感
Dimethicone Copolyol	硅氧烷	乳化剂,有润肤功效
Dimonium Chloride Phosphate		乳化剂
Dioxybenzone		化学性防晒成分,属苯甲酮类
Dipotassium Glycyrrhiziate	甘草酸钾	预防过敏
Disodium EDTA	乙二胺四乙酸二钠	水质处理,有抗氧化功效,当作防腐剂使用,亦可防止钙镁离子沉淀
Disodium Laureth Sulfosuccinate	磺基琥珀酸酯	一种界面活性剂,清洁用起泡剂
Distilled Water	蒸馏水	基质,产品调制时所需的水分
Dmdm Hydantoin		防腐剂,会释放甲醛会刺激皮肤,长期使用有致癌之虞
Edera Extract	长春藤	具抗氧化作用代谢废物、排泄毒素
Elastin	弹力素	增加弹性、保湿
Elder	接骨木	温和紧肤、美白祛斑作用;兼能舒缓颜面神经紧张,舒缓肌肉僵硬
Ergocalciferol	维生素 D_2、骨化醇	刺激细胞再生
Erucamidopropyl Hydroxy Sultane		起泡剂
Ethyl Paraben	乙酯	防腐剂
Ethylene	乙烯	一种植物性荷尔蒙,可促进细胞活化

230

INGREDIENTS(成分)	中文标示	简 介
Ethylene Diaminetetra Acetic Acid(EDTA)	乙烯二胺四乙酸	产品溶液沉淀防止剂、硬水软化剂
Ethylhexyl Methoxycinnamate	乙基乙基—甲氧基肉桂酸盐	化学性防晒成分
Euphrasia Officinalis Extract	小米草萃取	收缩,镇静
Evening Primerose Oil	月见草油、夜樱草油	促进肌肤血液循环,并提供保湿
Fatty Alcohol	脂肪醇混晶	一种界面活性剂,清洁起泡剂
FD&C、D&C	色素	常常含在一些化妆品、染发剂及去除头皮洗发精里
Fennel	茴香	对清洁、紧肤、毛孔粗大、防皱有很好的效果
Ferulic Acid	阿魏酸	抗氧化
Floraesters 10	脂衍	Jojoba萃取液,保湿、预防松弛
Formaldehyde	甲醛	防腐剂,有致癌之虞,已被禁止使用
Forsythia Suspensa(Thunb.)Vahl Extract	连钱草萃取	消肿
Fragrance	香精	产品添加之化学香味
Geranium Essential Oil	天竺葵精油	收敛、抑菌,能调节内分泌腺
Germaben II		防腐剂
Ginger	姜	促进细胞生长、活化肌肤
Ginkgo Biloba	银杏	预防细胞老化、增进新陈代谢,并可达白皙效果
Ginkgo Biloba Leaf Extract	银杏叶萃取	抗氧化、抗紫外线、增加血液循环、促进细胞再生
Ginseng Extract	人参萃取液	滋养、消除疲劳、预防皱纹、促进血液循环等功效
Glycerin	甘油	保湿、滋润肌肤
Glycerol Mono Stearate	单硬脂酸甘油酯	乳化剂
Glyceryl Cocoate		乳化剂
Glyceryl PABA		化学性防晒成分,属对氨基苯甲酸盐类,常致过敏反应,现多不为采用
Glyceryl Polymethacrylate		润滑剂、保湿剂

INGREDIENTS(成分)	中 文 标 示	简 介
Glyceryl Stearate	甘油硬脂酸酯	乳化剂
Glycolic Acid	甘醇酸	常用的果酸成分,去除老废角质、增加肌肤新陈代谢
Glycoproteins	糖蛋白	强化细胞修复、代谢能力
Glycyrrhetinic Acid	甘草酸	具良好之防敏感效果,可使眼部肌肤挥别黯沉
Glycyrrhizin Acid	甘草次酸	预防肌肤敏感现象,安抚、舒缓受刺激的肌肤
Grape Seed Extract	葡萄籽萃取	含高成分葡萄多酚,可预防自由基及细胞氧化功能
Grapefruit Essential Oil	葡萄柚精油	调节皮脂分泌,具良好流动性,可增加体内水分代谢
Grapeseed Oil	葡萄籽油	富含维生素,矿物质及蛋白质,抗氧化的效果是维生素 C 的 20 倍,维生素 E 的 50 倍
Green Tea Extract	绿茶萃取	舒缓、抗自由基
Hamamelis	金缕梅	去淤消肿
Hawthorn Extract	山楂萃取	抗发炎
Hazel Leaves	榛叶	促进血液循环,提升细胞含氧量,辅助肌肤代谢,增加肌肤的免疫功能
Hectorite	贺客多力士	乳化剂,是一种含硅酸镁、硅酸锂的黏土
Helichryse Extract	永久花萃取	促进细胞再生
Hispagel	生化糖醛酸	保湿
Homosalate		化学性防晒成分,属水杨酸盐类
Horse Chestnut Extract	马栗树,七叶树萃取	预防发炎,预防微血管曲张
Horsetail Extract	木贼萃取	促进肌肤细胞中胶原蛋白的合成
Hyaluronic Acid	玻尿酸,糖醛酸	属于非油脂性滋润剂,能吸收比本身重量多 500～1000 倍的水分,在皮肤细胞之间锁住水分
Hyasol		保湿剂
Hybrid Safflower Oil	红花子油	滋润剂
Hydrocotyle Extract	天胡荽萃取	去脂肪,可作为瘦身用途;另可防过敏,增加皮肤愈合力
Hydrogenated Lecithin	氢化卵磷脂	滋润、预防老化
Hydrogenated Polyisobutene		油脂剂,作为基质

INGREDIENTS(成分)	中文标示	简 介
Hydrogenated Soy Glyceride	氢化大豆甘油酯	润肤剂
Hydrolyzed Glycosaminoglycans		滋润、保湿剂
Hydrolyzed Protein	水解蛋白	水解蛋白质,具保湿、增加肌肤弹性
Hydrolyzed Collagen Protein	水解胶原蛋白	维持肌肤紧实及弹性,分子比胶原蛋白小,较易为皮肤吸收
Hydroquinone(HQ) Illuminex	对苯二酚	高效美白去斑成分,列为药物管制制黑剂,含维生素 A、C、E、K
Imidazolidinyl Urea	眯坐丁尿酸	防腐剂,会释放甲醛（Formaldehyde）,刺激皮肤,长期使用有致癌之虞
Iniferine		是一种抗自由基之天然复合物,能抗拒因外来因素之分子与铜离子之结合以避免铜离子之氧化作用而防止黑色素之形成
Iodopropynyl Butylcarbamate		抗菌剂
Iron Oxide	氧化铁	色料
Isodecane	异癸烷	舒缓（可由大茴香、奶油酸、柠檬油、菩提树油中萃取）
Iso-Flavones	植物性荷尔蒙、异黄素	延缓肌肤老化,减少细纹产生
Isohexadecane	异十六烷	增添质感(可由甜胡椒、大茴香、白菖根、芹菜籽、奶油酸、咖啡、茶等萃取)
Isopropyl Alcohol	异丙醇	乳化剂
Isopropyl Myristate	十四酸异丙酯,肉豆蔻盐	化学合成油脂剂,易致暗疮
Isopropyl Palmitate	十六酸异丙酯,棕榈油盐	化学合成油脂剂,易致暗疮
Isositearoyl Hydrolyzed Collagen	氢化骨胶原	润肤
Isostearic Acid	异硬脂酸	饱和脂肪酸,用于调节稠度及外观质感
Isostearyl Alcohol	异十八醇	乳化剂

INGREDIENTS(成分)	中文标示	简介
Ivy extract	常春藤萃取	具去脂、抗水肿,分解脂肪,收敛及镇静作用,促进代谢循环、消除蜂窝组织
Jojoba Ester	霍霍巴酯	滋润、保湿
Jojoba Oil	霍霍巴油	滋润、保湿
Kaolin	白陶土	中国土,用做颜料
Ketoconazole	克多可那挫	抗霉菌剂,用来治疗因皮屑芽孢菌感染的脂溢性皮肤炎或头皮屑效果很好
Kiwi	奇异果	内含多种维生素,可使肌肤白皙、活化细胞
Kohakuhi	桑白皮	白皙、淡化斑点
Kojic Acid	曲酸	抑制黑色素形成,使麦拉宁色素代谢正常,卫生署公布有效美白成分之一
Kukui Nut Oil	夏威夷核油	含多种脂肪酸,有极佳的渗透性及滋润效果
Lactic Acid	乳酸	角质软化及保湿作用
Laminaria Digtatitat	海藻萃取液	柔软肌肤、提升肌肤免疫力、加强肌肤弹力与光泽 Laniline Alcohol 蜂蜡醇
Lanolin	羊毛脂	滋润
Lanoline Alcohol	羊毛脂醇	乳化剂,天然油脂,可作为基质
Lappa Extract	牛蒡萃取	预防粉刺、抗菌,抑制头皮屑
L-Ascorbic acid	左旋维生素 C	抗氧化作用
L-Ascorbic Acid Phosphate Magnesiom Salt N-nydrate (MAP)	维生素 C 磷酸镁复合物	维生素 C 衍生物,具有美白功效,为卫生署公布之有效美白成分
Lauroyl Lysine	氨基酸月桂醇酯	一种改质剂,轻滑、柔顺、高亮泽度,除可使粉体较亲油、增强保湿性外,亦可增加产品的稳定性
Lauryl Betaine		界面活性剂,起泡剂
Lauryl Diethanolamide		界面活性剂,起泡剂
Lavender Extract	熏衣草萃取	抗菌、消炎、镇静皮肤
Lecithin	卵磷脂	保湿及抗氧化功能
Lemon Extract	柠檬萃取	美白、滋润、抗炎

INGREDIENTS（成分）	中 文 标 示	简　　介
Lemongrass Essential Oil	柠檬香茅精油	缓和肌肤不适感、抑菌、消除肌肉酸痛、可作为防菌剂
Lesser Celandine Extract	白屈菜萃取	预防过敏,增加抵抗力
Licorice Extract	甘草萃取	保护敏感肌肤
Licorice Root	甘草根	预防发炎
Ligusticum Chuanxiong Hort Extract	川芎萃取	增加细胞代谢
Lily Extract	百合萃取	镇静、抗炎
Lime Extract	莱姆树萃取	含丰富的植物氨基酸,能活化细胞组织及再生能力
Lime Fruit Extract	莱姆萃取	平衡油脂分泌
Linden Extract	菩提萃取	具安抚、舒缓肌肤功效
Linoleic Acid	亚麻仁油酸,维生素 F	不饱和脂肪酸,防止表皮水分流失,滋润皮肤
Lipase	脂肪脢,酵素	增加肌肤新陈代谢
Liposome	微脂体	结构与人体细胞类似,可以非常容易被人体所吸收,可增加皮肤之保湿平滑性
Liquid Paraffin	液态石蜡	润肤
Luffa Cylindrica	丝瓜萃取	保湿,镇静
Macadamia Nut Oil	澳洲胡桃油	对皮肤的血液循环及毒素排除有一定的效果,防止自由基生成,抗老化、紫外线
Magnesium Aluminum Silicate		乳化剂,安定剂,可加强溶液浓度
Magnesium Ascorbylphosphate(MAP)	维生素 C 磷酸镁复合物	维生素 C 衍生物,具有美白功效,为卫生署公布之有效美白成分
Malic Acid	苹果酸	由苹果中萃取出来,为果酸的一种,可加速皮肤代谢老废角质
Mallow Extract	锦葵萃取	含丰富的植物氨基酸,能活化肌肤细胞组织及再生能力
Marigold Oil	金盏花油	抗发炎、清洁、收敛、活血散瘀,增加皮肤愈合力
Marjoram Extract	马郁兰萃取	对扩张动脉、微血管扩张、散瘀有帮助
Marshmallow Extract	药蜀葵萃取	含黏质美容成分;可放松肌肤,安抚日晒后的各种不适现象

INGREDIENTS(成分)	中 文 标 示	简　　介
Matricaria Extract	洋甘菊萃取	抗炎、防过敏
Meadowfoam Seed Oil	小白花,绣线菊籽油	滋润、抗敏
Meadowsweet Extract	绣线菊萃取液	具有预防刺激、舒缓、收敛肌肤功效
Melawhite	美拉白	抑制黑色素沉淀及淡化色斑
Melissa Extract	香蜂草萃取	肌肤油水平衡,增强抵抗力,预防感染
Menaquinones	维生素 K	去瘀、消肿
Menthol	薄荷脑	清洁、杀菌
Meristem Extract	被子植物萃取	预防发炎过敏
Methyl Anthranilate		化学性防晒成分
Methyl Hydroxybenzoate	甲基羟苯酸酯	防腐剂
Methyl Paraben Methyl Parahydroxybenzoate(MethylParaben)	苯甲酸甲酯 苯甲酸甲酯	防腐剂 防腐剂
Methyl Salicylate	水杨酸甲酯,冬青油	抗发炎
Mexoryl	麦光素滤光环	化学性防晒成分
Mica	云母	通常加入化妆品中增加使用后的质感与肤触
Microcrystalline Wax	微粒蜡	微粒化之蜡,用做基质
Milk Protein	牛奶蛋白	具保湿、嫩白作用
Mineral Oil	矿物油	基质
Monoethanolamine Lauryl Sulfate		界面活性剂,清洁力过强,常导致皮肤干燥
Montmorillonite(green)	绿土	可吸收过多油脂达到收敛、抗菌及抗炎等作用
Mulberry Extract	桑葚萃取	含氨基酸及黄碱素,捕捉自由基,对于肌肤有抗氧化及白皙作用
Musk Extract	麝香萃取液	减少过多油脂分泌,收缩粗大毛孔,柔细肌肤
Myricl Alcohol	羊毛脂醇	天然油脂
Myristyl Alcohol	蜂蜡醇	乳化剂
Myristyl Lactate		合成油脂剂,可使肌肤触感柔软
NA-PCA(NaPCA,Sodium Pyrrolidone Carboxylate)	钠羟基皮酪烷酮	为一自然水溶性亲子基因子,用来作为保湿剂
Natural Moisturising Factor(N. M. F.)		为一自然水溶性亲子基因子,用来作为保湿剂

236

INGREDIENTS（成分）	中文标示	简 介
Neroli Extract	橙花萃取	促进细胞再生,预防敏感
Nicotinamide	烟碱酰胺,维生素 B_3 衍生物	防止皮肤对阳光有过烈的反应,修补阳光对皮肤造成的伤害
Nitrosamines	亚硝胺	化妆品常用的次要成分,非常毒
Nylon Fiber	尼龙纤维	通常用在睫毛膏中,增加使用时的增长效果
Nylon-12	尼龙-12	经过特别研制的尼龙粉底,可作为滑石粉的替代品,其微细圆粒,能让涂敷粉底更容易
Octyl Dimethy PABA	对氨基苯甲酸盐	紫外线吸收剂,防晒成分,但容易引致敏感
Octyl Methoxycinnamate（OMC）	桂皮酸盐	化学性防晒成分,可防御 UVB
Octyl Palmitate	棕榈酸辛酯	有长效保湿功用,使肌肤柔嫩光滑
Octyl Salicylate	水杨酸盐	化学性防晒成分
Octyldodecanol		油脂剂,作为基质
Oleic Acid	油酸	由植物中萃取之成分可帮助产品的渗透
Oligo Extract	寡糖萃取	增强肌肤新陈代谢
Olive Oil	橄榄油	保湿、滋润、抗皱、超级抗老化作用、并能保持毛孔畅通、洁净
Orange Essential Oil	橙橘精油	富含维生素 A、B、C
Oxybenzone	二苯甲酮	化学性防晒成分,可防御 UVA,属苯甲酮类
Ozokerite	地蜡	天然矿物蜡,为保养品基剂
PABA	对氨基苯甲酸盐	化学性防晒成分,常致过敏反应,现多不为采用
Padimate O(PadimateA)		化学性防晒成分,属对氨基苯甲酸盐类,常致过敏反应,现多不为采用
Paeonia Suffruticosa Root Extract	牡丹根萃取	活络血液循环
Palmaria Palmata	红藻萃取	可促进微血管循环,去除水肿
Palmitic Acid	棕榈酸,软脂酸	油脂剂
Palmitoleic Acid	棕榈油酸	不饱和脂肪酸,防止表皮水分流失,柔润皮肤
Panthenol	维生素 B_5,泛先醇	保湿剂

INGREDIENTS(成分)	中文标示	简 介
Papaya Enzyme	木瓜酵素	清除代谢老废的角质细胞、促进细胞组织更新
Para-aminobenzoic Acid (PABA)	对氨基苯甲酸盐	紫外线吸收剂,化学防晒成分,主要是防 UVB,但容易引致敏感,现已极少采用
Paraffin	石蜡	基质,可加强溶液浓度
PARA-Hydroxy Benzoic Acid Ester	对-羟基苯甲酸酯	防腐剂
Parahydroxybenzoate(Paraben)		防腐剂,长期使用有引起接触性皮肤之虞
Parsol 1789		化学性防晒成分,罕见过敏反应
Pear Power	珍珠粉	含有十八种对人体有益的氨基酸,具有美白、润肤、修护的效果
Pearl Pigment	珍珠颜料	用在化妆品中以增加光泽
PEG-60 Hydrogenated Castor Oil	氢化蓖麻油	为天然植物性油脂,具肌肤柔润作用
PEG8-Bees Wax	蜜蜡	基质,可增强产品浓度
Pentavitin	泛维他	保湿剂
Peppermint Extract	薄荷萃取	镇静、清洁毛孔
Perfume	香精	产品添加之化学香味
Petrolatum	石蜡油,凡士林	润滑剂、保湿剂
Phenol	防腐剂	
Phenolic acid	酚酸	抗氧化剂
Phenoxyethanol	苯氧基乙醇	杀菌剂
Phylloquinone	维生素 K_1	去瘀、可用来去除黑眼圈
Phytoplacenta	植物胎盘素	预防老化、活化细胞弹力
Phyto-Placentol	植物性胎盘素	预防老化、活化细胞弹力
Pigment	色素	
Pinecone Extract	松果萃取	
Placenta	胎盘素	提供各种肌肤所需的氨基酸、弹力蛋白、使肌肤富弹性
Placental Protein	胎盘蛋白	刺激麦拉宁色素由角质层剥落
Placentol	胎盘素	提供各种肌肤所需的氨基酸、弹力蛋白、使肌肤富弹性
Plantain	车前草	含熊果素,可淡斑、美白
Polybutene	聚异丁烯	赋型剂,加强浓度

INGREDIENTS(成分)	中文标示	简 介
Polyethylene	聚乙烯	酒精之脱水产物,用以控制产品变干的时间
Polyglucan	聚葡萄糖	保湿,预防过敏,舒缓红肿
Polyglucuronic Acid	聚多糖酸	防止老化、促进新陈代谢
Polyglyceryl-3	聚甘油二酯	润滑剂
Polygonum Multiflorum Thunb Extract	何首乌萃取	增加血液循环,活络细胞
Polymethyl Methacrylate (PMMA)	聚甲基丙烯酸甲酯	可使修容粉长效不易脱落,亲肤性更佳
Polyoxyethylene	聚乙二醇	天然非离子接口活性剂,清洁
Polyoxyethylene Lauryl Ether	聚氧乙烯月桂醚	阴离子系合成之界面活性剂,洗净力强
Polypeptides	寡胜	是氨基酸的一种,能呵护受损的细胞
Polyquaterium-6	聚季铵盐-6	柔软剂
Polysorbate 20	多己二烯酸 20	乳化剂
Polysorbate 60	多己二烯酸 60	乳化剂
Polysorbate 80(Tween 80)	多己二烯酸 80	乳化剂
Polyvinyl Alcohol	聚乙烯醇	高分子聚合胶,属植物性胶体,可吸附深层毛孔中的污垢及粉刺
Potassium Sorbate	山梨酸钾	防腐剂
Propyl Allate		防腐剂
Propyl Hydroxybenzoate	丙基羟苯酸酯	防腐剂
Propyl Paraben	羟苯甲酸丙酯	防腐剂,较为安全
Propylene Glycol	丙二醇、丙烯甘醇	保湿剂
Protelnase	蛋白胺	清洁柔软促进活化振奋振乏的细胞
Psoralea Corylifolia L Extract	补骨脂	滋润
Purified Water	纯水	基质,载体
Pyridoxine HCl	维生素 B$_6$	是一种共同酵素,增加代谢
Pyrrolidone Carboxylic Acid (Sodium PCA)	角质素	保湿
Quatenarium-18	夸特宁-18	纤维萃取,用做结合之媒介
Quaternium 15	聚季铵盐-15	防腐剂,会释放甲醛,会刺激皮肤,长期使用有致癌之虞

INGREDIENTS（成分）	中 文 标 示	简 介
Radix Angelicae Dahuricae	白芷	美白、保湿、供给皮肤养分
Retinoic Acid	维生素 A 酸	具有去角质、促进代谢、调理油脂分泌的功能,可以改善、治疗青春痘、粉刺
Retinoids	维生素 A 素	促进皮肤新陈代谢,减少粉刺,治疗暗疮、减少细纹
Retinol	维生素 A	高效除皱成分
Retinyl Palmitate	棕榈酸维生素 A	具有滋润功效,减少细少纹路及修护肌肤作用
Revitalin	植物再生素	修护受损肌肤
Riboflavin	维生素 B_2、核黄素	增强代谢,促进皮肤、指甲、及头发的健康生长
Ricinoleic Acid	蓖麻油酸	润滑、保湿
Rose Essence Oil	玫瑰精油	润白、保湿
Rose Extract	玫瑰萃取	保湿、防皱、美白、软化、收敛舒缓、抗老、深层细胞补充水分、防止皮肤干燥、促进女性荷尔蒙分泌
Rose Hip	玫瑰果	富含维生素 C,可美白、滋润肌肤
Rosemary Essence Oil	迷迭香精油	帮助血液循环、平衡神经系统、强化敏感肌肤
Rosemary Extract	迷迭香萃取	收敛毛孔、紧实皮肤
Saccharideisomerate		一种植物性糖类聚合物,有保湿功效
Safflower Oil	红花油	基质,润肤成分
Sage Extract	鼠尾草萃取	收敛、抗炎、镇静,平衡油脂,促进细胞再生
Salicylates	水杨酸盐类	化学性防晒成分
Salicylic Acid	水杨酸	有去角质的功能,能去除粉刺。（另可做为防腐剂用途）
Scutellaria Baicalensis Extract	黄芩萃取	镇静、抗菌
SD Alochol 40	酒精	保养品、化妆品用酒精
Seamollient	海藻黏多糖体	保湿剂
Seaweed Extract	海藻萃取	柔软肌肤、提升肌肤免疫力、加强肌肤弹力与光泽
Sericite	绢云母	用作化妆品,增加质感

INGREDIENTS(成分)	中 文 标 示	简　　介
Serum Protein	血清蛋白	促进细胞再生,促使真皮层中纤维母细胞制造弹力蛋白
Sesame Oil	芝麻油	滋润剂
Shiconix Extract	紫根萃取	舒缓红肿肌肤,增加抗体
Silica	硅、石英	色料及保护剂,多为化妆品添加剂
Silicon Oil	硅油	防氧化,对肌肤不刺激,添加于保养品中 1%～5% 的浓度,可改变皮肤的触感,增加柔软度
Silk Amino Acid	丝氨基酸	润肤
Silk Protein	丝蛋白	活化细胞,增加肌肤弹性
Sliver-Birch	白桦	含维生素 C、钠与磷、具有促进血液循环、收敛、抗感染
Sodium Alginate	海藻胶	保湿剂
Sodium Ascorbate	维生素 C	抗氧化
Sodium Benzoate	苯甲酸钠,安息香酸钠	产品溶液缓冲剂,亦为产品防腐剂
Sodium Citrate	柠檬酸钠	产品溶液缓冲剂,让产品型态更为安定
Sodium Cocoyl Sarcosinate		界面活性剂,刺激性较低的清洁成分
Sodium Hyaluronate	玻尿酸钠	天然保湿因子
Sodium Hydroxide	氢氧化钠,苛性钠	碱性,可用来调整酸碱度
Sodium Laureth Sulfate (SLEs)	聚氧乙烯烷基硫酸钠	阴离子界面活性剂,易起泡性易溶于水中
Sodium PCA (Pyrrolidone Carboxylic Acid)	角质素	保湿
Sodium Pyrolidone Carboxylate(NA-PCA)	钠羟基酪烷酮	为一自然水溶性亲子基因子,用来作为保湿剂
Sodium Sorbate	山梨酸钠	防腐剂
Sorbic Acid	己二烯酸,山梨酸	防腐剂
Sorbitan Stearate		乳化剂
Sorbitol	山梨醇	保湿剂
Soybean Protein	大豆蛋白	刺激细胞新生,产生胶原纤维及弹力纤维,增强肌肤支撑组织的弹性与紧实
Squalene	角鲨烯,海鲛鱼油	含有丰富的胶质成分,易于皮肤吸收,并可促进皮脂再生,具有清爽不油腻的独特感觉,滋润皮肤

241

INGREDIENTS(成分)	中文标示	简 介
ST. John's Wort	小连翘	能修复伤口、柔软肌肤
Stearic Acid	硬脂酸	油脂剂
Stearyl Alcohol	十八烷醇,硬脂醇	乳化剂,但不会起泡
Stearyl Glycyrrhetinate	甘草酸硬脂酯	具有预防肌肤受刺激、降低敏感的功能
Sterocare	植物性荷尔蒙	抗老化
Sulfur	硫磺剂	有消炎、干燥的功效,常用来治疗青春痘肌肤
Sulisobenzone		化学性防晒成分,属苯甲酮类
Sweet Almond Oil	甜杏仁油	含有维生素 D、维生素 E,对面疱有调理作用,还具有隔离紫外线的作用
Talc	滑石粉	物理性防晒功能,为天然矿石萃取
Tartaric Acid	酒石酸	由葡萄酒中萃取出来,为果酸的一种,可加速皮肤代谢老废角质
Tea Tree Essential Oil	茶树精油	天然的抑菌剂,可平衡油脂、预防感染
Tetrasodium EDTA	乙二氨四乙酸四钠	化妆品溶液中的隔离剂,可做为产品中的抗菌剂(防腐剂)
Thiamine Mononitrate (Thiamine HCI)	维生素 B$_1$,硫胺素	增加代谢
Thiostim		是种温和的含硫化合物,可以保护肌肤天然酵素免于因氧化所带来的伤害
Thyme Extract	百里香萃取	具抗菌、防腐、镇静、收敛等作用
TiO$_2$	二氧化钛	物理性防晒成分,可改善肤色
Titanium Dioxide	二氧化钛	物理性防晒成分,可改善肤色
Tocopherol	维生素 E,生育醇	抗自由基、预防老化
Tocopheryl Acetate	维生素 E	抗氧化剂
Toluene	甲苯	常是指甲油与去除剂的成分
Trehalose	海藻多糖体	具有保湿及柔软作用
Tretinoin	维生素 A 酸	具有去角质、促进代谢、调理油脂分泌的功能,可以改善、治疗青春痘、粉刺,但有光敏感性,白天最好不要使用
Trichlorosan	三氯沙	有杀菌的功效,常用来治疗青春痘
Triclosan	玉洁新	抗菌,可抑制痤疮

INGREDIENTS(成分)	中 文 标 示	简　　介
Triethanolamine	三乙醇胺	酸碱值调节剂
Triethanolamine（TEA）Lauryl Sulfate		界面活性剂,清洁力过强,常导致皮肤干燥
Trolamine salicylate		化学性防晒成分,属水杨酸盐类
Tween 20	吐温 20	乳化剂
Tween 80	吐温 80	乳化剂
Ultramarines	群青	色料
Urea	尿素	保湿、收敛
Vaseline	凡士林	润滑剂
Vc-PMG（Magnesium Ascorbyl Phosphate,MAP）	维生素 C 磷酸镁复合物	为一极为安定之维生素 C 衍生物
Vitamin A Acid	维生素 A 酸	具有去角质、促进代谢、调理油脂分泌的功能,可以改善、治疗青春痘、粉刺
Vitamin A Palmitate	棕榈酸维生素 A	具有滋润功效,减少细少纹路及修护肌肤作用
Vitamin C	维生素 C	美白、抗斑
Vitamin E	维生素 E	抗自由基、天然保存剂、保湿剂
Vitamin E Oil	维生素 E 油	抗氧化、保湿、滋润
Vitamin F	维生素 F	保湿
Vitamin K	维生素 K	帮助血循、淡化黑眼圈
Wax Esters	蜡酯	基质,润肤成分
Waxes	蜡	化妆品之基质
Wheat Germ Oil	小麦胚芽油	含丰富维生素 E,是天然抗氧化剂
Wheat Protein	小麦蛋白	水解蛋白质,低敏感性,有抗氧化作用
White Lily Extract	百合萃取	柔软肌肤、消毒、治疗伤口
Wild Yam Extract	山药萃取	具有修护、保湿及增加肌肤弹力功效
Witch Hazel Extract	金缕梅萃取	抗炎、去红肿、平衡油脂分泌
Wool Fat	羊毛脂	滋润皮肤
Yarrow Extract	蓍草萃取	平衡油脂,促进细胞再生
Yeast	酵素	含有碳水化合物、乳酸、重要的矿物质及维生素群,可以促进皮肤及黏膜的细胞机能,并能迅速分解污垢、促进肌肤新陈代谢
Yellow Gentian Extract	黄龙胆根萃取	可预防雀斑、有滋养作用

INGREDIENTS(成分)	中文标示	简　介
Ylang-Ylang Essential Oil	依兰精油	平衡油脂分泌,适合油性肌肤使用
Yogurt	优格	修护肌肤、嫩白
Zinc Oxide	氧化锌	物理性防晒剂
Zostera Marina Pectin	海草胶	保湿
Zthylhexyl p-methoxycinnamate		化学性防晒成分,属桂皮酸盐类
β-Glucan	β-聚葡萄糖	滋养、保湿、预防老化

APPENDIX Ⅲ　参考文献英文刊名的缩写规则

本文参考国际标准 ISO 4—1984《文献工作——期刊刊名缩写的国际规则》。

1. 单个词组成的刊名不得缩写

部分刊名由一个实词组成,如 Adsorption, Aerobiologia, Radiochemistry, Biomaterials, nature, science 等均不得缩写。

2. 刊名中单音节词一般不缩写

英文期刊中有许多单音节词,如 FOOD, CHEST, CHILD, 这些词不得缩写。如医学期刊 hear and lung, 缩写为 Heart Lung, 仅略去连词 and, 但少数构成地名的单词, 如 NEW, SOUTH 等, 可缩写成相应首字字母。如 New England Journal of Medcine, 可缩写为 N Engl J Med, 不应略为 New Engl J Med, South African Journal of Surgery 可缩写为 S Afr J Surg, 不可缩写为 South Afr J Surg. 另外, 少于 5 个字母 (含 5 个字母) 的单词一般不缩写, 如 Acta, Heart, Bone, Joint 等均不缩写。

3. 刊名中的虚词一律省略

国外学术期刊刊名中含有许多虚词,如 the, of, for, and, on, from, to 等, 在缩写时均省去。如 Journal of chemistry 缩写为 J chem, Archives of Medical Research 缩写为 Arch Med Res.

4. 单词缩写应省略在辅音之后，元音之前

英文单词缩写一般以辅音结尾，而不以元音结尾。如 American 省略为 Am，而不省略为 Ame 或 Amer，Medicine 或 Medical 缩写为 Med，European 缩写为 Eur 等。但 Science 例外，缩写为 Sci，可能是因为元音 I 之后又是元音 E 的缘故。缩写刊名每个词首字母必须大写，而不可全部都用大写或小写。

5. 压缩字母法

仅个别单词采用压缩字母方式缩写，如 Japanese 缩写为 Jpn 而不是 Jan，National 应缩写为 Natl 而不是 Nat 等。经常有读者将 Japanese 写成 Jan 是参考文献著录中常见的错误。如 Japanese Journal of Ophthalmology，应缩写为 Jpn J Ophthalmol，National Cancer Institute Research Report 缩写为 Natl Cancer Inst Res Rep. 而 Nat 是 Nature 和 Natural 的缩写，如 Nature Medicine，Nature biotechnology 分别缩写为 Nat Med，Nat Biotechnol. 另外 CN 是中国的国别代码，期刊缩写刊名中，ChinaChinese 不得缩写为 CN，而应缩写为 Chin. 采用压缩写法是为了避免与其他常用缩写混淆。如 Japanese 不能缩写为 Jan，可能是 Jan 是 January 的固定缩写形式，National 缩写为 Natl 而不缩写为 Nat，可能是 Nat 是 Nature 和 Natural 的缩写。

6. 学科名称缩写

刊名中学科名称缩写很常见，因而了解学科名缩写规则非常必要。凡以 -ogy 结尾的单词，一律将词尾 -ogy 去掉，如 Cardiology 缩写为 Cariol，Biology 缩写为 Biol，以 -ics 结尾的学科名词，缩写时将 -ics 或连同其前面若干字母略去。如 Physics，缩写为 Phys，以 -try 结尾的词，缩写时将 -try 连同前面若干字母略去。如 chemistry 缩写为 Chem，其中也包括其他形容词的缩写。

7. 刊名中常用词和特殊单词的缩写

期刊名中有些常用单词可以缩写为一个字母，如 Journal 缩写为 J，Quarterly 缩写为 Q，Royal 缩写为 R，New 缩写为 N，South 缩写为 S 等。

8. 刊名首字母组合

有些杂志名称缩写采用首字母组合，而且已被固定下来，一般都是国际上有较大影响的期刊，并得到国际上众多索引性检索工具的认同。如 The Journal of American Medical Association 缩写为 JAMA，British Medical Journal 缩写为 BMJ 等。

9. 国家名称的缩写

刊名中国家名称的缩写分为两种情况。如国家名称为单个词汇，缩写时常略去词尾或词的后部分若干字母。如 American 缩写为 Am，British 缩写为 Br，Chinese 缩写为 Chin 等。而国家名称由多个词组组成时，常取每个词的首字母，如 United States of America 缩写为 USA 或 US 等。

以上只是一些英文刊名缩写的一般规则，具体到一个刊名的缩写，很多检索工具后都有缩略刊表。请对照。

APPENDIX Ⅳ 化学常用词头和词尾的含义

词头或词尾	含　　义	词头或词尾	含　　义
-acetal	醛缩醇	-ase	酶
acetal-	乙酰	-ate	含氧酸的盐、酯
acid	酸	-atriyne	三炔
-al	醛	azo-	偶氮
alcohol	醇	benxene	苯
-aldehyde	醛	bi-	在盐类前表示酸式盐
alkali-	碱	bis-	双
alkoxy-	烷氧基	-borane	硼烷
allyl	丙烯基	bromo-	溴
-amide	酰胺	butyl	丁基
-amidine	脒	-caboxylic acid	羧酸
-amine	胺	-carbinol	甲醇
amino-	氨基的	carbonyl	羰基
-ane	烷	centi-	10^{-2}
anhydride	酐	chloro-	氯代
anilino-	苯氨基	cis-	顺式
aquo-	含水的	condensed	缩合的、冷凝的

词头或词尾	含义	词头或词尾	含义
cyclo-	环	meta-	间,偏
deca-	十	methoxy-	甲氧基
deci	10^{-1}	methyl	甲基
di-	二	micro-	10^{-6}
-dine	啶	milli-	10^{-3}
dodeca-	十二	mono(mon-)	一,单
-ene	烯	nano-	10^{-9}
epi-	表	nitro-	硝基
epoxy-	环氧	nitroso-	亚硝基
-ester	酯	nona-	九
-ether	醚	nonadeca-	十九
ethoxy-	乙氧基	octa-	十八
ethyl	乙基	-oic	酸的
fluoro-	氟代	-ol	醇
-form	仿	-one	酮
-glycol	二醇	ortho-	邻,正,原
hemi-	半	-ous	亚酸的,低价金属
hendeca-	十一	oxa-	氧杂
hepta-	七	-oxide	氧化合物
heptadeca-	十七	-oxime	肟
hexa- 六	六	oxo-	酮
hexadeca-	十六	oxy-	氧化
-hydrin	醇	-oyl	酰
hydro-	氢或水	para-	对位,仲
hydroxyl	羟基	penta-	五
hypo-	低级的,次	pentadeca-	十五
-ic	酸的,高价金属无氧酸的盐,酰	per-	高,过
-ide	替…胺,酐	petro-	石油
-il	亚胺	phenol	苯酚
iodo-	碘代	phenyl	苯基
iso-	异,等,同	pico-	10^{-12}
-ite	亚酸盐	poly-	聚,多
keto	酮	quadri-	四
ketone	酮	quinque-	五
-lactone	内酯	semi-	半
mega-10^6	10^6	septi-	七
		sesqui-	一个半
		sexi-	六

词头或词尾	含　义	词头或词尾	含　义
sulfa-	磺胺	trideca-	十三
sym-	对称	tris-	三个
syn-	顺式,同,共	undeca-	十一
ter-	三	uni-	单,一
tetra-	四	unsym-	不对称的,偏位
tetradeca-	十四	-yl	基
tetrakis-	四个	-ylene	亚基(二价基,价在不同原子上)
thio-	硫代		
trans-	反式,超,跨	-yne	炔
tri-	三个		

APPENDIX Ⅴ　常用词头及词尾含义

词头及词尾	含　义	词头及词尾	含　义
ab-	脱离	deca-	十
-able	能…的	deci-	十分之一
ad-	添加	di-	二
anti-	反对,抗	dia-	通过,横过
auto-	自	dis-	不,无,解除
bi-	二,双	-en	加在形容词后,表"使…"
by-	附属的,次要的	en-	使,置于
centi-	百,百分之一	equi-	同等
circum-	环境,在周边	ex-	除去,离开,出自
co-	共,一齐	-fold	加在数词后,表示"…倍"
con-	共同,一起	-free	无…的
contra-	反对,相反	-ful	充满…的
counter-	逆,反	-graph	名词词尾,写、画的结果或用具
de-	除去		

词头及词尾	含　义	词头及词尾	含　义
hecto-	百	out-	超过,向外
hemi-	半	over-	超过,过分
heteo-	异,杂	pent-	五
hexa-	六	per-	高,过
homo-	同	peri-	周围,近,环境
hyddro-	水	phono-	声
hyper-	超越	photo-	光
hypo-	低,次	poly-	多,聚
-ician	名词词尾,精通者,…家	post-	在后,补充
-ics	名词词尾,…学	pre-	预先,在前
-ify	动词词尾,使…,…化	pro	向前
in-	在内,向内,不	-proof	防…的
inter-	在…之间,相互	quadr-	四
intro-	向内	quinque-	五
-ish	形容词词尾,略带…色的	radio-	放射,无线电
-ism	…学说	re-	再次,重复,反对,返回
-ist	…的信仰者	-scope	…镜
-ive	形容词词尾,易…的	semi-	半
-ize	动词词尾,…化,变成…	sept-	七
kilo-	千	sex-	六
-less	无…的	sub-	次于,在下,低,稍微
-logy	…学	super-	在上,超
mega-	大,兆,百万	syn-或sym-	或sym
-meter	…计,…表	tele-	远
micro-	微,小,百分之一	tetra-	四
mid-	中	-tight	紧密的
milli-	千分之一,毫	trans-	横过,转移
mis-	误	tri-	三
mono-	单,一	ultra-	超,极端
multi-	多	un	不,未
non-	非,不	under-	不足,在…下
nona-	九	uni-	单,一
oct-,octa-	八	with-	反对,返回

APPENDIX Ⅵ 化学上常见的缩略语

A. P.	analytically pure 分析纯	equiv.	equivalent 等价的
ab.	Absolute 绝对的	et. al.	and others 以及其他的
addn.	addition 添加	etc.	et cetera 等等
alc.	alcohol 醇	expt.	experimental 实验的
alk.	alkali 碱	fig.	figure 图
amt.	amout 量	h. p.	hoiling point 沸点
app.	apparatus 装置	hyd.	hydrous 水的
approx.	approximate 大约	ibid.	in the same place 在同一地方
aqu.	aqueous 水的	L. R.	laboratory reagent 实验试剂
asym.	asymmetric 不对称的	lab.	laboratory 实验室
atm.	atmospheric 大气压	liq.	liquid 液体
av.	average 平均的	m. p.	melting point 熔点
C. P.	chemically pure 化学纯	manf.	manufacture 制造
ca.	about 大约	max.	maximum 最大的
cal.	caloric 卡路里	min.	minute 最小的
calc.	calculate 计算	mixt.	mixture 混合物
cf.	compare 比较	mol. wt.	modecular weight 分子量
chem.	chemistry 化学	org.	organic 有机的
compd.	compound 化合物	ppm.	parts per million 百万分之一
conc.	Concentrated 浓缩的	ppt.	preipitated 沉淀的
const.	constant 常数	Prep.	prepare 制备
contg.	containing 含有…的	Resp.	respectively 分别地
cryst.	crystalline 分解	sec.	second 第二
decomp.	decompose 分解	soln.	solution 溶液
deriv.	derivative 衍生	solv.	solvent 溶剂
detn.	determination 测定	sp. gr	specific gravity 比重
dil.	dilute 稀释的	sq.	square 平方
distd.	distillad 蒸馏的	sub.	sublime 升华
e. g.	for example 例如	susp.	suspended 悬浮地
eavp.	eavporation 蒸发	tech.	technical 技术的
elec.	electric 电的	Tech. P.	technically pure 技术纯
eq.	equation 方程	vol.	volume 体积
equiv.	equivalent 平衡	wt.	weight 重量

250

APPENDIX Ⅶ 化工常用英文缩写

缩写	全 称	缩写	全 称
A/MMA	丙烯腈/甲基丙烯酸甲酯共聚物	AS	丙烯腈-苯乙烯共聚物
AA	丙烯酸	ASA	丙烯腈-苯乙烯-丙烯酸酯共聚物
AAS	丙烯酸酯-丙烯酸酯-苯乙烯共聚物	ATT	靛蓝
		AU	聚酯型聚氨酯橡胶
ABFN	偶氮(二)甲酰胺	AW	6-乙氧基-2,2,4-三甲基-1,2-二氢化喹啉
ABN	偶氮(二)异丁腈		
ABPS	壬基苯氧基丙烷磺酸钠	BAC	碱式氯化铝
ABR	聚丙烯酸酯	BACN	新型阻燃剂
ABS	苯乙烯-丙烯腈-丁二烯共聚物	BAD	双水杨酸双酚 A 酯
		BAL	2,3-巯(基)丙醇
ABVN	偶氮(二)异庚腈	BBP	邻苯二甲酸丁苄酯
AC	偶氮(二)碳酰胺	BC	叶酸
ACB	2-氨基-4-氯苯胺	BCD	β-环糊精
ACNU	嘧啶亚硝脲	BCG	苯顺二醇
ACP	三氧化铝	BCNU	氯化亚硝脲
ACR	丙烯酸酯共聚物	BD	丁二烯
ACS	苯乙烯-丙烯腈-氯化聚乙烯共聚物	BE	丙烯酸乳胶外墙涂料
		BEE	苯偶姻乙醚
ACTA	促皮质素	BFRM	硼纤维增强塑料
ADC	偶氮甲酰胺	BG	丁二醇
ADCA	偶氮二甲酰胺	BGE	反应性稀释剂
AE	脂肪醇聚氧乙烯醚	BHA	特丁基-4-羟基茴香醚
AES	脂肪醇聚氧乙烯醚硫酸酯钠盐	BHT	二丁基羟基甲苯
		BL	丁内酯
AI	酰胺-酰亚胺(聚合物)	BLE	丙酮-二苯胺高温缩合物
AK	醇酸树脂	BLP	粉末涂料流平剂
AM	丙烯酰胺	BMA	甲基丙烯酸丁酯
AN	丙烯腈	BMC	团状模塑料
AN-AE	丙烯腈-丙烯酸酯共聚物	BMU	氨基树脂皮革鞣剂
ANM	丙烯腈-丙烯酸酯合成橡胶	BN	氮化硼
AP	多羟基氨基聚醚	BNE	新型环氧树脂
APP	无规聚丙烯	BNS	β-萘磺酸甲醛低缩合物
AR	丙烯酸酯橡胶	BOA	己二酸辛苄酯

251

缩写	全　称	缩写	全　称
BOP	邻苯二甲酰丁辛酯	CFM	碳纤维密封填料
BOPP	双轴向聚丙烯	CFRP	碳纤维增强塑料
BP	苯甲醇	CLF	含氯纤维
BPA	双酚 A	CMC	羧甲基纤维素
BPBG	邻苯二甲酸丁(乙醇酸乙酯)酯	CMCNa	羧甲基纤维素钠
BPF	双酚 F	CMD	代尼尔纤维
BPMC	2-仲丁基苯基-N-甲基氨基酸酯	CMS	羧甲基淀粉
		CN	硝酸纤维素
BPO	过氧化苯甲酰	CNA	α-蒎烯树脂
BPP	过氧化特戊酸特丁酯	COPP	共聚聚丙烯
BPPD	过氧化二碳酸二苯氧化酯	CP	丙酸纤维素
BPS	4,4'-硫代双(6-特丁基-3-甲基苯酚)	CPE	氯化聚乙烯
		CPL	己内酰胺
		CPPG	聚氯醚
BPTP	聚对苯二甲酸丁二醇酯	CPVC	氯化聚氯乙烯(过氯乙烯)
BR	丁二烯橡胶	CR	氯丁橡胶
BRN	青红光硫化黑	CS	酪蛋白塑料(酪素塑料)
BROC	二溴(代)甲酚环氧丙基醚	CSPE	氯磺化聚乙烯
BS	丁二烯-苯乙烯共聚物	CTA	三醋酸纤维素
BS-1S	新型密封胶	CTEE	三氟氯乙烯(氯化三氟乙烯)
BSH	苯磺酰肼	CUP	铜氨纤维
BSU	N,N'-双(三甲基硅烷)脲	CV	黏胶纤维
BT	聚丁烯(热塑性塑料)	DAF	富马酸二烯丙酯
BTA	苯并三唑	DAIP	间苯二酸二烯丙酯
BTX	苯-甲苯-二甲苯混合物	DAM	马来酸二烯丙酯
BX	渗透剂	DAP	间苯二酸二烯丙酯
BXA	己二酸二丁基二甘酯	DATBP	四溴邻苯二甲酸二烯丙酯
BZ	二正丁基二硫代氨基甲酸锌	DBA	己二酸二丁酯
		DBEP	邻苯二甲酸二丁氧乙酯
CAB	醋酸-丁酸纤维素	DBP	邻苯二甲酸二丁酯
CAN	醋酸-硝酸纤维素	DBR	二苯甲酰间苯二酚
CAP	醋酸-丙酸纤维素	DBS	癸二酸二癸酯
CBA	化学发泡剂	DCCA	二氯异氰脲酸
CDP	磷酸甲酚二苯酯	DCCK	二氯异氰脲酸钾
CF	甲醛-甲酚树脂,碳纤维	DCCNa	二氯异氰脲酸钠
CFE	氯氟乙烯	DCHP	邻苯二甲酸二环乙酯

缩写	全称	缩写	全称
DCPD	过氧化二碳酸二环乙酯	DOZ	壬二酸二辛酯
DDA	己二酸二癸酯	DPA	二苯胺
DDP	邻苯二甲酸二癸酯	DVB	二乙烯基苯
DEAE	二乙氨基乙基纤维素	E/EA	乙烯/丙烯酸乙酯共聚物
DEP	邻苯二甲酸二乙酯	E/P	乙烯/丙烯共聚物
DETA	二亚乙基三胺	E/P/D	乙烯/丙烯/二烯三元共聚物
DFA	薄膜胶黏剂	E/TEE	乙烯/四氟乙烯共聚物
DHA	己二酸二己酯	E/VAC	乙烯/醋酸乙烯共聚物
DHP	邻苯二甲酸二己酯	E/VAL	乙烯/乙烯醇共聚物
DHS	癸二酸二己酯	EAA	乙烯-丙烯酸共聚物
DIBA	己二酸二异丁酯	EAK	乙基戊丙酮
DIDA	己二酸二异癸酯	EBM	挤出吹塑模塑
DIDG	戊二酸二异癸酯	EC	乙基纤维素
DIDP	邻苯二甲酸二异癸酯	ECB	乙烯共聚物和沥青的共混物
DINA	己二酸二异壬酯	ECD	环氧氯丙烷橡胶
DINP	邻苯二甲酸二异壬酯	ECTEE	聚（乙烯-三氟氯乙烯）
DINZ	壬二酸二异壬酯	ED-3	环氧酯
DIOA	己酸二异辛酯	EDC	二氯乙烷
DIOP	邻苯二甲酸二异辛酯	EDTA	乙二胺四乙酸
DIOS	癸二酸二异辛酯	EEA	乙烯-醋酸丙烯共聚物
DIOZ	壬二酸二异辛酯	EG	乙二醇
DIPA	二异丙醇胺	2-EH	异辛醇
DMA	二甲胺	EO	环氧乙烷
DMC	碳酸二甲酯	EOT	聚乙烯硫醚
DMEP	邻苯二甲酸二甲氧基乙酯	EP	环氧树脂
DMF	二甲基酰胺	EPI	环氧氯丙烷
DMP	邻苯二甲酸二甲酯	EPM	乙烯-丙烯共聚物
DMS	癸二酸二甲酯	EPOR	三元乙丙橡胶
DMSO	二甲基亚砜	EPR	乙丙橡胶
DMT	对苯二甲酸二甲酯	EPS	可发性聚苯乙烯
DNA	己二酸二壬酯	EPSAN	乙烯-丙烯-苯乙烯-丙烯腈
DNP	邻苯二甲酸二壬酯		共聚物
DNS	癸二酸壬酯	EPT	乙烯丙烯三元共聚物
DOP	邻苯二甲酸二辛酯	EPVC	乳液法聚氯乙烯
DOPP	对苯二甲酸二辛酯	EU	聚醚型聚氨酯
DOS	癸二酸二辛酯	EVA	乙烯-醋酸乙烯共聚物
DOTP	对苯二甲酸二异辛酯	EVE	乙烯基乙基醚

缩写	全称	缩写	全称
EXP	醋酸乙烯-乙烯-丙烯酸酯三元共聚乳液	HEDP	1-羟基乙叉-1,1-二膦酸
		HFP	六氟丙烯
F/VAL	乙烯/烯醇共聚物	HIPS	高抗冲聚苯乙烯
F-23	四氟乙烯-偏氯乙烯共聚物	HLA	天然聚合物透明质胶
F-30	三氟氯乙烯-乙烯共聚物	HLD	树脂性氯丁胶
F-40	四氟氯乙烯-乙烯共聚物	HM	高甲氧基果胶
FDY	丙纶全牵伸丝	HMC	高强度模塑料
FEP	全氟(乙烯-丙烯)共聚物	HMF	非干性密封胶
FNG	耐水硅胶	HOPP	均聚聚丙烯
FPM	氟橡胶	HPC	羟丙基纤维素
FRA	纤维增强丙烯酸酯	HPMC	羟丙基甲基纤维素
FRC	阻燃黏胶纤维	HPMCP	羟丙基甲基纤维素邻苯二甲酸酯
FRP	纤维增强塑料		
FRPA-101	玻璃纤维增强聚癸二酸癸胺(玻璃纤维增强尼龙1010树脂)	HPT	六甲基磷酸三酰胺
		HS	六苯乙烯
		HTPS	高冲击聚苯乙烯
FRPA-610	玻璃纤维增强聚癸二酰乙二胺(玻璃纤维增强尼龙610树脂)	IEN	互贯网络弹性体
		IHPN	互贯网络均聚物
		IIR	异丁烯-异戊二烯橡胶
FWA	荧光增白剂	IO	离子聚合物
GF	玻璃纤维	IPA	异丙醇
GFRP	玻璃纤维增强塑料	IPN	互贯网络聚合物
GFRTP	玻璃纤维增强热塑性塑料促进剂	IR	异戊二烯橡胶
		IVE	异丁基乙烯基醚
GOF	石英光纤	JSF	聚乙烯醇缩醛胶
GPS	通用聚苯乙烯	JZ	塑胶胶黏剂
GR-1	异丁橡胶	KSG	空分硅胶
GR-N	丁腈橡胶	LAS	十二烷基苯磺酸钠
GR-S	丁苯橡胶	LCM	液态固化剂
GRTP	玻璃纤维增强热塑性塑料	LDJ	低毒胶黏剂
GUV	紫外光固化硅橡胶涂料	LDN	氯丁胶黏剂
GX	邻二甲苯	LDPE	高压聚乙烯(低密度)
GY	厌氧胶	LDR	氯丁橡胶
H	乌洛托品	LF	脲
HDI	六亚甲基二异氰酸酯	LGP	液化石油气
HDPE	低压聚乙烯(高密度)	LHPC	低替代度羟丙基纤维素

缩写	全 称	缩写	全 称
LIM	液体浸渍模塑	MNA	甲基丙烯腈
LIPN	乳胶互贯网络聚合物	MPEG	乙醇酸乙酯
LJ	接体型氯丁橡胶	MPF	三聚氨胺-酚醛树脂
LLDPE	线性低密度聚乙烯	MPK	甲基丙基甲酮
LM	低甲氧基果胶	M-PP	改性聚丙烯
LMG	液态甲烷气	MPPO	改性聚苯醚
LMWPE	低分子量聚乙烯	MPS	改性聚苯乙烯
LN	液态氮	MS	苯乙烯-甲基丙烯酸甲酯树脂
LRM	液态反应模塑		
LRMR	增强液体反应模塑	MSO	石油醚
LSR	羧基氯丁乳胶	MTBE	甲基叔丁基醚
MA	丙烯酸甲酯	MTT	氯丁胶新型交联剂
MAA	甲基丙烯酸	MWR	旋转模塑
MABS	甲基丙烯酸甲酯-丙烯腈-丁二烯-苯乙烯共聚物	MXD-10/6	醇溶三元共聚尼龙
		MXDP	间苯二甲基二胺
MAL	甲基丙烯醛	OBP	邻苯二甲酸辛苄酯
MBS	甲基丙烯酸甲酯-丁二烯-苯乙烯共聚物	ODA	己二酸异辛癸酯
		ODPP	磷酸辛二苯酯
MBTE	甲基叔丁基醚	OIDD	邻苯二甲酸正辛异癸酯
MC	甲基纤维素	OPP	定向聚丙烯(薄膜)
MCA	三聚氰胺氰脲酸盐	OPS	定向聚苯乙烯(薄膜)
MCPA-6	改性聚己内酰胺(铸型尼龙6)	OPVC	正向聚氯乙烯
		OT	气溶胶
MCR	改性氯丁冷粘鞋用胶	PA-1010	聚癸二酸癸二胺(尼龙1010)
MDI	3,3'-二甲基-4,4'-二氨基二苯甲烷		
		PA-11	聚十一酰胺(尼龙11)
MDI	二苯甲烷二异氰酸酯	PA-12	聚十二酰胺(尼龙12)
MDPE	中压聚乙烯(高密度)	PA-6	聚己内酰胺(尼龙6)
MEK	丁酮(甲乙酮)	PA-610	聚癸二酰乙二胺(尼龙610)
MEKP	过氧化甲乙酮		
MES	脂肪酸甲酯磺酸盐	PA-612	聚十二烷二酰乙二胺(尼龙612)
MF	三聚氰胺-甲醛树脂		
M-HIPS	改性高冲聚苯乙烯	PA-66	聚己二酸己二胺(尼龙66)
MIBK	甲基异丁基酮	PA-8	聚辛酰胺(尼龙8)
MMA	甲基丙烯酸甲酯	PA-9	聚9-氨基壬酸(尼龙9)
MMF	甲基甲酰胺	PAA	聚丙烯酸

缩写	全 称	缩写	全 称
PAAS	水质稳定剂	PCT	聚己内酰胺
PABM	聚氨基双马来酰亚胺	PCTEE	聚三氟氯乙烯
PAC	聚氯化铝	PD	二羟基聚醚
PAEK	聚芳基醚酮	PDAIP	聚间苯二甲酸二烯丙酯
PAI	聚酰胺-酰亚胺	PDAP	聚对苯二甲酸二烯丙酯
PAM	聚丙烯酰胺	PDMS	聚二甲基硅氧烷
PAMBA	抗血纤溶芳酸	PE	聚乙烯
PAMS	聚 α-甲基苯乙烯	PEA	聚丙烯酸酯
PAN	聚丙烯腈	PEAM	苯乙烯型聚乙烯均相离子交换膜
PAP	对氨基苯酚		
PAPA	聚壬二酐	PEC	氯化聚乙烯
PAPI	多亚甲基多苯基异氰酸酯	PECM	苯乙烯型聚乙烯均相阳离子交换膜
PAR	聚芳酰胺		
PAR	聚芳酯（双酚 A 型）	PEE	聚醚酯纤维
PAS	聚芳砜（聚芳基硫醚）	PEEK	聚醚醚酮
PB	聚丁二烯-[1,3]	PEG	聚乙二醇
PBAN	聚（丁二烯-丙烯腈）	PEHA	五亚乙基六胺
PBI	聚苯并咪唑	PEN	聚萘二酸乙二醇酯
PBMA	聚甲基丙烯酸正丁酯	PEO	聚环氧乙烷
PBN	聚萘二酸丁醇酯	PEOK	聚氧化乙烯
PBR	丙烯-丁二烯橡胶	PEP	对-乙基苯酚聚全氟乙丙烯薄膜
PBS	聚（丁二烯-苯乙烯）		
PBS	聚（丁二烯-苯乙烯）	PES	聚苯醚砜
PBT	聚对苯二甲酸丁二酯	PET	聚对苯二甲酸乙二酯
PC	聚碳酸酯	PETE	涤纶长丝
PC/ABS	聚碳酸酯/ABS 树脂共混合金	PETP	聚对苯二甲酸乙二醇酯
		PF	酚醛树脂
PC/PBT	聚碳酸酯/聚对苯二甲酸丁二醇酯弹性体共混合金	PF/PA	尼龙改性酚醛压塑粉
		PF/PVC	聚氯乙烯改性酚醛压塑粉
PCD	聚癸二酰亚胺	PFA	全氟烷氧基树脂
PCDT	聚（1,4-环己烯二亚甲基对苯二甲酸酯）	PFG	聚乙二醇
		PFS	聚合硫酸铁
PCE	四氯乙烯	PG	丙二醇
PCMX	对氯间二甲酚	PGEEA	乙二醇（甲）乙醚醋酸酯
PCT	聚对苯二甲酸环己烷对二甲醇酯	PGL	环氧灌封料
		PH	六羟基聚醚

缩 写	全 称	缩 写	全 称
PHEMA	聚(甲基丙烯酸-2-羟乙酯)	PPO	聚苯醚(聚 2,6-二甲基苯醚)
PHP	水解聚丙烯酰胺	PPOX	聚环氧丙烷
PI	聚异戊二烯	PPS	聚苯硫醚
PIB	聚异丁烯	PPSU	聚苯砜(聚芳碱)
PIBO	聚氧化异丁烯	PR	聚酯
PIC	聚三聚氰酸酯	PROT	蛋白质纤维
PIEE	聚四氟乙烯	PS	聚苯乙烯
PIR	聚三聚氰酸酯	PSAN	聚苯乙烯-丙烯腈共聚物
PL	丙烯	PSB	聚苯乙烯-丁二烯共聚物
PLD	防老剂 4030	PSF(PSU)	聚砜
PLME	1∶1 型十二(烷)酸单异丙醇酰胺	PSI	聚甲基苯基硅氧烷
		PST	聚苯乙烯纤维
PMA	聚丙烯酸甲酯	PT	甲苯
PMAC	聚甲氧基缩醛	PTA	精对苯二甲酸
PMAN	聚甲基丙烯腈	PTBP	对特丁基苯酚
PMCA	聚 α-氧化丙烯酸甲酯	PTEE	聚四氟乙烯
PMDETA	五甲基二乙烯基三胺	PTMEG	聚醚二醇
PMI	聚甲基丙烯酰亚胺	PTMG	聚四氢呋喃醚二醇
PMMA	聚甲基丙烯酸甲酯(有机玻璃)	PTP	聚对苯二甲酸酯
		PTX	苯(甲苯、二甲苯)
PMMI	聚均苯四甲酰亚胺	PU	聚氨酯(聚氨基甲酸酯)
PMP	聚 4-甲基 1-戊烯	PVA	聚乙烯醇
PNT	对硝基甲苯	PVAC	聚醋酸乙烯乳液
PO	环氧乙烷	PVAL	乙烯醇系纤维
POA	聚己内酰胺纤维	PVB	聚乙烯醇缩丁醛
POF	有机光纤	PVC	聚氯乙烯
POM	聚甲醛	PVCA	聚氯乙烯醋酸酯
POP	对辛基苯酚	PVCC	氯化聚氯乙烯
POR	环氧丙烷橡胶	PVDC	聚偏二氯乙烯
PP	聚丙烯	PVDF	聚偏二氟乙烯
PPA	聚己二酸丙二醇酯	PVE	聚乙烯基乙醚
PPB	溴代十五烷基吡啶	PVF	聚氟乙烯
PPC	氯化聚丙烯	PVFM	聚乙烯醇缩甲醛
PPD	防老剂 4020	PVI	聚乙烯基丁醚
PPG	聚醚	PVK	聚乙烯基咔唑

缩写	全称	缩写	全称
PVM	聚烯基甲醚	TAC	三聚氰酸三烯丙酯
PVP	聚乙烯基吡咯烷酮	TAME	甲基叔戊基醚
PX	二甲苯	TAP	磷酸三烯丙酯
PXL	对二甲苯	TBE	四溴乙烷
PZ	二甲基二硫代氨基甲酸锌	TBP	磷酸三丁酯
RE	橡胶胶黏剂	TCA	三醋酸纤维素
RF	间苯二酚-甲醛树脂	TCCA	三氯异氰脲酸
RFL	间苯二酚-甲醛乳胶	TCEF	磷酸三氯乙酯
RP	增强塑料	TCF	磷酸三甲酚酯
RP/C	增强复合材料	TCPP	磷酸三氯丙酯
RX	橡胶软化剂	TDI	甲苯二异氰酸酯
S/MS	苯乙烯-α-甲基苯乙烯共聚物	TEA	三乙胺
SAN	苯乙烯-丙烯腈共聚物	TEAE	三乙氨基乙纤维素
SAS	仲烷基磺酸钠	TEDA	三乙二胺
SB	苯乙烯-丁二烯共聚物	TEFC	三氟氯乙烯
SBR	丁苯橡胶	TEP	磷酸三乙酯
SBS	苯乙烯-丁二烯-苯乙烯嵌段共聚物	TFE	四氟乙烯
		THF	四氢呋喃
SC	硅橡胶气调织物膜	TLCP	热散液晶聚酯
SDDC	N,N-二甲基硫代氨基甲酸钠	TMP	三羟甲基丙烷
		TMPD	三甲基戊二醇
SE	磺乙基纤维素	TMTD	二硫化四甲基秋兰姆(硫化促进剂 TT)
SGA	丙烯酸酯胶		
SI	聚硅氧烷	TNP	三壬基苯亚磷酸酯
SIS	苯乙烯-异戊二烯-苯乙烯嵌段共聚物	TPA	对苯二甲酸
		TPE	磷酸三苯酯
SIS/SEBS	苯乙烯-乙烯-丁二烯-苯乙烯共聚物	TPS	韧性聚苯乙烯
		TPU	热塑性聚氨酯树脂
SM	苯乙烯	TR	聚硫橡胶
SMA	苯乙烯-顺丁烯二酸酐共聚物	TRPP	纤维增强聚丙烯
		TR-RFT	纤维增强聚对苯二甲酸丁二醇酯
SPP	间规聚苯乙烯		
SPVC	悬浮法聚氯乙烯	TRTP	纤维增强热塑性塑料
SR	合成橡胶	TTP	磷酸二甲苯酯
ST	矿物纤维	U	脲
		UF	脲甲醛树脂

258

缩写	全　称	缩写	全　称
UHMWPE	超高分子量聚乙烯	VC/VAC	氯乙烯/醋酸乙烯酯共聚物
UP	不饱和聚酯	VCM	氯乙烯(单体)
VAC	醋酸乙烯酯	VCP	氯乙烯-丙烯共聚物
VAE	乙烯-醋酸乙烯共聚物	VCS	丙烯腈-氯化聚乙烯-苯乙
VAM	醋酸乙烯		烯共聚物
VAMA	醋酸乙烯-顺丁烯二酐共	VDC	偏二氯乙烯
	聚物	VPC	硫化聚乙烯
VC	氯乙烯	VTPS	特种橡胶偶联剂
VC/CDC	氯乙烯/偏二氯乙烯共	WF	新型橡塑填料
	聚物	WP	织物涂层胶
VC/E	氯乙烯/乙烯共聚物	WRS	聚苯乙烯球形细粒
VC/E/MA	氯乙烯/乙烯/丙烯酸甲酯	XF	二甲苯甲醛树脂
	共聚物	XMC	复合材料
VC/E/VAC	氯乙烯/乙烯/醋酸乙烯酯	YH	改性氯丁胶
	共聚物	YM	聚丙烯酸酯压敏胶乳
VC/MA	氯乙烯/丙烯酸甲酯共聚物	ZE	玉米纤维
VC/MMA	氯乙烯/甲基丙烯酸甲酯	ZH	溶剂型氯化天然橡胶胶
	共聚物		黏剂
VC/OA	氯乙烯/丙烯酸辛酯共聚物	ZN	粉状脲醛树脂胶

APPENDIX Ⅷ　颜色词汇中英文对照（彩妆用）

橄榄黄	olive yellow	深黄	deep yellow
稻草黄	straw yellow	棕黄	tan
芥末黄	mustard	青黄	bluish yellow
杏黄	broze yellow	灰黄	sallow　　grey yellow
蛋黄	york yellow egg yellow	米黄	cream
藤黄	rattan yellow	嫩黄	yellow cream
象牙黄	nude	鲜黄	cadmium yellow
日光黄	sunny yellow earth yellow	鹅黄	light yellow
	yellowish	中黄	midium yellow　　light
土黄	brown		yellow　　pale yellow
砂黄	sand yellow	浅黄	buff
金黄	golden yellow　　gold	淡黄	primrose　　jasmine

红色	red	宝石红	ruby red
朱红	vermeil ponceau	玛瑙红	agate red
粉红色	pink;soft red rose bloom	珊瑚红	coral
		金红	bronze red
梅红	plum crimson	铁红	iron oxide red
玫瑰红	rose	铁锈红	rust red
桃红	peach blossom	铬红	chrome red
樱桃红	cherry	砖红	brick red
橘红色	salmon pink	土红	reddle
石榴红	garnet	紫红(酒红)	purplish red wine red
枣红色	purplish red date red	深紫红	prune mulberry
莲红色	lotus red	棕红	henna
浅莲红	fuchsia pink	暗红	dark red dull red
豆红	bean red		fresh red blood red
辣椒红	capsicum red		bright
高粱红	Kaoliang red	鲜红	red
芙蓉红	poppy red	绯红	scarlet
胭脂红	lake rouge red	米红	silver pink
鲑鱼红	salmon	深红	deep red
玳瑁红	hawksbill turtle red	淡红	light red
海螺红	cadmium orange		

REFERENCES

［1］ 胡鸣，刘霞. 化学工程与工艺专业英语. 北京：化学工业出版社，2004.

［2］ 李维屏，祝祖耀. 新编现代化工英语. 上海：华东理工大学出版社，1993.

［3］ 张铭德等. 英语化学化工词分析. 北京：科学普及出版社，1985.

［4］ 魏高原. 化学专业基础英语知识（Ⅰ）. 北京：北京大学出版社，2001.

［5］ http：//www. fda. com. cn/

［6］ http：//www. fda. com/

［7］ http：//www. pg. com. cn/

［8］ http：//world. std. com/

［9］ http：//www. ultimate-cosmetics. com/

［10］ http：//www. wildaboutmakeup. com/eye-make-up-tips

［11］ Margaret Morrison. "HYPOALLERGENIC" COSMETICS. U. S. Food and Drug Administration FDA CONSUMER：1978，4.

［12］ Kyoko Joichi，Katsuki Ogawa，Kazuhisa Ohno，Akio Nasu. United states Patent 6749838 2004 06-15